Connectionist Symbol Processing

Special Issues of Artificial Intelligence: An International Journal

The titles in this series are paperback, readily accessible editions of the Special Volumes of *Artificial Intelligence: An International Journal*, edited by Daniel G. Bobrow and produced by special agreement with Elsevier Science Publishers B.V.

Qualitative Reasoning about Physical Systems, edited by Daniel G. Bobrow, 1985.

Geometric Reasoning, edited by Deekpak Kapur and Joseph L. Mundy, 1989.

Machine Learning: Paradigms and Methods, edited by Jaime Carbonell, 1990.

Artificial Intelligence and Learning Environments, edited by William J. Clancey and Elliot Soloway, 1990.

Connectionist Symbol Processing, edited by G. E. Hinton, 1991.

Connectionist Symbol Processing

edited by

G. E. Hinton

A Bradford Book
The MIT Press
Cambridge, Massachusetts
London, England

First MIT Press edition, 1991

© 1990 Elsevier Science Publishers B.V.
Amsterdam, the Netherlands

Reprinted from *Artificial Intelligence: An International Journal*, Volume 46, Numbers 1–2, 1990. The MIT Press has exclusive license to sell this English-language book edition throughout the world.

Printed and bound in the Netherlands.

Library of Congress Cataloging-in-Publication Data

Connectionist symbol processing / edited by G.E. Hinton. — 1st MIT Press ed.
     p.   cm.
    "A Bradford book."
    "Reprinted from Artificial intelligence, an international journal, volume 46, numbers 1–2, 1990"—T.p. verso.
    Includes bibliographical references and index.
    ISBN 0-262-58106-X (pbk.)
    1. Connection machines. 2. Neural networks (Computer science) I. Hinton, Geoffrey E.
QA76.5.C61939 1991
006.3—dc20   90-28969
                                                CIP

CONTENTS

Preface to the Special Issue on Connectionist Symbol Processing

Geoffrey E. Hinton

Department of Computer Science, University of Toronto,
10 Kings College Road, Toronto, Canada M5S 1A4

Connectionist networks are composed of relatively simple, neuron-like processing elements that store all their long-term knowledge in the strengths of the connections between processors. In the last decade there has been considerable progress in developing learning procedures for these networks that allow them to automatically construct their own internal representations [6–8, 10]. The learning procedures are typically applied in networks that map input vectors to output vectors via a few layers of "hidden" units. The network learns to dedicate particular hidden units to particular pieces or aspects of the input vector that are relevant in determining the output. The network generally learns to use distributed representations [5] in which each input vector is represented by activity in many different hidden units, and each hidden unit is involved in representing many different input vectors.

Within the connectionist community, there has been a long and unresolved debate between those who favor localist representations in which each processing element corresponds to a meaningful concept [3, 11] and those who favor distributed representations. The major criticism of distributed representations has been that they cannot handle structured knowledge properly and this criticism has motivated many of the papers in this issue. Another criticism has been the unintelligibility of distributed representations. As soon as there are several hidden layers, it becomes very difficult to say what each hidden unit is representing. Other things being equal, it is clearly desirable to understand *how* a system performing a task such as medical diagnosis arrives at a particular conclusion and to provide this information to the user. A large pattern of activities or set of learned weights is not a convincing explanation. If, however, the large set of weights performs consistently better than an alternative system that can explain its reasoning, it might be better to settle for the system that works best. Under certain conditions, we can be quite justified in trusting a system even if we have very little understanding of how it arrives at a particular conclusion. Using the probably approximately correct framework developed in [12], Baum and Haussler [1] have shown that if a neural network can be

Artificial Intelligence **46** (1990) 1–4

adapted to produce the correct answer for a number of training cases that is large compared with the size of the network, it can be trusted to respond correctly to previously unseen cases provided they are drawn from the same population using the same distribution as the training cases. This remarkable result undermines the common idea that explanations are a *necessary* feature of trustworthy systems.

Unfortunately, the kinds of networks in which the learning procedures have generally been applied lack some properties that AI researchers working within the symbolic paradigm consider to be essential in a general-purpose information processing system [4]. The ability to represent complex hierarchical structures efficiently and to apply structure sensitive operations to these representations seems to be essential. Most connectionist researchers accept this, though they expect that this ability may be implemented in ways that have not been anticipated within the standard symbol-processing tradition. Moreover, they hope that the connectionist approach will be far better at dealing with interactions between levels. Many of the challenging phenomena in language, for example, have to do with cross-over phenomena, in which details at one level have consequences for details at another. Such phenomena are often difficult to capture within the more traditional framework.[1]

Most connectionist researchers are aware of the gulf in representational power between a typical connectionist network and a set of statements in a language such as predicate calculus. They continue to develop the connectionist framework not because they are blind to its current limitations, but because they aim to eventually bridge the gulf by building outwards from a foundation that includes automatic learning procedures and/or massively parallel computation as essential ingredients. Subject to these hard constraints, they aim to progressively improve representational power. The papers in this special issue should be interpreted from that perspective. It is not the standard AI perspective in which the ability to succinctly represent and efficiently apply complex knowledge is viewed as a more important consideration than automatic learning.

There have been important battles in the past between symbolic AI researchers who focussed on representational power and other researchers who nailed their flag to automatic learning procedures. The perceptron battle was a resounding victory for symbolic AI. A single layer of adaptive linear threshold units was just too limited, and no effective learning procedure was then known for multilayer networks. The subsequent speech recognition battle between symbolic AI and those who believed in adaptive hidden Markov models (HMMs) is not as commonly mentioned in AI circles. It turned out that the complex, hand-designed representations and rules in systems like HEARSAY [9] were no match for HMMs even though HMMs, being a variety of finite

---

[1] Elman, Personal communication.

state machine, are clearly very limited in representational power. The outcomes of these two battles suggest that as the learning procedures become more sophisticated the advantage of automatic parameter tuning may more than outweigh the representational inadequacies of the restricted systems that admit such optimization techniques. An optimal member of a class of incorrect models may work much better than a far from optimal member of a class that contains the right model. Clearly, the ultimate goal is efficient learning procedures for representationally powerful systems. The disagreement is about which of these two objectives should be sacrificed in the short term.

Current connectionist learning procedures such as backpropagation are comparable in power to the learning procedure for HMMs. Indeed, one kind of backpropagation network is equivalent to one kind of hidden Markov recognizer [2]. As further theoretical progress is made, we can expect the optimization techniques used for connectionist learning to become much more efficient and, if these techniques can be applied in networks with greater representational abilities, we may see artificial neural networks that can do much more than just classify patterns. But for now, the problem is to devise effective ways of representing complex structures in connectionist networks without sacrificing the ability to learn the representations. My own view is that connectionists are still a very long way from solving this problem, but the papers in this issue suggest some interesting directions to pursue.

REFERENCES

1. E.B. Baum and D. Haussler, What size net gives valid generalization? *Neural Comput.* **1** (1989) 151–160.
2. J.S. Bridle, Alpha-nets: A recurrent "neural" network architecture with a hidden Markov model interpretation, Tech. Rept. SP Research Note 104, Royal Signals and Radar Establishment, UK (1989); also *Speech Communication* (to appear) Special *Neurospeech* Issue.
3. J.A. Feldman, Neural representation of conceptual knowledge, Tech. Rept. TR189, Department of Computer Science, University of Rochester, Rochester, NY (1986).
4. J.A. Fodor and Z.W. Pylyshyn, Connectionism and cognitive architecture: A critical analysis, *Cognition* **28** (1988) 3–71.
5. G.E. Hinton, J.L. McClelland and D.E. Rumelhart, Distributed representations, in: D.E. Rumelhart, J.L. McClelland and the PDP Research Group, eds., *Parallel Distributed Processing: Explorations in the Microstructure of Cognition* **1**: *Foundations* (MIT Press/Bradford Books, Cambridge, MA, 1986) 77–109.
6. G.E. Hinton and T.J. Sejnowski, Learning and relearning in Boltzmann machines, in: D.E. Rumelhart, J.L. McClelland and the PDP Research Group, eds., *Parallel Distributed Processing: Explorations in the Microstructure of Cognition* **1**: *Foundations* (MIT Press/Bradford Books, Cambridge, MA, 1986) 282–317.
7. T. Kohonen, Self-organized formation of topologically correct feature maps, *Biol. Cybern.* **43** (1982) 59–69.
8. J. Moody and C. Darken, Fast learning in networks of locally-tuned processing units, *Neural Comput.* **1** (1989) 281–294.
9. D.R. Reddy, L.D. Erman, R.D. Fennell and R.B. Neely, The hearsay speech understanding system: An example of the recognition process, in: *Proceedings IJCAI-73*, Stanford, CA (1973) 185–194.

10. D.E. Rumelhart, G.E. Hinton and R.J. Williams, Learning internal representations by back-propagating errors, *Nature* **323** (1986) 533–536.
11. L. Shastri, A connectionist approach to knowledge representation and limited interference, *Cognitive Sci.* **12** (1988) 331–392.
12. L.G. Valiant, A theory of the learnable, *Commun. ACM* **27** (1984) 1134–1142.

BoltzCONS: Dynamic Symbol Structures in a Connectionist Network

David S. Touretzky

School of Computer Science, Carnegie Mellon University, Pittsburgh, PA 15213, USA

ABSTRACT

BoltzCONS is a connectionist model that dynamically creates and manipulates composite symbol structures. These structures are implemented using a functional analog of linked lists, but BoltzCONS employs distributed representations and associative retrieval in place of a conventional memory organization. Associative retrieval leads to some interesting properties, e.g., the model can instantaneously access any uniquely-named internal node of a tree. But the point of the work is not to reimplement linked lists in some peculiar new way; it is to show how neural networks can exhibit compositionality and distal access (the ability to reference a complex structure via an abbreviated tag), two properties that distinguish symbol processing from lower-level cognitive functions such as pattern recognition. Unlike certain other neural net models, BoltzCONS represents objects as a collection of superimposed activity patterns rather than as a set of weights. It can therefore create new structured objects dynamically, without reliance on iterative training procedures, without rehearsal of previously-learned patterns, and without resorting to grandmother cells.

1. Introduction

BoltzCONS[1] is a neural network that dynamically creates and manipulates composite symbol structures, such as stacks and trees. In LISP, these structures are represented as linked lists. In BoltzCONS, we investigate what a parallel, distributed version of linked lists might look like. The goal is not to arrive at some peculiar new version of LISP, or to suggest that any representation as impoverished as cons cells might actually exist in the brain. Rather, it is to address the issues of compositionality, cited by Fodor and Pylyshyn [5], and what Newell [14] calls distal access, that help to distinguish symbol processing from lower-level cognitive functions like pattern recognition.

"Compositionality" is the recursive combining of symbol structures into larger, more complex structures. It is an essential feature of language. "Distal access" is the ability to reference a structure in some remote, abbreviated way, such as via a pointer or symbolic tag. Without this ability, concepts would have

---

[1] The name is a play on Boltzmann machines [9] and CONS, the first MIT LISP Machine [6].

Artificial Intelligence **46** (1990) 5–46

0004-3702/90/$03.50 © 1990 — Elsevier Science Publishers B.V. (North-Holland)

to be written out in full detail everywhere they were referenced. Limited resources, and the circularity of semantic representations, preclude this. Compositionality therefore requires distal access. These issues are fundamental ones which connectionist systems must deal with if they are to address the full range of human cognitive phenomena, rather than being limited to pattern recognition and associative memory [25].

It is an open question whether symbolic data structures such as frames, parse trees, and semantic nets have any cognitive validity. Presently, though, it is difficult to imagine a comprehensive cognitive theory without such structures. BoltzCONS is an attempt at reconciling the functional properties of these data structures with the implementational constraints of PDP models [22]. Not all connectionists concede the necessity of such a reconciliation. For example, Rumelhart and McClelland's verb learning model [18] maps input strings to output strings in a way that captures both the rules of English past tense formation and the many classes of exceptions, yet they explicitly deny that the model has symbolic rules or a lexicon. Pinker and Prince [15] refer to this as "eliminative connectionism," because it eliminates the symbolic level as a valid level of description. Symbolic theories, according to the eliminativists, are no more than crude approximations to what really takes place in the brain. They are not a truthful high-level description of the neurological facts in the way that the source listing of a Pascal program can be a truthful description of the machine language version. This anti-symbolic view is controversial, but it has yet to be effectively refuted.

McClelland, Rumelhart, and Hinton [12], in arguing against the validity of symbol structures, suggest that what we perceive introspectively to be symbolic processes are mere epiphenomena of an underlying subsymbolic system. Smolensky [20] characterizes the subsymbolic level as a continuous dynamical system. The evolution of its states through time may be well-approximated by a discrete symbolic theory,[2] but complete accuracy would only be achievable by descriptions phrased as numerical differential equations. He goes on to suggest that what we consciously experience as discrete throughts may be snapshots of the dynamical state vector taken when a number of processing units have remained stable for a few tens of milliseconds.

If the extreme eliminativist view is correct, the long struggle to symbolically axiomatize such things as deep and surface-level linguistic structure, episodic memory, goals, beliefs, and so forth, can never succeed. At the other extreme, one could adopt the "implementationalist" stance [15] that discrete symbolic representations are perfectly adequate, and that connectionist networks are just another implementation technology, not a new theoretical approach. I don't see how either of these views can be correct. My goal is to explore how the properties of a connectionist implementation influence our understanding

---

[2] This admission separates him from the radical eliminativist camp.

of what symbol processing is about.

Despite their support elsewhere for an eliminativist view, Hinton, Rumelhart and McClelland [9, p.78] warn that "it would be wrong to view distributed representations as an *alternative* to representational schemes like semantic networks or production systems . . . ." Instead they suggest that parallel, distributed processing models can implement these schemes in ways that have important emergent properties. These properties would distinguish connectionist networks from other implementations of symbol processing theories. In Pinker and Prince's taxonomy [15], this position is called "revisionist-symbol-processing connectionism." BoltzCONS is an example of this approach.

Many of the differences between the way BoltzCONS and a von Neumann machine process data are due to the use of parallel associative retrieval. Associative retrieval is not unique to connectionist models. One can always duplicate its functionality (though not its efficiency) on a conventional computer using sequential search. And one can sometimes even obtain the same efficiency, by using hash tables. There are, however, certain areas where the decision to use a connectionist architecture, as opposed to some other parallel model not constrained to resemble neurons, uniquely influences the choice of representations and the efficiency of primitive operations. Elucidating those influences is the primary contribution of this paper.

What distinguishes BoltzCONS from many earlier connectionist models is its ability to construct and modify composite symbol structures *dynamically*, by representing them as activity patterns rather than as weights. BoltzCONS is therefore not limited to retrieving one of a set of pre-existing patterns. It can create new ones "on the fly," without extensive training, without rehearsal of previously learned patterns to prevent their decay, and without resorting to grandmother cells.

The control of BoltzCONS is external to the model. While it would not be difficult to build a finite state machine from simulated neurons to issue the necessary control signals for copying activity patterns from one module to another, initiating an associative retrieval, and so on, this would add little of interest. The real issues the model addresses are issues of representation.

Internally, BoltzCONS uses coarse-coded, distributed representations for linked lists that are quite unlike von Neumann machine data structures. It includes a functional equivalent of pointers, but no notion of addresses. Its associative retrieval capabilities support primitives that are not available in conventional computer implementations of linked lists. One modest example is instantaneous access to the internal nodes of a tree, given a node label. But *connectionist* associative retrieval suggests much more powerful operations, such as rapidly accessing parts of a symbol structure based on closest match rather than exact match. This puts BoltzCONS-style models in the realm of truly revisionist symbol processing, pointing the way toward new computational theories that exploit the special strengths of PDP architectures.

2. Direct and Indirect Representations

Both stacks and trees are special cases of directed graphs. LISP offers a direct representation for a highly restricted class of graphs as analogous cons cell structures. By *direct representation* I mean that each element of the graph corresponds to either an atom or a cons, and the basic graph operations of finding the left or right child of a node, and constructing a new nonterminal node given its two children, correspond to the LISP primitives car, cdr, and cons. Only directed graphs whose nodes and links are unlabeled, and whose nonterminal nodes all have out-degree 2, can be represented this way. Stacks and binary trees fall in this category, but general tree structures do not.

Different versions of BoltzCONS also offer natural, direct representations for various kinds of graphs. The version primarily discussed in this article is called BoltzCONS-3. It can directly represent the same set of structures as LISP, although its repertoire of primitive operations is larger. Section 5.3 discusses another version of the model, called BoltzCONS-5, that has a richer direct representation.

In order to manipulate graphs for which no direct representation is available, programmers employ *indirect representations*. For example, one often needs to represent general (not strictly binary) trees. A common technique is to represent each nonterminal node by a linked list of its children, marking the cell that points to the last child by placing something special in its cdr. If nodes are labeled, then the first cell of the linked list holds the node label; the remaining elements point to the children. Interpreted LISP programs are represented as tree structures in precisely this way.

Following this convention, the tree of Fig. 1 would be represented in LISP by the list shown in Fig. 2. Internally, this list is a cons structure as shown in Fig. 3. The slashes in the cdrs of some cells indicate the termination of a cons cell chain. In LISP, the termination marker is the distinguished symbol **nil.**

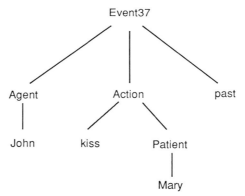

Fig. 1. A tree with labeled nonterminals.

(Event37
(Agent
John)
(Action
kiss
(Patient
Mary))
past)

Fig. 2. Linked list representation of the tree of Fig. 1.

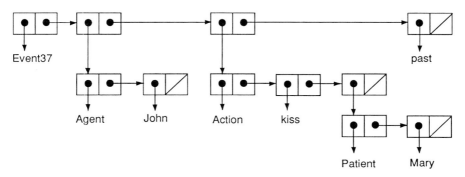

Fig. 3. Cons cell representation of the tree of Fig. 1.

The major disadvantage of this indirect representation for trees is that it limits the ways one can access the nodes. For example, on a von Neumann machine one cannot access the rightmost child of a node in constant time. Another problem is that given a pointer to an arbitrary node in a tree, one can find its descendants but not its parents or siblings, because von Neumann machines cannot follow pointers backward. LISP programmers are of course free to create more complex indirect representations that overcome these limitations, but doing so would increase the cost of representing and modifying the tree, and block the use of LISP's many built-in tree manipulation primitives.

3. Representing Linked Lists on an Associative Retrieval Machine

This and the two following sections give a high-level overview of the BoltzCONS architecture as an abstract associative retrieval machine. Section 6 then presents the connectionist implementation of BoltzCONS, including details of the distributed representation and the wiring patterns of the various modules.

TAG	CAR	CDR
(p	Event37	q)
(q	r	t)
(r	Agent	s)
(s	John	s)
(t	u	z)
(u	Action	v)
(v	kiss	w)
(w	x	w)
(x	Patient	y)
(y	Mary	y)
(z	past	z)

Fig. 4. The linked list structure of Fig. 3 encoded as tuples.

3.1. Encoding cells as tuples

We can represent one cell of a linked list as a three-tuple of symbols of form (**tag, car, cdr**). Tags serve as the targets of what would be called pointers in conventional computers. But tags are symbols, not addresses. In particular, they are not integer indices into a vector of sequential memory locations, as on a von Neumann machine. The memory of our abstract associative retrieval machine has nothing corresponding to discrete sequential addresses.

The symbols in the car and cdr fields of a tuple refer either to the tags of other cells, or to atoms (terminal nodes; objects without composite structure). No two cells may have the same tag. Figure 4 shows one way the linked list structure of Fig. 3 could be encoded as tuples. Other ways are possible, since the assignment of tags is arbitrary. This encoding strategy does not use **nil** to mark the end of chains, due to a property of the distributed memory representation, to be described later.

3.2. An architecture for associative retrieval

A general outline of the BoltzCONS architecture is shown in Fig. 5. Tuple Memory contains the set of tuples that encode the graph structures BoltzCONS creates. Tuple Buffer holds only a single tuple, known as the "current tuple." Sometimes it is empty. The individual components of the current tuple, if there is one, are also represented in the three symbol spaces labeled TAG, CAR, and CDR. These spaces can be clamped (meaning their state is frozen) and used to drive associative retrievals from Tuple Memory via the buffer. For example, if Tuple Memory contains the set of tuples in Fig. 4, then clamping the symbol p into TAG space and performing an associative retrieval would cause (p, **Event37**, q) to appear in the Tuple Buffer. Simultaneously, **Event37** and q would appear in the CAR and CDR spaces, respectively. (The actual simulation uses just the symbols A through Y. I use symbols like John and Event37 here to distinguish atoms from tags, and to suggest that atoms might

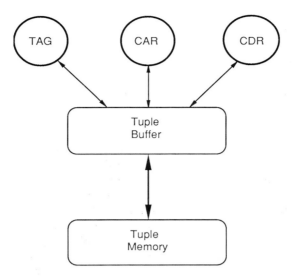

Fig. 5. The BoltzCONS architecture.

have semantic content, even though BoltzCONS itself does not rely on this content.)

3.3. Pointer traversal

Pointer traversal by associative retrieval is straightforward. We assume there is a current tuple in the Tuple Buffer, with its components represented in TAG, CAR, and CDR spaces. LISP's car function is implemented by copying the symbol currently in CAR space into TAG space, clamping TAG space, clearing the CAR and CDR spaces and the Tuple Buffer, and performing an associative retrieval. This fetches the triple with the specified TAG value into the Tuple Buffer; simultaneously, its second and third components are fetched into CAR and CDR space, respectively.

At this point it will be convenient to introduce a notation for sequences of these operations. The retrieval just described consists of two steps in this notation:

        GetCAR =
          {$CAR→TAG;
          $Retrieve.by.TAG}

The first step of the GetCAR sequence is to issue a control signal causing the symbol in CAR space to be copied into TAG space. This destroys the previous contents of TAG space. The second step issues a control signal that initiates an associative retrieval, with TAG space providing the retrieval cue. The units in

TAG space are clamped so they cannot change during the retrieval. The BoltzCONS implementation of LISP's cdr function is similar:

```
GetCDR =
  {$CDR → TAG;
   $Retrieve.by.TAG}
```

To use pointer traversal to go from the **Event37** node of Fig. 1, represented by the tuple (p, **Event37**, q), to the Action node, represented by (u, **Action**, v), a sequence of two cdrs followed by a car is required. A suitable composition of the GetCAR and GetCDR procedures is easily constructed, since each procedure leaves its result in the Tuple Buffer and associated symbol spaces, where it may serve as the argument to the next procedure.

With associative retrieval one is not limited to following pointers in the forward direction. We can go from the **Agent** node of Fig. 1, represented by the tuple (r, **Agent**, s), to its parent node, by performing an un-car operation. The first step is to copy the symbol r from TAG space to CAR space. An associative retrieval with CAR space clamped then yields the tuple (q, r, t). We have followed a pointer backward from the cons cell r to the cons cell q. Next an un-cdr is performed. The symbol q is copied from TAG space and clamped into CDR space, and after a second associative retrieval, (p, **Event37**, q) appears in the Tuple Buffer.

```
un-CAR =
  {$TAG → CAR;
   $Retrieve.by.CAR}

un-CDR =
  {$TAG → CDR;
   $Retrieve.by.CDR}
```

These little procedures are in some ways analogous to Ullman's notion of visual routines [30]. They are short, simple routines, with direct hardware implementations, that form the primitives from which more complex processing operations are built.

3.4. Detecting atoms and list termination

There are several ways one might distinguish terminals from nonterminals (or atoms from cells). One way is to *a priori* divide the set of symbols into those that may be used as tags for composite objects and those that may not. The latter class may then be used to refer to atoms. A minor drawback to implementing this approach is that the model must somehow be able to tell which class each symbol is in.

A second approach is to note that a symbol associated with an atom is not the tag of any composite object, so it will never appear as the first component of any tuple. An associative retrieval with that symbol clamped into TAG space will fail, i.e., whatever it retrieves will not match the specified tag. Thus the model can determine whether a symbol refers to a composite object by attempting one associative retrieval. The drawback to this method is that extra associative retrivals waste time, and performing one will destroy the state of the unclamped symbol spaces. If the retrieval fails, their state may need to be restored before the next step of the computation can proceed.

A third approach is to represent atoms as tuples with a special marker in all but the first field, e.g., the symbol John could be represented by the tuple (**John**, ∗, ∗). The model can simply check for the presence of the ∗ marker after a tuple is retrieved to determine whether it represents an atom. But this method would not work well in BoltzCONS due to the model's coarse-coded, distributed memory representation. In a phenomenon called local blurring, when a distinguished symbol appears in the same position in many tuples, it reduces the accuracy of the distributed memory. This is one of the ways in which the connectionist implementation influences the design of the model.

A fourth approach represents atoms as tuples whose car and cdr fields contain the atom's own tag. This eliminates the local blurring problem, since each atom will have unique car and cdr values. In this scheme, John would be coded as (**John**, **John**, **John**). It is easy to detect when a tuple represents an atom: the model simply compares the tag, car, and cdr fields to see if they are identical.

In applying BoltzCONS to various problems, both the first and fourth methods for distinguishing atoms have been used.

A related concern is the method of marking termination of linked lists. Although **nil** could be used as a terminator, following the LISP convention, it would have to appear many times in highly-branched structures, which raises the probability of local blurring interfering with the accuracy of retrieval. An alternative is to mark the last cell in a chain by having its cdr point to itself, as in Fig. 4. The model can easily detect a cell marked this way because its tag and cdr components are equal. If this convention is used for list termination, then one of the other three conventions must be used to distinguish atoms from composite objects. In the example in Fig. 3, we assume that the symbol space has been divided *a priori* into symbols that denote atoms and symbols that may be used as tags for cells.

3.5. Creating new structure

We create new list cells by adding tuples to Tuple Memory. The first step in adding a tuple is to clamp values into the TAG, CAR, and CDR spaces. These are then assembled into a new tuple in the Tuple Buffer. Any previous value in the Tuple Buffer is discarded. Finally, the pattern in the Tuple Buffer is added to the contents of Tuple Memory.

In the procedure MakeCell below, certain operations can proceed in parallel because they involve independent modules or transmission paths. These operations appear on the same line, separated by ampersands, to highlight the potential parallelism. The parameters x and y represent inputs from external symbol spaces that are not part of the BoltzCONS model, but are connected to it in the context of some larger information processing architecture. An example of such an architecture is given in [23].

```
MakeCell(x, y) =
    {$x → CAR  &  $y → CDR  &  $NewTag → TAG;
    $Assemble.tuple.in.buffer;
    $Store.tuple}
```

The problems of avoiding collisions when choosing tags for new tuples, and reclaiming tags no longer in use (garbage collection), will be addressed in Section 7.

3.6. Modifying structures

LISP destructively modifies cells by storing new pointers into the car or cdr half with the rplaca and rplacd operations, respectively. In BoltzCONS the equivalent effect can be achieved by deleting the tuple and storing another with the modified components. For example, to change the agent of Fig. 1 from John to Bill, the tuple (s, **John,** s) would be called into the Tuple Buffer and then deleted from Tuple Memory. Then the triple (s, **Bill,** s) would be assembled in the buffer and stored in the memory. Due to the distributed representations BoltzCONS uses for its Tuple Memory, the order of these operations is important: the delete operation should take place before the store. The procedures below assume that the tuple to be modified is the one currently represented in the Tuple Buffer, with its components represented in the TAG, CAR, and CDR spaces.

```
ReplaceCAR(x) =
    {$Delete.tuple.from.memory  &  $x → CAR;
    $Assemble.tuple.in.buffer;
    $Store.tuple}

ReplaceCDR(x) =
    {$Delete.tuple.from.memory  &  $x → CDR;
    $Assemble.tuple.in.buffer;
    $Store.tuple}
```

The delete operation in the above procedures can be done in parallel with the transfer of a new symbol into CAR or CDR space, because deletion is performed by the Tuple Buffer and only affects the state of Tuple Memory.

4. Associative Stacks

This and the following section present associative versions of two familiar recursive data structures: stacks and trees.[3] In both cases the use of associative retrieval leads to slightly different algorithms with different performance characteristics than LISP on von Neumann machines.

Stacks may be represented as linked lists. The top of the stack resides in the Tuple Buffer, and also in the TAG, CAR, and CDR spaces. The stack is popped by taking its cdr, i.e., deleting the tuple currently in the Tuple Buffer from Tuple Memory, copying the symbol in CDR space to TAG space, and doing an associative retrieval with TAG space clamped. The new top of the stack then appears in the Tuple Buffer. An empty stack may be denoted by a tuple with a special "top of stack" marker as its car component. This tuple will always be the last one in the chain. The procedures below do not check for empty stack or stack full conditions.

```
StackPush(x) =
    {$TAG→CDR & $x→CAR;
     $NewTag→TAG;
     $Assemble.tuple.in.buffer;
     $Store.tuple}

StackPop =
    {$Delete.tuple.from.memory & $CDR→TAG;
     $Retrieve.by.TAG}
```

Notice that a **NewTag** operation is used by the stack push procedure to generate a new tag for the cons that is about to become the top of the stack. One way to avoid the problem of generating new tags dynamically when building stacks is to construct a static linked list that is as long as the maximum desired stack depth. The cell that is the top of the stack is maintained in the Tuple Buffer, as before. (The initial contents of the Tuple Buffer will be the *last* cell of the chain.) To push a new object onto this fixed stack, we use associative retrieval to find the cell that points to the current one, make it current, and store the new object into its car:

```
FixedStackPush(x) =
    {un-CDR;
     ReplaceCAR(x)}

FixedStackPop =
    {GetCDR}
```

---

[3] A recursive data structure is one whose instances are of the same type as their components. Trees are recursive because their branches are trees. Stacks are recursive because their tails are stacks.

Associative retrieval permits another interesting stack operation: associative stack pop. This operation pops the stack back to the point where a specified element is the top, in constant time. If the element appears on the stack more than once, an instance can be picked at random. The items above the one being sought are not deleted, so one can find the top of the stack again by repeatedly un-popping it until the un-pop operation fails. In order to detect when a retrieval has failed, we introduce a "verify" operation to confirm that the retrieval has found a tuple whose specified component exactly matches the cue supplied.

```
AssocPop(x) =
  {$x → CAR;
   $Retrieve.by.CAR}

UnPop( ) =
  {un-CDR}

FindStackTop =
  {loop
     unPop;
     $Verify.CDR.retrieval;
     if $Retrieval.failed        — unpopped once too many;
       then exit-loop            — TAG and CAR hold garbage
     endloop;
     GetCDR}                     — CDR still valid; undo the failed UnPop
```

This technique for returning to the top of the stack won't work for fixed stacks because cells aren't deleted when the stack is popped; the current top of stack must be marked somehow before an associative stack pop in order to permit it to be found again. Any number of marking conventions may be employed. For example, cells above the current top of the stack may have their car set equal to their tag, so the sequential unpop operation can tell when it has gone too far.

5. Associative Trees

In describing operations on tree structures, one must be careful to distinguish between trees with direct representations (i.e., binary trees whose internal nodes are unlabeled), and more general sorts of trees. We will consider each type in turn.

5.1. Traversing binary trees

Associative retrieval allows one to nondestructively traverse binary trees of

unbounded depth without a control stack. LISP cannot do this.[4] The procedures shown below are tail-recursive, and hence can be implemented by a finite
state machine. The top level procedure, Traverse, traverses a binary tree and
outputs the symbols at the terminal nodes in left-to-right order. (A neural
network can "output" a symbol by transmitting its activity pattern to some
external module to which the network is connected.)

The Traverse procedure assumes that the root of the tree is initially the
current tuple, and that atoms are represented by conses whose cdrs point to
themselves. The details of how the root is remembered so the algorithm knows
when to exit are omitted; a simple marking convention or an auxiliary register
may be used.

```
Traverse =
  {$Remember.root;
   DownCAR}

DownCAR =
  {if $TAG.neq.CDR then   — at a nonterminal node
     GetCAR;
     DownCAR
   else                   — at a terminal node
     $Transmit.CAR;
     Backup
   endif}

DownCDR =
  {if $TAG.neq.CDR then   — at a nonterminal node
     GetCDR;
     DownCAR
   else                   — at a terminal node
     $Transmit.CAR;
     Backup
   endif}

Backup =
  {un-CAR;
   $Verify.CAR.retrieval;
   if $Retrieval.succeeded then   — was parent's car
     DownCDR
   else                           — wasn't parent's car, so
```

---

[4] We assume one-way pointers, as in normal LISP lists. If destructive operations are allowed,
then LISP can traverse binary trees without a control stack; this is the basis of certain sophisticated
garbage collection algorithms.

```
$CAR→CDR;                    — must be parent's cdr
$Retrieve.by.CDR;
if $TAG.eql.root then        — quit if parent is root
   exit
else                         — continue backing up
   Backup
endif
endif}
```

One subtlety in the above algorithm is the method of backing up from a terminal node. The algorithm cannot know whether the current cell is the left or right child of its parent. If it is the left child, its tag will appear as the second element of its parent's tuple; if a right child its tag will appear as the third element. Backing up is therefore a two-step operation. The Backup procedure begins by assuming the current cell is a left child. It performs an un-car operation, and then verifies that the retrieval succeeded. If so, the assumption was correct, and the algorithm can now proceed to examine the cdr of the parent cell. If the retrieval failed, the terminal node must have been a right child rather than a left child. The contents of TAG and CDR spaces are now invalid, but CAR space, which was clamped during the retrieval, still holds the tag of the child. After copying the contents of CAR space into CDR space, a new retrieval can be run with CDR space clamped to find the correct parent.

Whenever it backs up from a node that is a right child, the algorithm performs the backup procedure again. It will continue doing so until it either backs up from a node that is a left child, or it backs up to the root from a right child. In the latter case the entire tree has been visited, so the algorithm terminates.

Figure 6 shows a sample binary tree, and Fig. 7 gives its representation as a set of triples. A complete list of steps the traversal algorithm goes through when applied to this tree is shown in Table 1.

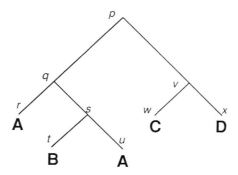

Fig. 6. A binary tree. Tags used for the tuple encoding are shown in italics.

```
                 TAG        CAR        CDR

            (    p          q          v     )
            (    q          r          s     )
            (    r          A          r     )
            (    s          t          u     )
            (    t          B          t     )
            (    u          A          u     )
            (    v          w          x     )
            (    w          C          w     )
            (    x          D          x     )
```

Fig. 7. The encoding of Fig. 6 as a set of triples.

Table 1
Steps in traversing the tree of Fig. 6.

Step	Retrieval cue	Retrieved tuple	Action or comment
Traverse		(p, q, v)	*Remember root is* p.
DownCAR	$(q, \_, \_)$	(q, r, s)	
DownCAR	$(r, \_, \_)$	(r, A, r)	transmit "A"
Backup	$(\_, r, \_)$	(q, r, s)	
DownCDR	$(s, \_, \_)$	(s, t, u)	
DownCAR	$(t, \_, \_)$	(t, B, t)	transmit "B"
Backup	$(\_, t, \_)$	(s, t, u)	
DownCDR	$(u, \_, \_)$	(u, A, u)	transmit "A"
Backup	$(\_, u, \_)$	$\ldots$	*Associative retrieval failed.*
	$(\_, \_, u)$	(s, t, u)	
Backup	$(\_, s, \_)$	$\ldots$	*Associative retrieval failed.*
	$(\_, \_, s)$	(q, r, s)	
Backup	$(\_, q, \_)$	(p, q, v)	
DownCDR	$(v, \_, \_)$	(v, w, x)	
DownCAR	$(w, \_, \_)$	(w, C, w)	transmit "C"
Backup	$(\_, w, \_)$	(v, w, x)	
DownCDR	$(x, \_, \_)$	(x, D, x)	transmit "D"
Backup	$(\_, x, \_)$	$\ldots$	*Associative retrieval failed.*
	$(\_, \_, x)$	(v, w, x)	
Backup	$(\_, v, \_)$	$\ldots$	*Associative retrieval failed.*
	$(\_, \_, v)$	(p, q, v)	*At root, so done.*

5.2. General tree manipulation

General trees, in which interior nodes are labeled and may have any number of descendants, must be represented indirectly if one is using linked lists. As mentioned previously, interpreted LISP programs are trees of this form. An associative retrieval machine can manipulate general trees the same way LISP does. For example, imagine that the parse tree of Fig. 8 is represented as a linked list. Each node of the tree is a cons cell chain; the car of the first cell holds the node label, and the remaining cells hold the tags of the node's

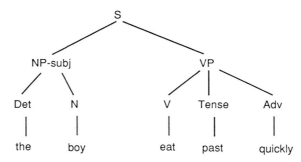

Fig. 8. Parse tree for "The boy ate quickly."

children. We assume that terminal nodes are represented as chains with no
children, i.e., in parenthesis notation the tree would be written:

```
(Sent
  (Subject-NP
    (Det (the))
    (N (boy)))
  (VP
    (Verb (eat))
    (Tense (past))
    (Adv (quickly))))
```

The following procedure locates a particular child of a parent node, given
the child's label as input. For example, if the current node were VP, Find
NamedChild("Tense") would make the second child of the VP node be the
current node. We assume that the tuple representing the parent node (i.e., the
tuple for the head cell in the parent node's cons cell chain) resides in the Tuple
Buffer when the procedure is invoked.

```
FindNamedChild(x) =
  {loop
    GetCDR;              — find next child
    GetCAR;              — fetch child's label
    if $CAR.eql.x then   — if this is the child we want
      exitloop           — then exit
    else
      un-CAR;            — else back up to the parent chain
    endif                — and iterate to check next child
  endloop}
```

If node labels are unique, associative retrieval eliminates the need to search
a tree sequentially. For example, we can access any node of Fig. 8 in constant

time with the following procedure:

```
FindNamedNode(x) =
    {$x→CAR;
     $Retrieve.by.CAR}
```

The next procedure finds the parent of the current node by using associative retrieval to follow pointers backward. It assumes that the model is able to distinguish between symbols that are used as atoms and symbols that are used as tags for composite objects. Only symbols denoting atoms can serve as node labels.

```
FindParent =
    {un-CAR;                          — back up to parent's chain
     loop
         un-CDR;                      — back up to previous child
         if $CAR.is.atomic.then       — here's the parent's node label
             exitloop
     endloop}
```

5.3. A richer representation for general trees

We now consider a richer representation for trees that allows access to a node's parent or any of its siblings or descendants with a single associative retrieval. Each node will be a five-tuple:

$$(\textbf{tag, label, parent, rsib, lchild})\,.$$

The tag field, as before, serves as a unique id for the tuple. The label field contains the node's label. A tree might have several nodes with the same label, but they would have different tags. The parent field holds the tag of the parent of this node. The rsib field holds the tag of the node that is the right sibling of this node. (If a node is a rightmost child, its rsib field will contain the parent's tag.) The lchild field holds the tag of the node's leftmost child, or the node's own tag if it has no children. Figure 9 shows part of a tree represented this way, and Fig. 10 shows the architecture of a hypothetical BoltzCONS network called BoltzCONS-5 for supporting this richer tree representation.

Using this representation, the procedures for finding a node's parent, right sibling, and leftmost child are straightforward associative retrievals similar to the ones we've seen before. Certain other retrievals are a little more complex. To find a node's left sibling, we look for a tuple with the same parent as the current node, and the current node's tag in its rsib field. This search combines two cues into a single associative retrieval by clamping two symbol spaces simultaneously:

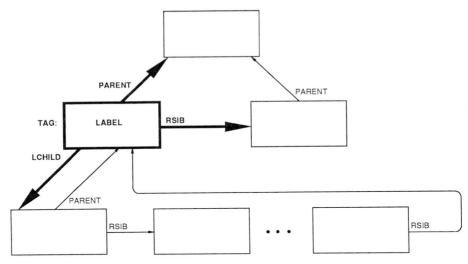

Fig. 9. A richer representation for tree structures.

GetLeftMostSib =
   {$TAG→RSIB;
    $Retrieve.by.PARENT.&.RSIB}

To find a node's rightmost child we can exploit the fact that sibling chains terminate by pointing back to the parent node. We simply search for a tuple

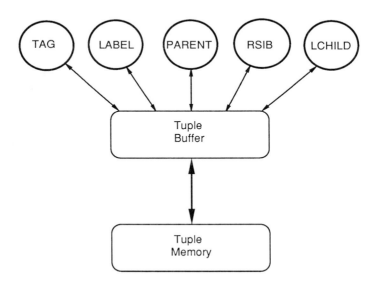

Fig. 10. A version of BoltzCONS that could support richer tree representations.

with this node's tag in both the parent and rsib fields:

```
GetRightMostChild =
    {$TAG→PARENT & $TAG→RSIB;
    $Retrieve.by.PARENT.&.RSIB}
```

To locate an arbitrary named child of the current node, we search for the tuple with this node as parent and the specified label; there is no problem if other nodes in the tree have the same label as long as they have a different parent.

```
GetNamedChild(x) =
    {$TAG→PARENT & $x→LABEL;
    $Retrieve.by.PARENT.&.LABEL}
```

It should be clear from these examples that associative retrieval models are not limited to reproducing the functionality of LISP cons cells. Any computational architecture based on pointers and structured objects is potentially implementable this way.

6. Connectionist Implementation

The low-level organization of BoltzCONS is similar to that of DCPS, Touretzky and Hinton's distributed connectionist production system [24, 28, 29]. It is constructed from essentially the same modules, hooked together in a different way. This section gives an overview of the model's wiring and principles of operation.

6.1. Distributed memory representation

The organization of Tuple Memory is similar to the Working Memory of DCPS. I will describe the simplest version of BoltzCONS with only three symbol spaces. Extension to more elaborate versions is straightforward.

Starting with a 25-symbol alphabet, there are $25^3 = 15,625$ triples that might appear in the tuple memory. We assume that the memory is very sparse, so that only a small fraction of these triples, typically one half to two dozen, will be present at any one time. Since the memory is extremely sparse, coarse coding (explained below) can be used to reduce the number of units required while adding a measure of redundancy and fault tolerance to the representation [10, 17].

Tuple Memory consists of 2000 units, each of which has a randomly-generated 6×3 receptive field table such as the one shown in Fig. 11. The table has three columns because we are encoding triples. The choice of six rows is not critical; it yields good performance (as measured by memory capacity, noise immunity, and amount of real memory required by the simulator), but five or seven rows would also work.

C	A	B
F	E	D
M	H	J
Q	K	M
S	T	P
W	Y	R

Fig. 11. An example of a randomly-generated receptive field table for a Tuple Memory unit. The receptive field of the unit is determined by the cross product of the three columns.

The receptive field of a unit is the set of triples generated by the cross-product of the three columns of its receptive field table. A receptive field contains $6 \times 6 \times 6 = 216$ triples, so each receptor covers approximately 1.4% of the space of all possible triples. Receptors are therefore "coarsely tuned"; hence the term "coarse coding." This is also an example of a distributed representation, because triples average $(6/25)^3 \times 2000 = 27.648$ receptors each. Activity in any one receptor does not constitute a representation of any particular triple. Only a collective pattern of activity across a set of receptors corresponds to a triple.

To store a triple in Tuple Memory one turns on all the units in whose receptive field it falls. If we stored the triple (F, A, B), for example, we would turn on the unit depicted in Fig. 11 because it has an F in column 1, an A in column 2, and a B in column 3. We would also turn on roughly 27 other units that also meet these specifications. If we then stored (F, C, D), its activity pattern, which also contains about 28 units, would be superimposed (via inclusive-or) on top of the previous pattern. The result is shown in Fig. 12, in which 55 of the 2000 units are active.

An external observer can tell whether a triple is present by checking the percentage of its receptors that are active. If the percentage is large enough, e.g., at least 75%, the triple may be deemed to be present. BoltzCONS does not actually compute these percentages; the relative activation strengths of triples determine which ones will be found when an associative retrieval is performed. However, for debugging purposes it can be useful to display the percentages of the most highly activated triples. Table 2 provides this information for the case where (F, A, B) and (F, C, D) have just been stored. There is a clear gap between present and absent triples; the strongest triple not actually present has only 40% activation. As the memory fills up, this gap gradually narrows.

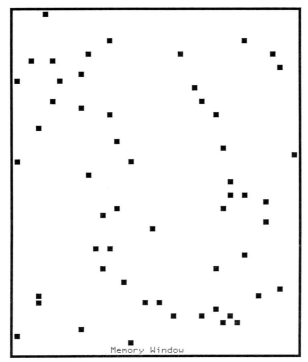

Fig. 12. The state of Tuple Memory after the triples (F, A, B) and (F, C, D) have both been stored. There are 55 units active out of 2000. There is no significance to the positions of these units.

Table 2
The first dozen triples with the strongest representations when (F, A, B) and (F, C, D) have been stored in memory

Triple	Levels of triple activation		
	Percent active	Active receptors	Total receptors
(F, A, B)	100%	28	/28
(F, C, D)	100%	28	/28
(F, A, D)	40%	11	/27
(F, B, D)	38%	10	/26
(F, A, X)	37%	11	/29
(S, A, B)	37%	10	/27
(F, Q, D)	37%	10	/27
(F, C, N)	37%	10	/27
(F, C, B)	37%	10	/27
(F, C, M)	35%	10	/28
(F, T, D)	35%	10	/28
(N, C, D)	34%	10	/29

Figure 13 is a graph of the activation levels of all 15,625 triples after (F, A, B) and (F, C, D) have been stored. The dots in this figure are associated with triples, not with Tuple Memory units. Triple (A, A, A) is in the upper left-hand corner, and (Y, Y, Y) in the lower right. The size of a dot indicates the number of active Tuple Memory units whose receptive field includes that triple. The dark horizontal band in the top quarter of the figure, called the "F-band," is an artifact of our storing two triples that both begin with F. The two darkest spots in this band correspond to (F, A, B) and (F, C, D). A moderate thresholding operator applied to this figure produces Fig. 14, where the triples with the highest activity levels stand out more clearly.

The 216 triples in a unit's receptive field are not chosen independently. They are generated by a Cartesian product of three sets, thereby forming a Cartesian subspace of the entire symbol space. Similar triples will therefore tend to share receptors. This is important for associative retrieval (in particular, it allows the TAG, CAR and CDR spaces to extract the components of a triple), but it can also lead to interference effects if the memory fills up, or if many similar triples are stored. Table 3 shows the expected number of receptors two triples share as a function of the number of components they have in common, c. The

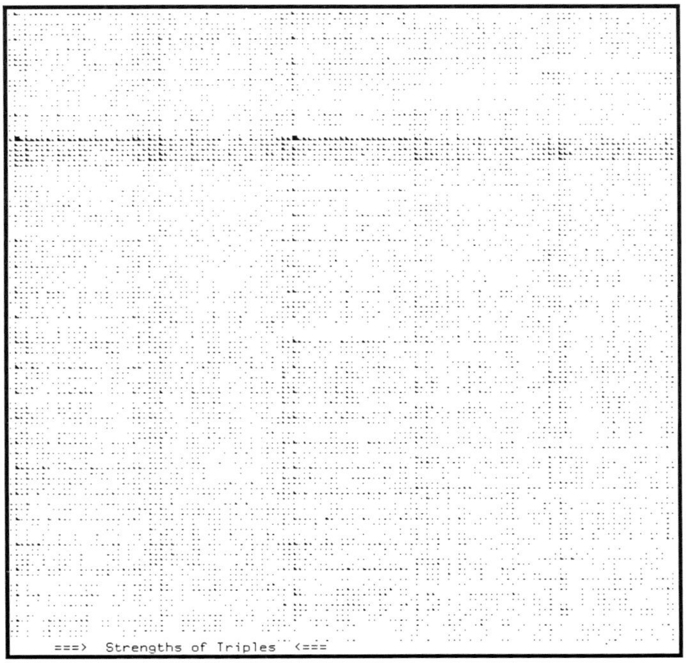

Fig. 13. The levels of support for all 15,625 triples after (F, A, B) and (F, C, D) have been stored in the Tuple Memory, represented by the 55 active units in Fig. 12.

Fig. 14. A moderately thresholded version of Fig. 13, where the (F, A, B) and (F, C, D) spots stand out more clearly.

expected fraction of overlap between receptors of two triples is $(\frac{5}{24})^{3-c}$; the number of shared receptors is therefore $(\frac{5}{24})^{(3-c)} \times (\frac{6}{25})^3 \times 2000$.

When several very similar triples are stored, a phenomenon called "local blurring" results. This is illustrated in Fig. 15. The four triples (F, A, A), (F, A, B), (F, A, C), and (F, A, D) have all been stored in Tuple Memory. Other triples in the same local neighborhood of Cartesian product space, such as (F, A, E), have a moderately high number of active receptors due to the overlapping representation. This makes it difficult to decide whether they are

Table 3
Degree of overlap between similar triples

Numer of symbols in common	Expected number of shared receptors	Expected percent of overlap
0	0.25	0.9%
1	1.20	4.3%
2	5.76	20.8%
3	27.65	100.0%

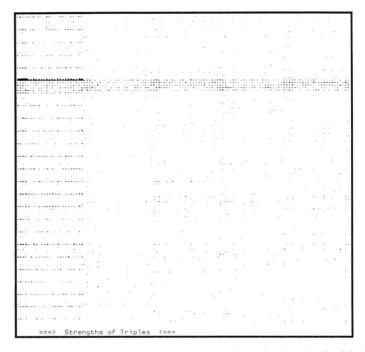

Fig. 15. An illustration of local blurring from storing four closely-related triples: (F, A, A), (F, A, B), (F, A, C), and (F, A, D). Other, similar triples receive a high degree of support, as shown by the dark (F, A, x) line at the beginning of the F-band and the weaker (x, A, y) lines in other bands. A light thresholding operator has been applied to enhance the image.

really present in the memory or not. But it is still clear that unrelated triples, such as (G, K, Q), are absent.

Two other interesting properties of the memory are worth mentioning. First, it has no fixed capacity; it does not "fill up" in the conventional sense. Rather, as more items are added, the gap between present and absent triples narrows. The result is a gradual decrease in retrieval accuracy, as the network finds it increasingly difficult to distinguish triples that were actually stored from those that emerged from overlaps with other triples. This sort of smooth performance degradation, rather than sudden failure when a limit is exceeded, is characteristic of connectionist models.

The second interesting property is the gradual decay of stored triples after a long sequence of deletions of other triples. The more closely related the deleted triples are to the stored one, the faster the fade out effect. This phenomenon is again a consequence of the overlapping representations that form a coarse-coded memory. One way to counteract the decay effect is to recall a triple before it completely fades away. We can then use the TAG,

CAR, and CDR spaces to regenerate the complete pattern for the triple in the Tuple Buffer, and store the completed pattern back into Tuple Memory.

A recent study of the mathematics of this coarse coded symbol representation indicates that it scales well and permits smooth tradeoffs among memory capacity (the number of items simultaneously representable), alphabet size, and accuracy of retrieval [17].

6.2. The Tuple Buffer

The Tuple Buffer serves two distinct purposes. It is used to associatively retrieve individual tuples from the Tuple Memory, given a cue from one of the TAG, CAR, or CDR spaces. It is also used to assemble new tuples by combining TAG, CAR, and CDR inputs. This section concentrates on just retrieval.

During retrievals, the Tuple Buffer acts as a *pullout network* that extracts one member from a collection of superimposed patterns, given some partial specification of the pattern desired. The term "pullout network" is due to Michael Mozer, who invented the concept independently at the same time as I was implementing it under the name "clause space" in DCPS. Mozer proposed the pullout network as a means for a perceptual system to attend to one object in a complex scene [13]. In DCPS, the two clause spaces extract elements from working memory such that together the two elements match the left-hand side of one production rule, and also satisfy a variable binding constraint common to all rules.

The three components of a pullout network as used in DCPS and BoltzCONS are: a one-one excitatory mapping between the units in some distributed memory and the units of the pullout network; a competitive or lateral inhibition mechanism that limits the total amount of activity in the pullout network to roughly enough to represent a single item; and finally, a set of excitatory biases from higher-level spaces that determine which item the network should pull out from memory. These components are illustrated in Fig. 16.

The Tuple Buffer of BoltzCONS consists of 2000 units, with one-one excitatory connections from the 2000 Tuple Memory units. The Tuple Buffer units have very high thresholds, counterbalanced by strong positive weights from Tuple Memory. The result is that no matter how much excitation a Tuple Buffer unit receives from the symbol spaces, it will not become active unless its corresponding Tuple Memory unit is also active. This assures that the Tuple Buffer can only retrieve existing tuples; it cannot hallucinate nonexistent ones. Top-down excitatory biases are supplied by units in the TAG, CAR, or CDR spaces, depending on which cue we are using for the retrieval.

The regulatory unit in Fig. 16 provides the lateral inhibition required by the pullout network. It receives excitatory inputs from all Tuple Buffer units; its

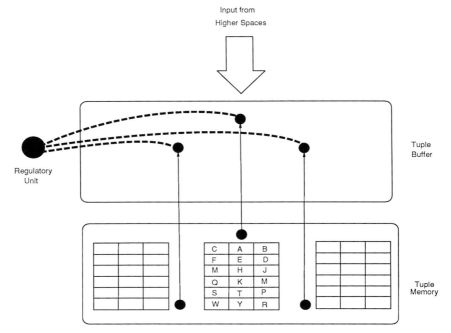

Fig. 16. The structure of the Tuple Buffer acting as a pullout network.

graded output is then fed back to the Tuple Buffer units via inhibitory connections. The amount of inhibition is set so that only about 28 units can remain active in the Tuple Buffer, which is just enough to represent one tuple. Exactly which tuple is chosen depends on the top-down biases the Tuple buffer receives from the symbol spaces.

The use of a regulatory unit with $2N$ asymmetric connections (N excitatory inputs and N inhibitory outputs, where N is the size of the Tuple Buffer) and a graded rather than binary response would appear to violate the definition of a Boltzmann machine. However, this structure is shown in [29] to be equivalent to a pure Boltzmann machine in which the regulatory unit is replaced by $\frac{1}{2} N^2$ bidirectional inhibitory links between pairs of Tuple Buffer units. The advantage of using a regulatory unit is that it implements lateral inhibition more efficiently. Similar regulatory functions have been ascribed to interneurons in real nervous systems.

6.3. Symbol spaces

The TAG, CAR, and CDR spaces are called symbol spaces because their global activity patterns represent individual symbols rather than tuples of symbols. Each space is organized as a coarse-coded, distributed winner-take-all network containing 25 cliques, one for each of the 25 symbols in the alphabet. See Feldman and Ballard [4] for a description of winner-take-all networks. Each clique has 72 units that vote for its symbol. Each unit, being coarse-coded, votes for three symbols. Thus, the symbol space contains $\frac{1}{3}(25 \times 72) = 600$ units.

The units within a clique support each other via excitatory connections, while units in rival cliques compete with each other via inhibitory connections, as shown in Fig. 17. (If two units have at least one symbol in common, the connection is excitatory.) The stable states of a symbol space are those where all the units in one clique are active, and all the units in rival cliques are inactive. Each of these stable states constitutes a global energy minimum when the symbol space is considered in isolation. In actuality, connections from units in other spaces bias the symbol space units so that one of the 25 stable states will become a deeper energy minimum than any of the others.

Just as the Tuple Buffer is used both for retrieving tuples and for creating new ones, the symbol spaces also play multiple roles. When a symbol space is clamped, its units are prevented from changing state, but those that are active supply top-down input to Tuple Buffer units via weighted connections between the two spaces. For example, suppose the symbol F is clamped into TAG space. During an associative retrieval, TAG units will supply excitatory inputs to those Tuple Buffer units having F in the first column of their receptive field tables. Each active Tuple Memory unit tries to turn on its corresponding Tuple Buffer unit, but lateral inhibition limits the number of active Tuple Buffer units to about 28. The bias supplied by the active TAG units will cause the Tuple Buffer to select only the active units from Tuple Memory whose receptive field tables contain F in the first column. Thus, given the retrieval cue $(F, \_, \_)$, the Tuple Buffer selects some tuple beginning with F.

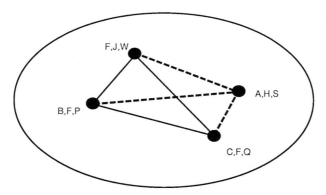

Fig. 17. Four nodes out of the 600 that make up a symbol space. Three of the nodes excite each other because they include F in their receptive field; they inhibit the fourth node, which does not vote for F. (Inhibitory connections are drawn as dashed lines.)

The CAR and CDR spaces are also connected to the Tuple Buffer. Suppose the tuple being retrieved from memory is (F, A, B). The units active in the Tuple Buffer will have an A in the second column of their receptive field table, and a B in the third column. Since the CAR and CDR spaces are not clamped, they are free to change state during the retrieval, and they are influenced by the pattern emerging in the Tuple Buffer. This will eventually cause the A clique to win the competition in CAR space. Its stable state has a deeper energy minimum than the other letters, due to the bias supplied by the pattern in the Tuple Buffer. Similarly, the B clique will win in CDR space.

The connections between symbol spaces and the Tuple Buffer are bidirectional, which means that even the unclamped symbol spaces will influence the behavior of Tuple Buffer units. During a retrieval with the cue $(F, \_, \_)$, if there are several items stored in memory, there will probably be more than just 28 active units that happen to have an F in their receptive field table, even if only one stored triple begins with F. The collective action of the CAR and CDR spaces helps the Tuple Buffer to home in on the roughly 28 active units that collectively code for a single tuple, such as (F, A, B), that all 28 units support.

6.4. Creating and deleting tuples

New tuples are created by clearing the Tuple Buffer and clamping the component symbols into their respective symbol spaces. The units in each symbol space will excite those Tuple Buffer units to which they have connections. The thresholds of the Tuple Buffer units can be manipulated (by shutting off input from Tuple Memory and supplying a nonspecific bias signal to all units in the buffer) so that only those tuple buffer units that receive excitation from the units in all three symbol spaces will become active. In effect, when creating a new tuple the buffer computes the intersection of the activation it receives from the TAG, CAR, and CDR units, as shown in Fig. 18.

After a new activity pattern has been established in the Tuple Buffer, it is copied into the Tuple Memory by the mechanism shown in the bottom half of Fig. 18. A set of gated one-one connections between the buffer and the memory allow each active Tuple Buffer unit to turn on its corresponding Tuple Memory unit. (Gating is implemented by multiplicative connections, drawn as triangles in Fig. 18.) The gate keeps the connection inactive most of the time, except when a store signal issued. At that time the activity pattern in the Tuple Buffer is transmitted to the Tuple Memory, where it is superimposed onto (that is, inclusive-ored with) any existing pattern there.

Multiplicative connections are not part of the normal Boltzmann machine model, although they are available in the "higher-order" Boltzmann machines defined by Sejnowski [19]. We need not be concerned with that here, however, because during an annealing, which is the only time we rely on the Boltzmann

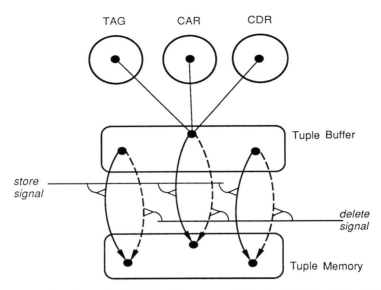

Fig. 18. Connections for storing/deleting the contents of the Tuple Buffer in Tuple Memory.

machine's properties, all gates are fixed. If the gate is open, a gated connection behaves like an ordinary connection; if the gate is closed, the model behaves as if the connection didn't exist.

Tuples are deleted from the Tuple Memory using a set of gated inhibitory connections, also shown in Fig. 18. First, the activity pattern of the tuple to be deleted must be set up in the Tuple Buffer. This is normally done by a retrieval, but it could also be done by assembling the tuple from individual components in the three symbol spaces. When the deletion gate is opened, each active Tuple Buffer unit turns off its corresponding Tuple Memory unit.

The Tuple Memory units do no processing on their own. They serve merely as latches to hold an activity pattern and apply it as input to the Tuple Buffer. The same effect could be achieved without a Tuple Memory if the Tuple Buffer units had modifiable rather than fixed thresholds.[5] Storing a pattern would be achieved by lowering the thresholds of selected Tuple Buffer units, making them more likely to come on.

On the other hand, storing tuples as activity patterns rather than as modified thresholds allows multiple parallel access to Tuple Memory, as shown in Fig. 19. Some BoltzCONS algorithms, such as those for permuting nodes in a tree, have faster and more straightforward implementations in a multiple-buffer architecture. For example, using the richer tree representation of Section 5.3, the algorithm below inserts a new node into a tree as a right sibling of the node

---

[5] This observation is due to Hinton.

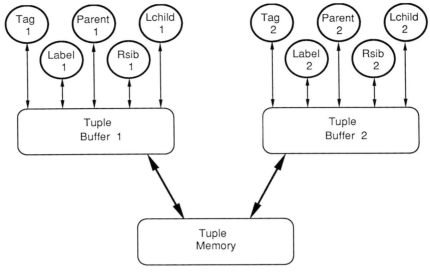

Fig. 19. A variant of BoltzCONS with multiple tuple buffers accessing the same memory.

currently in Tuple Buffer 1. We assume that the components of this tuple are also represented in the TAG1, LABEL1, PARENT1, RSIB1, and LCHILD1 spaces. The new node initially has no children:

```
InsertNode(x) =
    {$NewTag→ TAG2 &
        $x→ LABEL2 &
        $PARENT1→ PARENT2 &
        $RSIB1→ RSIB2 &
        $Delete.tuple.1.from.memory;
    $TAG2→ RSIB1 & $TAG2→LCHILD2;
    $Assemble.tuple.in.buffer.1 &
    $Assemble.tuple.in.buffer.2;
    $Store.tuple.1 & $Store.tuple.2}
```

6.5. Communication between symbol spaces

Following pointer chains requires copying the activity pattern representing a symbol from CAR or CDR space into TAG space. Other operations, such as following pointers backward, require copying in the opposite direction. Such transfers are trivial if each of the 600 symbol units in the destination space has the same three-letter receptive field as its counterpart in the source space. But even if this is not the case, the transfer of symbols between spaces is easily (and more robustly) achieved using many-to-many connections between units that have at least one letter in common. In this case the two spaces need not even be of the same size. The transfer method is illustrated in Fig. 20. Suppose the symbol *J* is represented in CAR space, meaning the first, second, and fourth units are active. To transfer this symbol to TAG space we turn off all the TAG units, hold the CAR units clamped so they cannot change state, and open the gate on the two-way connections between the two spaces. The first two TAG units in Fig. 20 will receive excitation from three connections each. The last TAG unit, which does not code for *J*, will receive excitation from only one connection; this spurious excitation comes from the fact that the last units in TAG and CAR space both happen to code for *P*. With a high enough threshold, the units that become active in TAG space will be only those that code for *J*. (Recall that the connections within TAG space will cause *J* units to excite their siblings and inhibit rival units, so any spurious activation from CAR units will be more than compensated for by intra-space lateral inhibition.)

The gate that controls this transfer is actually implemented by a set of multiplicative connections from a line carrying the "transfer" signal onto each of the connections between the two spaces. During an associative retrieval there is no transfer signal (i.e., the gate is closed), so these connections have no effect.

6.6. Associative retrieval by parallel constraint satisfaction

Associative retrieval in BoltzCONS is accomplished by parallel constraint satisfaction using the Boltzmann Machine simulated annealing algorithm. Assume that Tuple Memory holds the set of tuples shown in Fig. 4, and we wish to find the tuple whose tag is *p*. We begin by clamping the symbol *p* into TAG space, that is, we turn on all the TAG units that include *p* in their receptive field, and turn off the ones that don't include *p*. The states of the

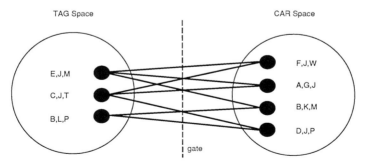

Fig. 20. Gated connections between symbol spaces allow symbols to be copied from one space to another. Using a many-to-many connection pattern, it isn't necessary for units in the two spaces to have identical receptive fields; the two spaces need not even be of the same size.

TAG units are then frozen so that they cannot change during the annealing. As the annealing begins, the active TAG units supply excitation to the Tuple Buffer units to which they are wired. At the same time, the active Tuple Memory units, representing the superimposed patterns of all eleven stored tuples, are exciting their corresponding Tuple Buffer units. Lateral inhibition in the Tuple Buffer prevents more than a few dozen Tuple Buffer units from being on simultaneously. The units that are most likely to be on are the ones receiving the highest activation, that is, the ones receiving input from Tuple Memory *plus* an extra boost from the clamped TAG space units. Therefore, the Tuple Buffer will tend to choose units that encode a tuple from the Tuple Memory that begins with p.

The CAR and CDR spaces, being unclamped, are free to wander about looking for an energy minimum. As the pattern in the Tuple Buffer develops toward the representation of one particular tuple, it exerts an influence on the CAR and CDR units. In CDR space, for example, units that vote for q will be getting a lot of excitatory input from active Tuple Buffer units representing (p, **Event7**, q). This tends to make the clique for q be the winner in CDR space.

Because BoltzCONS was built from the components of DCPS, it uses the same settling algorithm for associative retrieval. This algorithm does most of its work very quickly at a single temperature. It is more like rapid stochastic search than simulated annealing.

DCPS solves a much harder problem than BoltzCONS. DCPS must simultaneously retrieve two triples that jointly satisfy two independent constraints: the left-hand side pattern matching constraint and the variable binding constraint. See [24] for details. BoltzCONS, on the other hand, only retrieves one triple at a time, subject to a single constraint: the influence that the clamped symbol space exerts on the Tuple Buffer. Given the simplicity of the retrieval problem in BoltzCONS, it is likely that a simpler settling algorithm would give equally good results. In particular, the Hopfield and Tank model [11], which uses deterministic continuous-valued units instead of stochastic binary ones, seems an attractive alternative.

7. Managing a Distributed Memory

BoltzCONS might be viewed as a short term or working memory model for processing conceptual structures. Human short-term memory has a distinctly limited capacity. The few items present at any given time will quickly fade or be displaced unless some action is taken to retain them. In normal cognitive processing we may expect these items to be created, manipulated, and discarded at a rapid rate.

An acknowledgement of limited memory capacity leads to the question of how memory resources might be allocated and recovered. Too little is known about human information processing to support much speculation on this topic.

However, to pursue the basic pointer structure analogy that gave birth to BoltzCONS, I will sketch and compare some candidate mechanisms.

Let us define *allocation* as the process of finding a fresh tag, meaning a tag not in use by any currently-stored tuple. We define *reclamation* to mean deleting "garbage" tuples representing cells no longer pointed to by any of the concept structures currently in memory. To make this last idea more concrete—without making any psychological claims—we assume that working memory is organized as a tree whose root has a distinguished tag, and whose children, which are unordered, are individual conceptual structures. A structure can be converted to garbage by severing its connection to the root. Smaller bits of garbage might be generated as a side effect of performing minor surgery on graphs, such as deleting or permuting a few nodes. Thus, we expect that normal operations on symbol structures will continually produce garbage tuples that must be reclaimed to prevent the memory from filling up.

7.1. The allocation problem

Here are five increasingly sophisticated schemes for attacking the allocation problem:

(1) *Maintain a freelist*
This technique was used in early LISP implementations: all unallocated cells are strung together in a linked list. A pointer to the head of the list is maintained in a special register. New cells are allocated by popping them off the free list; in BoltzCONS this means deleting the tuple from Tuple Memory and then reusing its tag. The pop operation could be done efficiently in BoltzCONS without interfering with computations in progress by using a second Tuple Buffer with associated symbol spaces, as in Fig. 19. One problem with free lists is their inherent sequentiality. If there are multiple tuple buffers interacting with the Tuple Memory simultaneously to build new structures, maintenance of the freelist becomes a bottleneck.

(2) *Use a special marker for free cells*
Each unallocated cons cell could have a special marker in its car and cdr which could be picked up by associative retrieval. The problem with this approach is that if there are many free cells, local blurring will degrade the accuracy of the memory.

(3) *Mark free cells by setting their car and cdr fields to their tag*
This form of marking avoids local blurring. A constrained form of associative retrieval could be used to find such self-referential cells. However, this would interfere with some of the reclamation schemes proposed below.

(4) *Pick a tag at random and verify that it's unused*
We can use associative retrieval to verify that there is no stored tuple with the

given tag. If the memory is sparse, the first tag we pick will probably be free. If a tag is already in use, we can pick another tag at random and repeat the process. As memory fills up this scheme becomes less efficient. Processing time not only increases, it may also vary substantially depending on how lucky our random guesses turn out to be.

(5) *Use an inhibitory winner-take-all space*
This idea was suggested by David Chapman at the Massachusetts Institute of Technology. Create a special winner-take-all space whose units have inhibitory connections directly from the Tuple Memory; the connectivity is based on the first column of the receptive field table. The winner-take-all units will have negative thresholds (i.e., positive biases) which cause them to turn on in the absence of inhibition from Tuple Memory. The stable states of this network will then correspond to symbols that do not appear as the tag of any tuple present in Tuple Memory. We will also need excitatory connections within each clique of units and inhibitory connections between rival cliques, as in an ordinary winner-take-all space, to assure that only one symbol at a time is chosen as the winner.

7.2. The reclamation problem

Here are four schemes for removing tuples that are no longer accessible.

(1) *Activation decay of units in Tuple Memory*
If the activation levels of tuple memory units are made to decay slowly towards zero, the tuples those units represent will gradually fade from the memory. We can retain those tuples that continue to be accessed by having each Tuple Buffer unit refresh the activity level of its corresponding Tuple Memory unit at the end of every associative retrieval. One problem with this approach is that, since the components of an object are represented by independent tuples, if we continually access only some parts of an object, the other parts might fade away, leaving an incomplete structure in memory. It would be impractical to traverse an entire tree to refresh its tuples any time we access any part of it. However, in architectures such as Touretzky and Geva's DUCS model [27], where composite objects are represented by a single large activity pattern that is always retrieved as a whole, the use of exponential decay with refresh-on-retrieval is feasible.

It's not really clear if this is the right kind of reclamation, though. If the system gets busy (i.e., is suddenly called upon to do a lot of processing), it will be generating and discarding new structures very rapidly. The decay mechanism might then be unable to reclaim these structures quickly enough to prevent memory from filling up. We could compensate for the higher processing speed by increasing the decay rate of Tuple Memory units, but this will force us to waste more processing resources on refresh. It would be better if garbage were displaced by new data rather than simply allowing garbage to decay.

Another source of decay comes from the effect of overlapping representations due to coarse coding. Even if units' activity levels remain constant, as we delete many triples, some will share units with triples that were not meant to be deleted. After many deletions, a triple can fade from memory unless it has been periodically refreshed.

(2) *Pick a tuple at random and see if no car or cdr points to its tag*
If so, delete it, then check its car. If nothing points to the car, reclaim it and continue along the car path; otherwise check the cdr. When we get to the end of a chain of reclaimed tuples we go back to random search again. If we use a dedicated Tuple Buffer for this purpose, reclamation can occur in parallel with, and completely independent of, the creation and manipulation of non-garbage structures.

(3) *Monitor deletions*
If the storage recovery mechanism is in random search mode when BoltzCONS deletes a tuple, it should immediately check the car and cdr of the deleted tuple to see if they are tags (rather than atoms), and if any tuples other than the one just deleted contain those tags. If not, it can begin following a reclamation path, starting with the subtree beginning with the now orphaned tag, as in case (2). If both the car and cdr point to now-orphaned subtrees, the storage recovery mechanism need only pursue one of them. The other will be picked up later by random search.

(4) *Detect garbage tuples directly*
One could perhaps design a special module to detect garbage tuples, i.e., tuples not pointed to by any other tuple. This would be yet another variant on the familiar winner-take-all network. A unit that votes for, say, the tag J, would have excitatory connections from Tuple Memory units with J in their tag fields, and also inhibitory connections from Tuple Memory units with J in either their car or cdr fields. Such a network should settle into a stable state representing the tag of a tuple that was stored in memory but not pointed to by any other stored tuple. One could then perform an ordinary associative retrieval to access the tuple with this tag and delete it from memory. This wouldn't detect circular garbage, however.

Although use of dedicated hardware might seem an expensive way to detect and reclaim garbage, recall that BoltzCONS is modeling processing in short-term or working memory, not long-term memory. Since the short-term memory contains only a few moderately complex structured objects at a time, and its contents are subject to rapid turnover, special storage recovery circuitry might not be unreasonable.

8. Discussion

In the course of this paper, BoltzCONS evolved from a parallel associative implementation of LISP cons cells into a more powerful and general purpose symbol processor. The full architecture supports direct representations of arbitrary tree structures based on a 5-tuple encoding, and it can perform complex pointer manipulations using multiple buffers operating simultaneously on its tuple memory. A variety of methods for dynamic allocation and reclamation of memory resources were also discussed. In this final section I will try to put the BoltzCONS model in perspective.

8.1. BoltzCONS and implementational connectionism

BoltzCONS joins many other connectionist models in addressing an important implementation question: How can intelligence emerge from the collective activity of a mass of neurons? One might approach this question at many levels. At an extremely abstract theory of computation level, idealized neurons function as boolean logic gates and latches, from which one can wire up a Turing machine or any digital computer. Of course this approach ignores many crucial biological constraints, such as the fact that individual neurons are unreliable devices, or the fact that the human genome does not contain enough information to specify precise point-to-point neural wiring for something as complex as a computer. At the other extreme, if fidelity to biology rather than theoretical simplicity is the main goal, one could try mapping proposed symbol processing architectures directly onto actual brain structures. Neuroscientists have had great success explaining the early stages of vision in terms of receptive fields, cortical maps, hypercolumns, and so forth, but this approach seems premature for symbol processing, which involves nonsensory, nongeometric representations.

Connectionist symbol processing theories therefore occupy a middle ground between purely abstract computational architectures and purely data-driven biological models. Connectionist modelers are concerned with computational questions more than biological ones, but they try to work within hailing distance of the biologists. BoltzCONS in particular obeys several important biological constraints. Its units are stochastic, and the failure of any one of them would have no observable effect on the model's behavior. Units have coarsely-tuned receptive fields; they do not encode discrete symbols as a grandmother cell would. And the mappings between modules (e.g., between the symbol spaces and the Tuple Buffer) are rich and highly redundant, as is the case in real neural systems.

I do not envision connectionist symbol processing moving closer to real biological explanations any time soon. There are too many layers of description between psychology and neuroscience where our understanding is extremely limited. Connectionists will have to content themselves with studying the computational properties of various abstract architectures, drawing inspiration from biology where possible. One hopes that at some point in the future these investigations will provide the necessary language for framing a biological explanation of cognition.

8.2. BoltzCONS and cognitive psychology

Like Anderson's ACT* model [1], BoltzCONS raises questions about mental representations. If there really are symbol structures in the brain, one can legitimately ask about their functional properties, i.e., properties defined at the level of an abstract associative retrieval machine. Suppose, for example, that a particular cognitive theory suggests that people manipulate tree structures in their heads. One can ask: Does the brain use a direct or indirect representation for these trees? What tree manipulation primitives does it provide? If nodes are ordered, is it possible to access the rightmost child of a node as quickly as the leftmost child? How much time does it take to perform various sorts of permutations on nodes? The answers can reveal a lot about the underlying cognitive architecture. BoltzCONS-5 is a good illustration of the way a slight architectural modification can turn a slow serial operation into a fast parallel one.

Of course, people probably have much richer and more complex structures than trees in their heads. The BoltzCONS approach can be extended to develop models of these structures and explore their computational properties. In contrast, if one talks only about manipulating symbol structures, without considering how they could be realized in neuron-like hardware, then it is not meaningful to ask whether certain operations necessarily take longer or require more resources than others.

8.3. Revisionist symbol processing

One of the most pressing questions facing connectionists is how the neuron-like implementation of their models influences their view of what symbol processing is about. If there were no influence, connectionism would merely be an implementation technology rather than an alternative to classical processing. If the influence proves to be fundamental, connectionist modeling could lead to an entirely new understanding of symbol processing. This has not happened yet to any great degree, but one must be patient.

In the case of BoltzCONS, there are several areas where the choice of a connectionist implementation impacts the model. They are: coarse coding, combination of multiple cues, and closest-match search.

Coarse coding is a particularly "neural" representation strategy. The desire to avoid local blurring ruled out certain conventions for marking atoms and the termination of chains in BoltzCONS that would have been perfectly acceptable in noncoarse coded architectures. In addition, coarse coding predicts particular types of error behavior as the memory fills up, and particular types of fading as items are deleted.

The latter two areas where the effects of a connectionist implementation are felt both involve associative retrieval. As mentioned in the introduction, associative retrieval is not unique to connectionist models. But the dividing line between fast and slow operations is drawn differently when one takes a connectionist approach. For example, for a conventional computer to perform the associative retrievals used in BoltzCONS-5, tuples would have to be stored redundantly in five hash tables keyed on the TAG, LABEL, PARENT, RSIB, and LCHILD fields. Given one component of a tuple, it is easy to fetch the entire tuple from the appropriate hash table in constant time, independent of the number of tuples that have been stored. But that is as far as we can push the hash table representation. Other operations that connectionist architectures perform quickly will not map neatly onto hash tables.

One example is the combination of multiple cues, as in Section 5.3, where we used both the PARENT and RSIB fields to constrain a retrieval. In general, supplying more constraints causes a connectionist model to settle faster. But a conventional machine using hash table representations will be slowed down. It will either be forced to intersect the sets of entries retrieved from the PARENT and RSIB hash tables (a serial process), or it will have to maintain additional hash tables keyed on all pairs of fields that might be used in a query. For more complex representations, where the number of ways of combining multiple cues would be much larger, this second approach would not be feasible.

Finally, connectionist associative retrieval architectures do more than retrieve exact matches to a query. If there is no exact match, they can retrieve the closest inexact match. Consider this example from DUCS, a connectionist frame system. Given a frame describing a bird, and a request for the "nose" of the bird, DUCS retrieves the closest slot to "nose," which is "beak." For an elephant frame, the closest matching slot would be "trunk." DUCS encodes slot names as binary feature vectors and uses Hamming distance to determine the closest match. Serial machines cannot access a closest matching item in constant time; hashing works only for exact matches.

In the current version of BoltzCONS symbols are atomic; they have no semantic features that could be usd to determine closest match. But one could easily imagine a version of BoltzCONS in which symbols were semantic feature vectors. For example, Dolan and Smolensky's tensor product production system TPPS (discussed further below), which does allow for semantic features, could be adapted to form TensorCONS, much as DCPS gave rise to BoltzCONS.

8.4. Comparison with other connectionist models

BoltzCONS occupies a unique point in the space of connectionist symbol processing models. Like Pollack's Recursive Auto-Associative Memories [16], it represents objects with fixed numbers of components occurring in fixed positions. This distinguishes these models from Derthick's μKLONE [2] and Touretzky and Geva's DUCS [27], which can represent objects with variable numbers of components, and in which component names are not tied to fixed positions in a vector. Another common point between BoltzCONS and RAAMs is that pointer following is their central operation. μKLONE performs more interesting sorts of retrievals—actually inferences—based on parallel constraint satisfaction. Following chains of pointers from one concept to another is not its major purpose.

BoltzCONS' primary advantage over μKLONE and RAAMs is that it can create new objects dynamically, by changing the activity pattern in its Tuple Memory. μKLONE's knowledge is fixed in advance by its wiring pattern, which is compiled from a symbolic-level description of the domain. Although it can incorporate a small amount of new information as part of each query, it cannot retain this knowledge from one query to the next, or record the results of its inferences. Hinton's connectionist implementation of semantic nets [7] could acquire new knowledge, but since the semantic net was encoded in weights that were trained by the perceptron convergence procedure, the model could only learn by repeated presentation of the entire set of training instances by some external teacher. When viewed as a short-term or working memory model, its knowledge was static.

RAAMs also have essentially static knowledge, as adding new structure requires laborious training with backpropagation. However, RAAMs have an interesting property: the "pointers" that backprop creates, rather than being meaningless symbols as in BoltzCONS, encode some features of the objects they point to. They can thus serve as what Hinton [8] calls "reduced descriptions" that allow certain inferences to be made directly from the pointers themselves, rather than from the objects the pointers designate.

Smolensky [21] has shown that the coarse-coded representation used in DCPS and BoltzCONS can be viewed as a subset of a tensor product representation, in which each of the component symbols of a triple is replaced by a vector. This is of more than theoretical interest, because it suggests that the pullout mechanism and annealing process might be replaced by a faster inner product operator that collapses a rank-3 tensor to a rank-2 tensor. (The annealing in BoltzCONS is already extremely fast, though; in fact it is more properly termed "quenching.") Dolan and Smolensky [3] recently reimplemented DCPS using tensor product machinery in place of the coarse coded memory, and report encouraging preliminary results. It remains to be seen whether this approach offers any advantage in terms of number of units and connections required, or accuracy of retrieval over the coarse-coded model.

Another way to exploit the tensor product representation would be to make the pointers meaningful instead of arbitrary. In other words, let part of each vector hold an arbitrary identifier, but use the other part to encode salient features of the object being pointed to. This would allow pointers to act as reduced descriptions, as they do in RAAMs. The hard problem that remains is finding the right encoding of the distal object so that the pointer tells us something useful. (This same problem was encountered in DUCS, which used bit vectors as pointers but did not focus on salient features, since it was domain-independent.) In a RAAM, backprop creates the encoding, but BoltzCONS would have to use another method in order to retain its dynamic qualities. One possibility would be to use backprop to build an encoding network, from general knowledge about a designated domain, that could produce a useful reduced description of any structure in that domain. The encoder could then be wired into BoltzCONS and used to generate meaningful reduced descriptions on the fly.

9. Conclusions

Compared to Rumelhart and McClelland's verb learning model, BoltzCONS does not venture terribly far from traditional notions of symbol processing. Rather than being an eliminative theory, it affirms the reality of the symbolic level. But on the other hand, it is not merely "LISP done with neurons." BoltzCONS shows how the choice of a connectionist implementation can influence one's view of symbol processing in subtle ways. With richer, more complex symbolic representations, the influence of connectionist architectures should be more profound.

In a 1987 paper [26], Mark Derthick and I argued that truly powerful connectionist symbol processors require features of both the BoltzCONS and µKLONE-style models, to combine dynamic flexibility with powerful inference capabilities. Recent progress on many fronts, including work reported in this volume, lends encouragement that this may be feasible.

ACKNOWLEDGEMENT

I thank Geoffrey Hinton, Paul Smolensky, Jordan Pollack, Mark Derthick, Roni Rosenfeld, Charles Dolan, and David Chapman for helpful discussions and suggestions. This work was supported by National Science Foundation grants IST-8516330 and EET-8716324, and by contract number N00014-86-K-0678 from the Office of Naval Research.

REFERENCES

1. J.R. Anderson, *The Architecture of Cognition* (Harvard University Press, Cambridge, MA, 1983).
2. M.A. Derthick, Mundane reasoning by settling on a plausible model, *Artificial Intelligence* **46** (1990) 107–157, this issue.
3. C.P. Dolan and P. Smolensky, Implementing a connectionist production system using tensor products, in: D.S. Touretzky, G.E. Hinton, and T.J. Sejnowski, eds., *Proceedings 1988 Connectionist Models Summer School* (Morgan Kaufmann, Los Altos, CA, 1988) 265–272.
4. J.A. Feldman and D.H. Ballard, Connectionist models and their properties, *Cognitive Sci.* **6** (1982) 205–254.

5. J.A. Fodor and Z.W. Pylyshyn, Connectionism and cognitive architecture: A critical analysis, *Cognition* **28** (1988) 3–71.
6. R.D. Greenblatt, T.F. Knight Jr, J. Holloway, D.A. Moon and D.L. Weinreb, The Lisp machine, in: D.R. Barstow, H.E. Shrobe, and E. Sandewall, eds., *Interactive Programming Environments* (McGraw-Hill, New York, 1984).
7. G.E. Hinton, Implementing semantic networks in parallel hardware, in: G.E. Hinton and J.A. Anderson, *Parallel Models of Associative Memory* (Erlbaum, Hillsdale, NJ, 1981).
8. G.E. Hinton, Mapping part–whole hierarchies onto connectionist networks, *Artificial Intelligence* **46** (1990) 47–75, this issue.
9. G.E. Hinton and T.J. Sejnowsksi, Learning and relearning in Boltzmann machines, in: D.E. Rumelhart, J.L. McClelland and the PDP Research Group, eds., *Parallel Distributed Processing: Explorations in the Microstructure of Cognition* **1**: *Foundations* (Bradford Books/MIT Press, Cambridge, MA, 1986).
10. G.E. Hinton, J.L. McClelland and D.E. Rumelhart, Distributed representations, in: D.E. Rumelhart, J.L. McClelland and the PDP Research Group, eds., *Parallel Distributed Processing: Explorations in the Microstructure of Cognition* **1**: *Foundations* (Bradford Books/MIT Press, Cambridge, MA, 1986).
11. J.J. Hopfield and D. Tank, "Neural" computation of decisions in optimization problems, *Biol. Cybern.* **52** (1985) 151–152.
12. J.L. McClelland, D.E. Rumelhart and G.E. Hinton, The appeal of parallel distributed processing, in: D.E. Rumelhart, J.L. McClelland and the PDP Research Group, eds., *Parallel Distributed Processing: Explorations in the Microstructure of Cognition* **1**: *Foundations* (Bradford Books/MIT Press, Cambridge, MA, 1986).
13. M.C. Mozer, The perception of multiple objects: A parallel, distributed processing approach, Doctoral Dissertation, University of California, San Diego, CA (1987).
14. A. Newell, Physical symbol systems, *Cognitive Sci.* **4** (1980) 135–183.
15. S. Pinker and A. Prince, On language and connectionism: analysis of a parallel distributed processing model of language acquisition, *Cognition* **28** (1988) 73–193.
16. J. Pollack, Recursive distributed representations, *Artificial Intelligence* **46** (1990) 77–105, this issue.
17. R. Rosenfeld and D.S. Touretzky, Coarse-coded symbol memories and their properties, *Complex Syst.* **2** (4) (1988) 463–484.
18. D.E. Rumelhart and J.L. McClelland, On learning the past tenses of English verbs, in: J.L. McClelland, D.E. Rumelhart and the PDP Research Group, eds., *Parallel Distributed Processing: Explorations in the Microstructure of Cognition* **2**: *Applications* (Bradford Books/MIT Press, Cambridge, MA, 1986).
19. T.J. Sejnowski, Higher-order Boltzmann machines, in: J.S. Denker, ed., *Neural Networks for Computing*, AIP Conference Proceedings **151** (American Institute of Physics, New York, 1986) 398–403.
20. P. Smolensky, On the hypothesis underlying connectionsm, *Behav. Brain Sci.* **11** (1) (1988).
21. P. Smolensky, Tensor product variable binding and the representation of symbolic structures in connectionist systems, *Artificial Intelligence* **46** (1990) 159–216, this issue.
22. D.S. Touretzky, BoltzCONS: Reconciling connectionism with the recursive nature of stacks and trees, in: *Proceedings Eighth Annual Conference of the Cognitive Science Society*, Amherst, MA (1986) 522–530.
23. D.S. Touretzky, Representing and transforming recursive objects in a neural network, or "Trees *do* grow on Boltzmann machines", *Proceedings International Conference on Systems, Man, and Cybernetics*, Atlanta, GA (1986) 12–16.
24. D.S. Touretzky, Analyzing the energy landscapes of distributed winner-take-all networks, in: D.S. Touretzky, ed., *Advances in Neural Information Processing Systems* **1** (Morgan Kaufmann, San Mateo, CA, 1989).

25. D.S. Touretzky, Connectionism and compositional semantics, in: J.A. Barnden and J.B. Pollack, eds., *Advances in Connectionist and Neural Computational Theory* **2**: *High Level Connectionist Models* (Ablex, Norwood, NJ, to appear).
26. D.S. Touretzky and M.A. Derthick, Symbol structures in connectionist networks: Five properties and two architectures, *Digest of Papers*: *COMPCON Spring 87, Thirty-Second IEEE Computer Society International Conference*, San Francisco, CA (1987).
27. D.S. Touretzky and S. Geva, A distributed connectionist representation for concept structures, in: *Proceedings Ninth Annual Conference of the Cognitive Science Society*, Seattle, WA (1987) 155–164.
28. D.S. Touretzky and G.E. Hinton, Symbols among the neurons: details of a connectionist inference architecture, in: *Proceedings IJCAI-85*, Los Angeles, CA (1985) 238–243.
29. D.S. Touretzky and G.E. Hinton, A distributed connectionist production system, *Cognitive Sci.* **12** (3) (1988) 423–466.
30. S. Ullman, Visual routines, in: S. Pinker, ed., *Visual Cognition* (MIT Press, Cambridge, MA, 1984).

Mapping Part–Whole Hierarchies into Connectionist Networks*

Geoffrey E. Hinton

*Department of Computer Science, University of Toronto,
Toronto, Ontario, Canada M5S 1A4*

ABSTRACT

Three different ways of mapping part–whole hierarchies into connectionist networks are described. The simplest scheme uses a fixed mapping and is inadequate for most tasks because it fails to share units and connections between different pieces of the part–whole hierarchy. Two alternative schemes are described, each of which involves a different method of time-sharing connections and units. The scheme we finally arrive at suggests that neural networks have two quite different methods for performing inference. Simple "intuitive" inferences can be performed by a single settling of a network without changing the way in which the world is mapped into the network. More complex "rational" inferences involve a sequence of such settlings with mapping changes after each settling.

1. Introduction

One reason why many AI researchers are sceptical about connectionist networks that use distributed representations is that it is hard to imagine how complex, articulated structures can be represented and processed in these networks. The approach would be far more convincing if it could come up with a sensible scheme for representing the meaning of a sentence such as: "She seems to be more at ease with her fellow students than with me, her adviser." (Drew McDermott, personal communication). This meaning is clearly composed of several major constituents with relationships between them, and each major constituent has its own, complex, internal structure. A representational scheme for dealing with meanings of this complexity must, at the very least, specify how it is possible to focus attention on the constituents of the whole and how it is possible, in some sense, to have the whole meaning in mind at once.

The example given above is typical of examples from many different domains. It appears that whenever people have to deal with complexity they

* This research was supported by grants from the Alfred P. Sloan Foundation and the Ontario Information Technology Research Center. The author is a fellow of the Canadian Institute for Advanced Research.

impose part–whole hierarchies in which objects at one level are composed of inter-related objects at the next level down. In representing a visual scene or an everyday plan or the structure of a sentence we use hierarchical structures of this kind. The main issue addressed in this paper is how to map complex part–whole hierarchies into the fixed hardware of a connectionist network. The main conclusion is that it is essential to use some form of timesharing so that a portion of the connectionist network is used, at different times, to represent different parts of the part–whole hierarchy.

Most existing connectionist simulations do not use timesharing of the connectionist apparatus because they focus on computations that can be performed rapidly by parallel constraint satisfaction, and they typically ignore the issue of how the real world gets mapped into the bottom level units in the network or how the results produced by the network are integrated over longer periods of time. These simulations are best viewed as investigations of the computations that can be done by one internally parallel module. At best, they give little insight into how complex part–whole hierarchies should be mapped into connectionist networks, and at worst they lend support to the naive idea that the entire part–whole hierarchy should be mapped simultaneously using a fixed, inflexible mapping (as described in Section 5 below).

Given any finite connectionist network, we can always design a task that is so difficult that it cannot all be done in parallel by a single settling of the network. The task can be designed to have subtasks that require the same knowledge to be applied to different data, and although we can replicate portions of the network so that some of these subtasks can be performed in parallel, we will eventually run out of hardware and will be driven to use time instead of space. So eventually we have to face the issue of timesharing a module of the network between different pieces of a single task. This inevitably leads to questions of how we implement a flexible mapping of pieces of the task into a module of the network, how we store the intermediate results produced by the module so that it can be liberated to solve the next subtask, and how we use intermediate results to determine which subtask is tackled next. These questions have been widely ignored within neural network research, particularly within the sub-areas that have been inspired by physics and biology.

2. Symbols and the Conventional Implementation of Hierarchical Structures

It will be helpful to begin by reviewing the standard way of implementing hierarchical data-structures in a conventional digital computer. There are obviously many minor variations, but a suitable paradigm example is the kind of record structure that is found in languages like C. Each instance of a record is composed of a pre-determined set of fields (sometimes called "slots" or "roles") each of which contains a pointer to the contents of the field which may be either another instance of a record, or a primitive object. Since the pointers can be arbitrary addresses, this is a very flexible way of implementing a hierarchical data-structure, but the flexibility is bought at the price of the von Neumann bottleneck: The addressing mechanism means that only one pointer can be followed at a time.[1]

The addresses act as symbols for expressions, and they illustrate the essence of a symbol: It is a small representation of an object that provides a "remote access" path to a fuller representation of the same object.[2] In general, this fuller representation is itself composed of small representations (e.g. the addresses of the structures that fill the fields of the record). Because a symbol is small, many symbols can be put together to create a "fully-articulated" representation of some larger structure and the size of this fully-articulated representation need not be any larger than the fully-articulated representations of its constituents.

When addresses are used as symbols, there is normally an arbitrary relationship between the internal structure of a symbol and the fully articulated representation to which it provides access. Looking at the individual bits in the symbol provides no information about what it represents. Occasionally this is not quite true. If, for example, one type of data-structure is kept in the top half of memory and another type in the bottom half, the first bit of a symbol reveals the type of the data-structure to which it provides access. So it is possible to check the type without following the pointer. This trick can obviously be extended so that many of the bits in a symbol convey useful information. A symbol can then be viewed as a "reduced description" of the object.

One conclusion of this paper is that patterns of activity in some parts of a connectionist network need to exhibit the double life that is characteristic of symbols. The patterns must allow remote access to fuller representations, but so long as the patterns are also reduced descriptions this remote access need only be used very occasionally (e.g. a few times per second in a person). Most of the processing can be done by parallel constraint satisfaction on the patterns themselves. One interesting consequence of using parallel constraint satisfaction as a powerful but somewhat inflexible inner loop in a sequential process is that it leads to two quite different ways of performing an inference.

3. Rational and Intuitive Inference

Given a parallel network, some inferences can be performed very efficiently by simply allowing the network to settle down into a stable state [28]. The states or external inputs of a subset of the units are fixed to represent the premises,

---

[1] Architectures such as the Connection Machine [8] use routing hardware that allows many pointers to be followed at once.

[2] There is, of course, much debate about the meaning of the word "symbol." The informal definition given here emerged from conversations with Allen Newell.

and when the network has settled down, the conclusion is represented by the states of some other subset of the units. A large amount of knowledge about the domain can influence the settling process, provided the knowledge is in the form of connection strengths. This method of performing inference by a single settling of a network will be called "intuitive inference." More complex inferences require a more serial approach in which parts of the network are used for performing several different intuitive inferences in sequence. This will be called "rational inference." The distinction between these two kinds of inference is not simply a serial versus parallel distinction. A network that is settling to a single stable state typically requires a series of iterations. Also, it may exhibit another emergent type of seriality during a single settling because easily drawn conclusions may emerge early in the settling. So even within one settling a network can exhibit something that looks like sequential inference [27]. This interesting phenomenon makes it clear that the crucial criterion for distinguishing rational from intuitive inference is not seriality. The defining characteristic of rational inference is that the way in which entities in the domain are mapped into the hardware changes during the course of the inference.

The distinction between these two types of inference applies quite well to a conventional computer. Intuitive inferences correspond, roughly, to single machine instructions and rational inferences correspond to sequences of machine instructions that typically involve changes in the way in which parts of the task are mapped into the CPU. Moreover, the very same inference can sometimes be performed in different ways. The task of multiplying two integers, for example, can be performed in a single instruction by dedicated hardware, or it can be performed by a sequential program. In the first case the inference is very fast but is limited in flexibility. It may work well for 32 bit numbers but not for 33 bit numbers.

The idea that the same inference can be performed in radically different ways is important in defending connectionist research against the claim of Fodor and Pylyshyn [6] that connectionist networks which do not implement classical symbol processing are simply a revival of discredited associationism. To characterize a multiplier chip as simply associating the input with the correct output is misleading. A chip that multiplies two N-bit numbers to produce a $2N$-bit number is able to use far less than the $O(2^{2N})$ components required by a table look-up scheme because it captures a lot of regularities of the task in the hardware. Of course, we can always render it useless by using bigger numbers, but this does not mean that it has failed to capture the structure of multiplication. A computer designer would be ill-advised to leave out hardware multipliers just because they cannot cope with all numbers. Similarly, a theoretical psychologist would be ill-advised to leave out parallel modules that perform fast intuitive inference just because such modules are not the whole story.

One big difference between computers and people is in the amount of computation that can be done in an intuitive inference. A computer typically breaks up a computation into very many, very small machine instructions that are executed in sequence. For the computations that people can do well, they typically use a few sequential steps each of which involves a computationally intensive intuitive inference. So we can think of people as "huge instruction set computers." This view is quite close to Fahlman's idea [5] that a network of simple processors could make important operations such as set intersection or transitive closure almost as fast as a single machine instruction. The enormous difference between people and conventional computers in the amount of computation that gets done by a single intuitive inference may explain why many psychologists and even some AI researchers find typical AI accounts of natural language processing so implausible and are attracted to connectionist accounts even though the performance of connectionist models is currently much worse. In a typical AI model, understanding a sentence involves an enormous amount of sequential symbol processing. To rephrase this in our new terminology, typical AI models use rational inference to do almost everything, probably because this is the convenient way to get things done on a conventional computer.

A further difference between people and computers is that a computer does not change its instruction set as it runs, whereas people seem to be capable of taking frequently repeated sequences and eliminating the sequential steps so that an inference that was once rational becomes intuitive. A sketch of how this could happen in a connectionist network is given in Section 7.4. Of course, it is also possible to model this process in software on a conventional computer. One example is the SOAR system [18]. Another example is a checkers program which may start by using a deep mini-max search in a particular situation, but after using the results of deep searches to learn a better evaluation function may be able to arrive at the same conclusions with a much shallower search [25]. Berliner [2] uses the terms "reasoning" and "judgment" to denote the two kinds of inference in the context of game playing programs.

A good example of a large computation that can be performed by a single intuitive inference in a connectionist network is the task of completing a schema when given a subset of the slot-fillers [4, 9]. In a familiar domain, there will be many constraints between the fillers of the various slots in a schema. If the appropriate representations are used, it is possible to express these constraints as connection strengths which all act in parallel to determine the most plausible fillers for unfilled slots. Section 4 gives a detailed example and shows how connectionist learning techniques can be used to discover both the constraints and the representations that allow these constraints to be expressed effectively. Sections 5, 6, and 7 then describe three alternative ways of mapping a part–whole hierarchy into a connectionist network.

4. Learning to Perform Intuitive Inference

This section illustrates the kind of inference that can be performed by a connectionist network in a single settling. The example shows that a single settling can do more than just associate an input with an output. It can perform a simple inference. The example was first described in [10] and uses the backpropagation learning procedure operating in a layered, feedforward network. The equivalent of "settling" in such a network is a single forward pass from the input to the output. To make this example more compatible with the recurrent networks that are implicitly assumed in the rest of this paper, it would be necessary to reimplement it using one of the gradient descent learning techniques for recurrent networks.[3]

4.1. The family trees task

Figure 1 shows two family trees. All the information in these trees can be represented in simple propositions of the form (person1, relationship, person2). These propositions can be stored as the stable states of activity of a neural network which contains a group of units for the role person1, a group for the role relationship and a group for the role person2. The net will also require further groups of units in order to achieve the correct interactions between the three role-specific groups. Figure 2 shows a network in which one further group

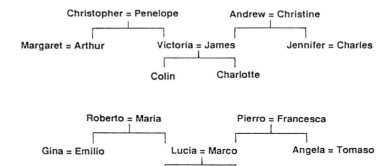

Fig. 1. Two isomorphic family trees. The symbol "=" means "married to."

[3] Rumelhart et al. [24] describe another version of the procedure which does not require a layered net. It works for arbitrary recurrent networks, but requires more complex units that remember their history of activity levels. Pineda [22] describes an alternative to backpropagation for recurrent networks that settle to stable states. Hinton [11] describes an efficient deterministic version of the Boltzmann machine learning procedure that could also be used for this task. These learning procedures for recurrent nets have not been tried on the family trees task.

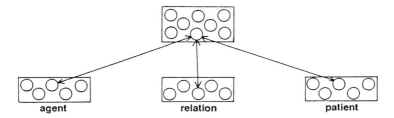

Fig. 2. An extra group of units can be used to implement higher-order constraints between the role-specific patterns.

has been introduced for this purpose. Units in this extra group detect combina-tions of features in the role-specific groups and can be used for causing appropriate completions of partial patterns. Suppose, for example, that one of the extra units becomes active whenever person1 is old and relationship requires that both people be the same age (e.g. the relationship has-husband in the very conventional domain we use). The extra unit can then activate the unit that represents the feature old within the person2 group. An extra unit that works in this way will be said to encode a micro-inference. It uses some of the features of some of the role-fillers to infer some of the features of other role-fillers and it is typically useful in encoding many different propositions rather than just a single one. By dedicating a unit to a micro-inference that is applicable in many different propositions, the network makes better use of the information carrying capacity of its activity levels and its weights than if it dedicated a single extra unit to each proposition. This is an example of the technique of coarse-coding described in [13]. In describing how a micro-inference could be implemented, we assumed that there was a single unit within the person1 group that was active whenever the pattern of activity in that group encoded an old person. This would not be true using random patterns, but it would be true using a componential representation.

Micro-inferences store propositions by encoding the underlying regularities of a domain. This form of storage has the advantage that it allows sensible generalization. If the network has learned the micro-inference given above it will have a natural tendency to make sensible guesses. If, for example, it is told enough about a new person, Jane, to know that Jane is old and it is then asked to complete the proposition Jane has-husband? it will expect the filler of the person2 role to be old. To achieve this kind of generalization of domain-specific regularities, it is necessary to pick a representation for Jane in the person1 role that has just the right active units so that the existing micro-inferences can cause the right effects in the other role-specific groups. A randomly chosen pattern will not do.

The real criterion for a good set of role-specific representations is that it makes it easy to express the regularities of the domain. It is sensible to dedicate a unit to a feature like old because useful micro-inferences can be expressed in terms of this feature. There is another way of stating this point which enables us to avoid awkward questions about whether the network really understands what old means. Instead of saying that activity in a unit means that the person is old, we can simply specify the set of people for which the unit is active. Each unit then corresponds to a way of partitioning all the people into two subsets, and good representations are ones for which these partitions are helpful in expressing the regularities. The search for good representations is then a search in the space of possible sets of partitions.[4]

4.2. Giving the network the freedom to choose representations

The network shown in Fig. 2 has the disadvantage that it is impossible to present a proposition to the network without already having decided on the patterns of activity that represent the people and relationships. We would like the network to use its experience of a set of propositions to construct its own internal representations of concepts, and so we must have a way of presenting the propositions that is neutral with respect to the various possible internal representations. Figure 3 shows how this can be done. The network translates a neutral input representation in which each person or relationship is represented by a single active unit into its own internal representation before making any associations. In the input representation, all pairs of concepts are equally

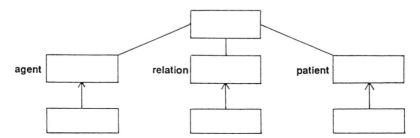

Fig. 3. The state of each role-specific group can be fixed via a special input group. By varying the weights between the special input groups and the role-specific groups the network can develop its own role-specific representations instead of being forced to use representations that are pre-determined.

---

[4] If the units can have intermediate activity levels or can behave stochastically, they do not correspond to clean cut partitions because there will be borderline cases. They are more like fuzzy sets, but the formal apparatus of fuzzy set theory (which is what defines the meaning of "fuzzy") is of no help here so we refrain from using the term "fuzzy." In much of what follows we talk as if units define clearcut sets with no marginal cases. This is just a useful idealisation.

similar. But we expect that the network will develop a hidden representation in which similar patterns of activity are used to represent people who have similar relationships to other people.

4.3. Distorting the task so that backpropagation can be used

To use the backpropagation learning procedure we need to express the task of learning about family relationships in a form suitable for a layered feed-forward network. There are many possible layered networks for this task and so our choice is somewhat arbitrary: We are merely trying to show that there is at least one way of doing it, and we are not claiming that this is the best or only way. The network we used is shown in Fig. 4. It has a group of input units for the filler of the person1 role, and another group for the filler of the relationship role. The output units represent the filler of the person2 role, so the network

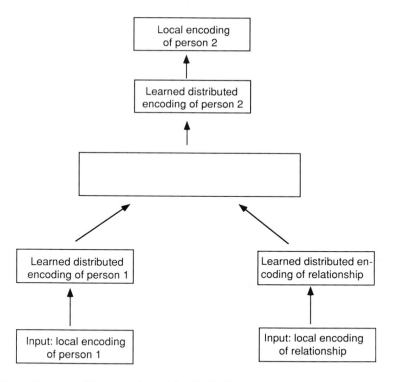

Fig. 4. The architecture of the network used for the family trees task. It has three hidden layers in which it constructs its own representations. The input and output layers are forced to use localist encodings.

can only be used to complete propositions when given the first two terms.[5] The states of the units in the input groups are clamped from outside and the network then determines the states of the output units and thus completes the proposition.

For some relationships, like uncle, there may be several possible fillers for the person2 role that are compatible with a given filler of the person1 role. In a stochastic network it would be reasonable to allow the network to choose one of the possibilities at random. In the deterministic network we decided to insist on an output which explicitly represented the whole set of possible fillers. This is easy to do because the neutral representation that we used for the output has a single active unit for each person and so there is an obvious representation for a set of people.

Using the relationships father, mother, husband, wife, son, daughter, uncle, aunt, brother, sister, nephew, niece there are 104 instances of relationships in the two family trees shown in Fig. 1. We trained the network on 100 of these instances. The details of the training are given in [10]. The training involved weight-decay which ensures that the final magnitude of a weight is proportional to the amount of work that it does in reducing the error in the output. This means that weights which are unimportant for the performance of the network shrink to near zero, which makes it much easier to interpret the weight displays. After 1500 sweeps through all 100 training examples the weights were very stable and the network performed correctly on all the training examples: When given a person1 and a relationship as input it always produced activity levels greater than 0.8 for the output units corresponding to correct answers and activity levels of less than 0.2 for all the other output units.

The fact that the network can learn the examples it is shown is not particularly surprising. Any associative memory or table look-up scheme could do that. The interesting questions are: Does it create sensible internal representations for the various people and relationships that make it easy to express regularities of the domain that are only implicit in the examples it is given? Does it generalize correctly to the remaining examples? Does it make use of the isomorphism between the two family trees to allow it to encode them more efficiently and to generalize relationships in one family tree by analogy to relationships in the other? If it does all these things, it seems reasonable to say that it is doing inference rather than mere association.

4.4. The representations

Figure 5 shows the weights on the connections from the 24 units that are used

---

[5] We would have preferred it to perform completion when given any two terms. This could have been done by using a bigger network in which there were three input groups and three output groups, but learning would have been slower in the larger network and so we opted for the simpler case.

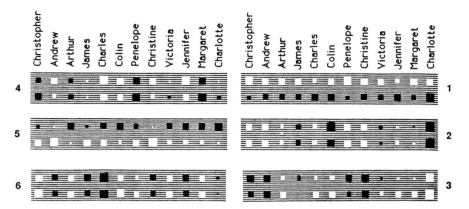

Fig. 5. The weights from the 24 input units that represent people to the 6 units in the second layer that learn distributed representations of people. White rectangles stand for excitatory weights, black for inhibitory weights, and the area of the rectangle encodes the magnitude of the weight. The weights from the 12 English people are in the top row of each unit. Beneath each of these weights is the weight from the isomorphic Italian.

to give a neutral input representation of person1 to the 6 units that are used for the network's internal, distributed representation of person1. These weights define the "receptive field" of each of the 6 units in the space of people. It is clear that at least one unit (unit number 1) is primarily concerned with the distinction between English and Italian. Moreover, most of the other units ignore this distinction which means that the representation of an English person is very similar to the representation of their Italian equivalent. The network is making use of the isomorphism between the two family trees to allow it to share structure and it will therefore tend to generalize sensibly from one tree to the other.

Unit 2 encodes which generation a person belongs to. Notice that the middle generation is encoded by an intermediate activity level. The network is never explicitly told that generation is a useful three-valued feature. It discovers this for itself by searching for features that make it easy to express the regularities of the domain. Unit 6 encodes which branch of the family a person belongs to. Again, this is useful for expressing the regularities but is not at all explicit in the examples.[6]

---

[6] In many tasks, features that are useful for expressing regularities between concepts are also observable properties of the individual concepts. For example, the feature male is useful for expressing regularities in the relationships between people and it is also related to sets of observable properties like hairyness and size. We carefully chose the input representation to make the problem difficult by removing all local cues that might have suggested the appropriate features.

It is initially surprising that none of the 6 units encodes sex. This is because of the particular set of relationship terms that was used. Each of the 12 relationship terms completely determines the sex of person2 so the sex of person1 is redundant. If we had included relationships like spouse there would have been more pressure to encode the sex of person1 because this would have been useful in constraining the possible fillers of the person2 role.

4.5. Generalization

The network was trained on 100 of the 104 instances of relationships in the two family trees. It was then tested on the remaining four instances. The whole training and testing procedure was repeated twice, starting from different random weights. In one case the network got all four test cases correct and in the other case it got 3 out of 4, where "correct" means that the output unit corresponding to the right answer had an activity level above 0.5, and all the other output units were below 0.5. In the test cases, the separation between the activity levels of the correct units and the activity levels of the remainder were not as sharp as in the training cases.

Any learning procedure which relied on finding direct correlations between the input and output vectors would generalize very badly on the family trees task. Consider the correlations between the filler of the person1 role and the filler of the person2 role. The filler of person1 that is used in each of the generalization tests is negatively correlated with the correct output vector because it never occurred with this output vector during training, and it did occur with other output vectors. The structure that must be discovered in order to generalize correctly is not present in the pairwise correlations between input units and output units.

4.6. Componential versus structuralist accounts of concepts

The family trees example sheds an interesting new light on a long-running controversy between rival theories of conceptual structure. There have been many different proposals for how conceptual information may be represented in neural networks. These range from extreme localist theories in which each concept is represented by a single neural unit [1] to extreme distributed theories in which a concept corresponds to a pattern of activity over a large part of the cortex [19]. These two extremes are the natural implementations of two different theories of semantics. In the structuralist approach, concepts are defined by their relationships to other concepts rather than by some internal essence. The natural expression of this approach in a neural net is to make each concept be a single unit with no internal structure and to use the connections between units to encode the relationships between concepts. In the componential approach each concept is simply a set of features and so a neural net can be made to implement a set of concepts by assigning a unit to each feature and setting the strengths of the connections between units so that each concept corresponds to a stable pattern of activity distributed over the whole network [15, 17, 33]. The network can then perform concept completion (i.e. retrieve the whole concept from a sufficient subset of its features). The problem with most componential theories is that they have little to say about how concepts are used for structured reasoning. They are primarily concerned with the similarities between concepts or with pairwise associations. They provide no obvious way of representing articulated structures composed of a number of concepts playing different roles within the structure.

The family trees example shows that componential reduced descriptions can be learned from structural information about how concepts go together within propositions. Given a sufficiently powerful learning procedure, the structuralist information can be converted into componential representations that facilitate rapid intuitive inference.

5. The Fixed Mapping

Perhaps the most obvious way to implement part–whole hierarchies in a connectionist network is to use the connections themselves as pointers. The simplest version of this uses localist representations, but once that version has been understood, it is easily converted into a version that uses distributed representations. Figure 6 shows a localist example taken from the work of McClelland and Rumelhart [21]. It is a network that recognizes a word when

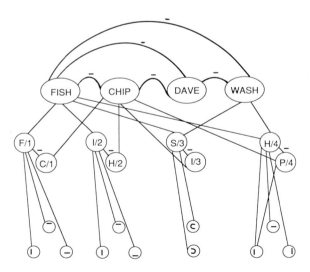

Fig. 6. Part of a network used for recognizing words. Only a few of the units and connections are shown. The connections between alternative hypotheses at the same level are inhibitory.

given partial information about the features of the letters in the word.[7] Because each relationship in the hierarchical tree-structure is implemented by its own dedicated connection, it is possible to do a lot of parallel processing during recognition. Simultaneously, many different letters can check whether the features they require are present, and many different words can check whether the letters they require are present.

One very important aspect of the McClelland and Rumelhart network is that each of the letter units has to be replicated for each possible position of a letter within the word. There are separate units for an H as first letter and an H as second letter. All the letter features and all the knowledge about which combinations of letter features make an H must also be replicated for each of the positions. This replication is a natural consequence of implementing part–whole relationships with pairwise connections. A part–whole relationship involves *three* different things: The part, the whole, and the role that the part plays within the whole. In the conventional implementation using pointers, the role is encoded by which field the pointer is in. A pairwise connection between neuron-like units does not have anything equivalent to a field, and so one of the two units is used to represent *both* the field and the contents of the field. Thus, instead of having a single role-independent representation of H which is pointed to from many different fields, we have many different "role-specific" representations. Activity in any one of these units then represents the *conjunction* of an identity and a role.

At first sight, the fixed mapping seems very wasteful because it replicates the apparatus for representing and recognizing letters across all the different roles. However, the replication has some useful consequences. It makes it possible to recognize different instances of the same letter in parallel without any of the contention that would occur if several different processes needed to access a single, central store of knowledge simultaneously. Also, when letters are used as cues for words, it is not just the letter identities that are important. It is the conjunction of the identity and the spatial role within the word that is the real cue. So it is very convenient to have units that explicitly represent such conjunctions.

5.1. The fixed mapping with distributed representations

The McClelland and Rumelhart network uses localist representations in which each entity is represented by activity in a single unit. Localist representations are efficient if a significant fraction of the possible entities are present on any one occasion or if the knowledge associated with each entity has little in common with the knowledge associated with other, alternative entities. Both

---

[7] We use this as the standard, concrete example of a part–whole hierarchy because it has clearly defined levels and the parts have convenient names, but this paper is not about word recognition.

these conditions hold quite well at the level of letter recognition. For the more natural part–whole hierarchies that occur in everyday scenes, neither condition holds. Only a tiny fraction of the possible objects are present on any one occasion, so if one unit is devoted to each possible object almost all the units will be inactive. This is a very inefficient way to use the representational capacity. Also, different objects, like a cup and a mug, may have similar appearances and may make similar predictions. This means that there can be a lot of useful sharing of units and connections. Most of what we know about cups and mugs could be associated with a unit that is active for either a cup or a mug. If this method of sharing is taken to its logical conclusion we arrive at distributed representations in which each object is represented by activity in many units and each unit is involved in the representation of many objects [13].

One way of viewing a distributed representation is as a *description* of an object in terms of a set of primitive descriptors. The description denotes the intersection of the sets of objects denoted by each of the individual descriptors. It is natural to assume that the individual units correspond to fixed primitive descriptors, but a more interesting possibility is that the primitive descriptors continually change their meanings. Each time a new object is encountered, many connection strengths change slightly and this causes slight changes in the circumstances in which each unit becomes active and in the effect that its activity has on the rest of the network. In the short term, the meanings of the primitive descriptors are fairly stable, but over a longer time scale they shift around and move towards a vocabulary that makes it easy to express the structure of the network's environment in the connection strengths [10].

One major advantage of using descriptions rather than single units as representations is that it is possible to create representations of novel objects (and also novel role-specific representations) by using novel combinations of the same set of primitive descriptors. This avoids the problem of having to find a suitably connected unit for each novel object.

5.2. Sharing units between similar roles

So far, we have assumed that each role within a structure has its own dedicated set of "role-specific" units. Each of these units may use "coarse-coding" in the space of possible identities for the role-filler, but it is entirely specific about the role. This way of localising the roles is reasonable if there are only a few possible roles (such as the four letter positions in the McClelland and Rumelhart model), but it has difficulty dealing with structures that have a large or indefinite number of potential roles. If, for example, we consider the semantic cases in English sentences, it is very hard to decide how many cases there really are, and it is also clear that some cases are very similar to others. In the sentences "Mary beat John at tennis" and "Mary helped John with his algebra" it is clear that tennis and algebra occupy similar but not quite identical semantic roles. A natural way to handle this phenomenon is to use conjunctive units that are coarse-coded in role-space as well as in identity space [9]. An instantiated structure then consists of a set of activations in these units, and each binding of an identity to a role is encoded by many of these coarse-coded units. Naturally, the representation becomes ambiguous if we simultaneously encode many bindings of similar identities to similar roles, but people also fail in these circumstances. Smolensky (this issue) gives a formal treatment of this type of representation using the formalism of tensor products.[8]

5.3. Disadvantages of the fixed mapping approach

The major problems of the fixed mapping approach are:

(1) Extra hardware is required to replicate the recognition apparatus across all roles.
(2) Extra learning time is required to train all the separate replicas of the same recognition apparatus.
(3) The replication raises the issue of how, if at all, different role-specific representations of the same entity are related to one another.
(4) The model presupposes some input apparatus for transforming the retinal image of a word into the primitive features that are used for recognition. As the word changes its position on the retina, the very same set of primitive feature units must remain active. It seems sensible to perform recognition by using a fixed network in which every connection implements a particular piece of knowledge about how things go together in good interpretations, but this can only work if there is a way of correctly mapping the external world into the bottom level units of the fixed network. Much of the difficulty of recognition lies in discovering this mapping.
(5) As we go down the hierarchy, there are fewer and fewer units available for representing each constituent. For relatively shallow, man-made hierarchies of the kind that are important in reading or speech recognition, it may be tolerable to always devote fewer units to representing smaller fragments of the overall structure. But for domains like normal visual scenes this strategy will not work. A room, for example, may contain a wall, and the wall may contain a picture, and the picture may depict a room. We need to be able to devote just as much apparatus to representing the depicted room as the real one. Moreover, the very same knowledge that is applied in recognizing the real room needs to be

---

[8] I suspect that extreme coarse-coding in role-space is a mistake. In a nonlinear system, it is probably easier to make use of the information about the fillers of roles if this information is localised (as it was in the family-trees example described in Section 4).

applied in recognizing the room in the picture. If this knowledge is in the form of connections and if the knowledge is not duplicated there must be a way of mapping the depicted room into an activity pattern on the very same set of units as are used for representing the real room.

6. Within-level Timesharing

Distributed representations provide a way of sharing units and connections between alternative objects or alternative role-specific representations. In this respect they work just like pointers in a conventional computer memory. Instead of using a separate bit for each possible object that could be pointed to, each bit is shared between many possible alternative objects. As a result, a word of memory can only point to one object at a time.[9] The following analysis of the functions performed by a role-specific representation suggests a quite different and complementary method of sharing which can be used to share connectionist apparatus between the different role-specific instances that occur within one whole.

In the McClelland and Rumelhart model each role-specific letter unit has three functions:

(1) It recognizes the occurrence of that letter in that spatial role. The recognition is accomplished by having appropriately weighted connections coming from units at the feature level.
(2) It contributes to the recognition of words. This is accomplished by its connections to units at the word level.
(3) Its activity level stores the results of letter recognition.

There is an alternative way of mapping the part–whole hierarchy into a connectionist network that uses role-specific letter units for functions (2) and (3), but not for function (1). Instead, the alternative method uses a single letter-recognition module which is applied to one position within the word at a time. Once the letter at the current position has been recognized, the combination of its identity and its position within the word activates a role-specific letter unit which acts as a temporary memory for the results of the recognition and also contributes to the recognition of the word (see Fig. 7.) This method is called "within-level" sharing because a single recognition module is shared across the entities within one level.

The letter-recognition module must be applied to one letter at a time and so there must be extra "attentional" apparatus that selects out one portion of the parallel input (which contains features of all the letters), maps this portion into

---

[9] Some ancient implementations of LISP actually use two separate role-specific representations within one word so that the first part of a word can point to one object and the second part can point to another.

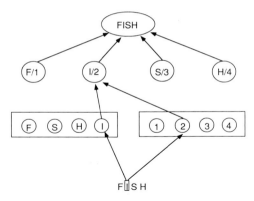

Fig. 7. Some of the apparatus required to store the sequence of outputs of a single, sequential letter-recognition module in order to recognize a word. The network is "attending" to the second letter of the word. Notice that the role-specific units do not need to be able to recognize letters. The apparatus required for mapping the appropriate part of the input into the letter recognition module is not shown.

the input of the letter-recognition module, and also creates an explicit representation of where the currently selected letter lies within the word. Actually, the McClelland and Rumelhart model implicitly presupposes that there is apparatus of a similar kind in order to pick out the features of one word within a sentence or to cope with changes in the position of a word. So the new model does not require any qualitatively new attentional apparatus, it merely requires it at the level of letters instead of at the level of words. Also, it makes explicit the requirement for attentional apparatus, storage apparatus, and control apparatus.

7. Between-level Timesharing

There is one limitation of within-level sharing that is unimportant in the domain of reading but is very important in most other domains where the same knowledge can be applied at many different levels. For reading, the knowledge is quite different at each level: Knowledge about the shape of a letter is quite different from knowledge about which sequences of letters make words, so there is little point in trying to use the same set of connections to encode both kinds of knowledge. In most natural domains, however, wholes and their parts have much in common. One example has already been given in which a room contains a picture that depicts a room. Another example is the sentence "Bill was annoyed that John disliked Mary." One of the constituents of this sentence, "John disliked Mary," has a lot in common with the whole sentence. The same kind of knowledge is needed for understanding the constituent as is needed for understanding the whole. This is also typical of natural visual scenes which generally have just as much richness at every level of detail.

To share the knowledge in the connections between different levels in the part–whole hierarchy, it is necessary to use flexible mappings between the entities in the part–whole hierarchy and the groups of units in the connectionist network. The hardware is viewed as a window that can be moved up and down (in discrete steps) over the part–whole hierarchy (see Fig. 8). One node in the hierarchy is chosen as the current whole and all of the units in the main network are then devoted to recognizing and representing this whole. Some units are used for describing the global properties of the whole, and others are used for role-specific descriptions of the major constituents of the whole. The entire pattern of activity will be called the "Gestalt" for the current whole.

The crucial property of the moveable window scheme is that the pattern of activity that represents the current whole is totally different from the pattern of activity that represents the very same object when it is viewed as being a constituent of some other whole.[10] In one case the representation of the object and its parts occupies all of the main network and in the other case it is a role-specific description that occupies only the units devoted to that role.

The idea that the very same object can be represented in different ways depending on the focus of attention is a radical proposal which violates the very natural assumption that each entity in the world has a unique corresponding representation in the network. Violating this assumption leads to so many obvious difficulties, that few researchers have considered it seriously, but these problems must be faced if we are to capture between-level regularities in a connectionist network. The problems include:

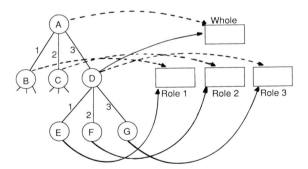

Fig. 8. The solid and dashed lines show two different ways of mapping a part–whole hierarchy (on the left) into the same connectionist hardware (on the right). Notice that node D in the hierarchy can be represented by two totally different activity patterns that have nothing in common.

[10] Charniak and Santos [3] describe a connectionist parser in which the hardware acts as a window that slides over the parse-tree, but they do not use the idea of reduced descriptions: To move the hardware window up the hierarchy they simply copy the representations from one hardware level to the next level down.

(1) When the mapping between the world and the network is changed in such a way that one constituent of the previous whole becomes the new focus of attention, what kind of internal operations are required to convert the previous, role-specific description of that constituent into a full description that occupies the whole of the main network?

(2) How is temporary information about recent Gestalts stored so that the network can return to them later? The information cannot be stored as the activity pattern that the network settles to when the Gestalt is created because the very same network is needed for creating the next Gestalt.

(3) How is the next mapping chosen? Is the choice made by a separate parallel computation, or can it be part of the same computation that is involved in forming the Gestalt? This is not a problem for the fixed mapping approach because all the parts of the hierarchy are represented simultaneously in a single large network.

The following subsections address these issues.

7.1. Moving up and down the part–whole hierarchy

Figure 9 shows some of the extra apparatus that might be required to allow a connectionist network to move down the part–whole hierarchy by expanding a role-specific, reduced description into a full description of the role-filler. This corresponds to following a pointer in a conventional implementation. Notice that it is a slow and cumbersome process. Moving back up the hierarchy is even more difficult. First, the full description of a part must be used to create the appropriate role-specific, reduced description of that part. This involves using the apparatus of Fig. 9 in the reverse direction. Then the role-specific, reduced description must be used to recreate the earlier full description of which it is a constituent. If the hierarchical structure is highly overlearned, it is possible to train a network to recover the full description [23], but if the hierarchy is a novel one, the only way to move back up it without additional external guidance is to use some kind of content-addressable working memory for earlier Gestalts. Traversing the part–whole hierarchy can be made simpler by using reduced descriptions whose microfeatures are systematically related to the microfeatures of the corresponding full descriptions. Even though the reduced and full descriptions correspond to quite different patterns of activity, it is much easier to generate one from the other if the patterns of activity are related in a non-arbitrary way.

The obvious way to implement the working memory required for recovering earlier Gestalts is to set aside a separate group of "working memory" units. If it is only necessary to remember one Gestalt at a time, this group can simply contain a copy of the pattern of activity in the network where Gestalts are formed. If several Gestalts need to be remembered at a time, several different

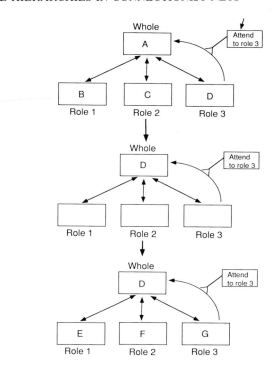

Fig. 9. One way of using some additional hardware to allow the network to access the full description of node D from a role-specific reduced description.

groups could be used. Alternatively, a single group could be used provided that the various patterns of activity that need to be stored are first recoded in such a way that they can be superimposed without confusing them with one another. Examples of such encodings are described in [29, 32]. Touretzky [30, 31] shows how this kind of working memory can be used to traverse and transform tree structures.

An interesting alternative implementation of working memory uses temporary modifications of the connection strengths in the network that is used for creating the Gestalt. Each internal connection in this network can be given two different weights: A long-term weight which changes relatively slowly and a short-term weight which is limited in magnitude, changes rapidly, and spontaneously decays towards zero. The effective connection strength at any time is simply the sum of the short-term and long-term weights. The long-term weights encode knowledge about which patterns of activity constitute good interpretations of the input to the network (i.e. familiar or plausible Gestalts). The short-term weights act as a contextual overlay[11] that encodes information about which patterns of activity occurred recently. If the network receives a rich external input which is incompatible with recently occurring Gestalts, it will settle to a new Gestalt and the short-term weights will act as noise (to which these networks are very resistant). If, however, parts of the external input are missing and the remainder fits some recently occurring Gestalt, the short-term weights will favor this Gestalt over other alternative Gestalts which would fit the partial input just as well if the short-term weights were not considered. So the short-term weights will implement a content-addressable memory for recent Gestalts.

Some unpublished simulations I performed in 1973 showed that short-term weights could be used to allow a network to return to a partially completed higher-level procedure after using between-level sharing to execute a recursive call of the same procedure in the same hardware. In these simulations desired states were specified for all the units at all times so there were no hidden units and a variation of the perceptron convergence procedure could be used to learn the appropriate long-term weights. The short-term weights were adapted by a simple local rule that combined a decay term with a term that increased the weight between two unit-states that occurred in close temporal proximity.

With the advent of the backpropagation learning procedure, it is now possible to use backpropagation through time to adapt the long-term weights of hidden units in such a way that a recurrent network can learn for itself how to store and retrieve temporary information in the short-term weights. This modification of the backpropagation procedure is rather complex, since it requires the backpropagated derivatives to take into account indirect effects of the following form: A change in a long-term weight at time t causes activity levels to change at time $t + 1$ which causes short-term weights to change at time $t + 2$ which causes activity levels to change at all subsequent times. A much simpler alternative is to ignore these complicated components of the derivatives and to rely on the fact that a simple hebbian rule for incrementing the short-term weights will typically cause these weights to store the information that is required a short time later. This simplification is similar to the simplification often used in recurrent nets in which derivatives are not back-propagated through time in a recurrent network. Instead, it is assumed that the hidden units will fortuitously encode the historical information that is subsequently required for performing the task [16].

7.2. Choosing mappings

Decisions about which parts of the world or the task should be mapped into

---

[11] A very different use of this contextual overlay is described in [14]. It can be used to approximately cancel out recent changes in the long-term weights, thus allowing earlier memories to be "deblurred."

which parts of the connectionist hardware are clearly of central importance and would form a major part of any account of how a particular network performed a particular rational inference. The purpose of this subsection is simply to point out that there is an interesting spectrum of possible ways in which a network might focus its attention on a particular piece of the domain. At one end of the spectrum, a separate "executive" module would select the current mapping without using any information about the representations that were then generated using that mapping. The choice of mapping would be based on previously generated representations, but not on the representation generated using the current mapping. At the other end of the spectrum, the desired mapping could be defined in terms of the representations it produced, so that the network would have to simultaneously settle on the mapping and the representation. Although this search might involve many iterations, it would not be sequential in the sense in which rational inference is sequential: It would not involve a sequence of *settlings*. So in the description of the rational inference, the network would just intuitively choose the appropriate mappings to generate the required representations at each step.

A working example of this way of choosing mappings is described in [12]. A network that is trying to locate a letter in an image that contains several letters can activate the desired shape representation and use this to select the correct mapping of the image onto the recognition apparatus.

7.3. An example of between-level sharing

So far, the discussion of between-level sharing has been rather abstract, mainly because there is no working implementation that properly illustrates the approach. Even without an implementation, however, the ideas may be clearer in the context of a specific task.

Consider a network that is trying to arrive at a plan of action that satisfies several goals such as arriving home on time with the TV guide, the wine and the pizza. Given enough units, it is possible to design a network in which all the possible choices and all the constraints between them can be simultaneously represented. Then, if the activities of some units are clamped to represent the satisfied goals, a single settling of this whole network can arrive at a set of choices that are consistent and that satisfy the goals. Given fewer units, however, this fixed mapping approach is not feasible and it is necessary to solve the overall task one piece at a time.

If there were no interactions between the subtasks, the serial computation would be relatively simple, and the connectionist implementation would be relatively uninteresting. But to arrive home on time, it may be necessary to choose a single store that sells several of the desired items, or a set of stores that are close to one another. Instead of solving the subtasks one at a time, it may be better to first settle on a rough overall plan, and to leave the details until later. The rough overall plan may contain reduced descriptions of the way each subtask will be solved. These reduced descriptions must have sufficient detail to ensure that the solutions to the subtasks fit together properly, but they do not require the full details of the solution. Of course, when the network later focusses its attention on a subtask, it may turn out to be impossible to fill in the details in a way that is consistent with the assumed solutions of the other subtasks, in which case a new overall rough plan will have to be formulated.

By sequentially re-using the same hardware for settling on the detailed solutions to the subtasks, the network can share the knowledge in the connections between these subtasks. However, the need to go back and reformulate the overall plan when its parts cannot be implemented consistently illustrates the major drawback of this kind of sharing: If the constraints are not all satisfied at the same time, it may be necessary to change the focus of attention many times before arriving at a solution which is consistent at all levels. For a network to avoid this kind of sequential "thrashing" it must use reduced descriptions of the subtasks that are compact enough to allow the global constraint satisfaction, but detailed enough to ensure that the parts of the global solution are locally feasible. For genuine puzzles, this may not be possible, but for normal common sense reasoning where there are many possible solutions it should be possible to learn appropriate reduced descriptions that allow large but friendly real-world constraint satisfaction problems to be hierarchically partitioned into manageable pieces. Whether this can actually be done remains to be seen.

7.4. Capturing regularities versus parallel recognition

The use of between-level sharing allows a connectionist network to capture certain kinds of regularity, but only by resorting to serial processing, and the loss of parallel processing seems like a very high price to pay. Connectionists would like their models to have all three of the following properties:

(1) All the long-term knowledge should be in the connection strengths.
(2) The network should capture the important regularities of the domain.
(3) Rapid recognition should be achieved by recognizing the major parts of a whole in parallel.

Unfortunately, it is very hard to achieve all three properties at once. If the knowledge is in the connections, and if the same knowledge is required to recognize several different parts of the same object (e.g. the letters in the word "banana") it seems as if we have to make an unpalatable choice. We can either capture the regularities in the appearances of different tokens of the same letter by sequentially re-using the very same connections to recognize the different instances of the letter "a," or we can achieve parallel recognition by replicating "a" recognizers across all the different positions in the word. McClelland [20] describes a clever but inefficient way out of this dilemma:

There is a single canonical representation of the knowledge whose weights are copied *during recognition* to produce the required parallel recognizers. An alternative way out of the dilemma is to use the learning process to transfer the knowledge from a canonical representation to a set of role-specific recognizers. The knowledge transfer is much slower than in McClelland's scheme, but it requires far fewer connections because weights are not transferred explicitly, and once the learning has been done, no transfer is required during recognition. This idea has strong similarities to a method that has been used by linguists to escape from the same dilemma. Some regularities of English that appear to require a context-sensitive grammar can actually be captured by generating sets of specific context-free rules from some underlying context-free meta-rules [7]. The whole system is context-free, and although there is great redundancy among sets of specific context-free rules, the regularity is nevertheless captured by the fact that the members of each set were all generated from the same underlying meta-rule.

Figure 7 suggests one way of using learning to transfer knowledge. The serial recognizers can be used to train the parallel, role-specific recognizers. A network that timeshares a serial recognizer already requires role-specific units for storing its successive outputs. If these role-specific units have some connections to the perceptual input, these connections can be trained by assuming that the outcome of the serial recognition is the desired outcome of the parallel recognition. The canonical, timeshared representation of the knowledge would then be acting as an internal local teacher for the parallel recognition hardware. This resembles the way in which the outcome of a serial mini-max tree search can be used to evaluate a position and hence to specify the desired outcome of a "parallel" board evaluation [25]. In the language of Section 3, rational inference can be used to train intuitive inference.

The usefulness of this method of transferring knowledge obviously depends on how much faster the learning is with an internal local teacher. This, in turn, depends on whether the canonical representations and the role-specific representations are distributed. If the representations are distributed, and if there is a non-arbitrary mapping between the canonical and the role-specific representations of the same entity, then the role-specific representations can be learned *much* faster because the canonical representations provide detailed information about what pattern of activity to use. This is equivalent to specifying desired values for the hidden units of a network. Connectionist learning is slow when it has to construct hidden representations and it is much faster when all units have their desired values specified.

8. Are These Just Implementation Details?

Proponents of the "classical" symbol processing approach to cognition have argued that many of the issues discussed in this paper are mere implementation details [6]. My view of this claim is best expressed by an analogy. Consider the theory that all locomotion requires wheels. A proponent of this theory could reasonably argue that people have wheels. Since people move over rough ground, they need very large diameter wheels with very springy suspension. They achieve this by implementing one spoke and one piece of rim for each wheel and then timesharing it. The only problem with this argument is that many of the "obvious" properties of wheels that we normally take for granted do not hold in this biological implementation. The timesharing removes the need for a fully revolving bearing, but it requires repeated accelerations and decelerations that make the system energetically inefficient at high speeds. Also, the timeshared spokes can be used in many other ways that do not at all resemble uses of normal wheels. If we insist on viewing connectionist networks as just a novel implementation of classical symbol processing, we should expect many of the standard intuitions we derive from classical systems to be equally misleading.

One major contribution of the connectionist approach is that it focusses attention on the distinction between rational and intuitive inference. Classical symbol processing takes rational inference as its paradigm. On a serial machine it is easy to program the kind of deliberate reasoning that occurs when a person sorts a list of numbers into ascending order. This is no coincidence: serial machines were designed to model this kind of deliberate reasoning, and so they are easy to program whenever a task can be reduced to straightforward deliberate reasoning. From the connectionist perspective, this is unsurprising and provides no justification for the idea that the kinds of inference which we make fast and intuitively should also be modeled by the same kind of symbol processing. The idea that fast intuitive inference is similar in form to conscious inference, but without the consciousness, seems to me to be a major psychological error. So long as we only consider serial machines, however, there is not much motivation for using a quite different model for fast intuitive inference, because the motivation comes from considerations about what kind of processing can be done fast in a connectionist network.[12]

A major weakness of the connectionist systems that have been sketched out in this paper is that they have great difficulty handling quantifiers and variable binding. A primitive scheme for variable binding is described in [32], but connectionist networks would be more convincing if they could rapidly construct complex, plausible scenarios in which many instantiated schemas fit together appropriately. Shastri [26] has recently described one way of doing this using localist representations. Each schema has its own dedicated hardware including dedicated hardware for representing the fillers of its slots. Shastri uses temporal phase as a temporary symbol for a slot-filler, but the same basic

---

[12] Tractability may also provide a motivation for some limited form of inference, but it is not clear why the same tractability argument should not also be applied to rational inference.

scheme could be implemented using reduced descriptions. This may allow fast, parallel, intuitive inference to do much more than simply completing the instantiation of a single schema.[13]

9. Summary of the Three Types of Mapping

If we consider how to map a part–whole hierarchy into a finite amount of parallel hardware there are three broad approaches: Fixed mappings, within-level timesharing, and between-level timesharing. These three approaches can be distinguished by abstract properties of the mappings involved:

(1) The fixed mapping uses a one-to-one mapping. Each object in the part–whole hierarchy is always mapped into a pattern of activity in the same set of units, and each set of units is always used to represent the same object.

(2) Within-level sharing uses a many-to-one mapping. Many different objects at the same level can be mapped into the same set of units in the serial recognition apparatus. But whenever one of these objects is recognized, it is represented in the same units.

(3) Between-level sharing uses a many-to-many mapping. It allows many different objects at the same level to be mapped into the same set of units, but it also allows the same object to be mapped into different sets of units depending on the level at which attention is focussed.

10. Conclusions

An important consequence of using role-specific reduced descriptions to implement pointers is that the relationship between a pointer and the thing it points to is not arbitrary. So computations, such as inferring the filler of one role when given the fillers of other roles, that would normally require a lot of sequential pointer-chasing, can be performed without accessing the full descriptions of the fillers. This means that the process of using a reduced description to gain access to the corresponding full description can be a relatively rare and slow event.

The combination of slow sequential access to full descriptions and fast parallel constraint-satisfaction using reduced descriptions is a style of computation that is well-suited to neural networks. The parallel inner loop allows the network to perform a great deal of computation by settling into a state that

---

[13] In [9] I rejected the idea of using separate hardware for each schema because I thought this would make it impossible to share common information between schemas. Now I can see a way out of the dilemma: For parallel inference, we give each schema its own hardware, but to capture the regularities among different schemas we have additional hardware for the fully-articulated representation of a schema. In this additional hardware, different schemas correspond to alternative activity patterns.

satisfies constraints that are encoded in the connections. So if the appropriate representations are known, a lot of useful computation can be done by a single intuitive inference. More elaborate computations which cannot be performed in a single settling using the current representations are performed by a sequence of settlings, and after each settling the mapping between the world and the network is changed. The ability to change the mapping is what allows the knowledge in any particular set of connections to be brought to bear on any part of the task, and thus provides the great flexibility that is characteristic of rational human thought.

ACKNOWLEDGEMENT

I thank Eugene Charniak, Jeffrey Elman, and David Plaut for helpful comments on an earlier draft. Many of the ideas described here were influenced by members of the PDP Research Group at San Diego, the Boltzmann group at Carnegie-Mellon and the Connectionist Research Group at Toronto.

REFERENCES

1. H.B. Barlow, Single units and sensation: A neuron doctrine for perceptual psychology? *Perception* **1** (1972) 371–394.
2. H.J. Berliner and D.H. Ackley, The QBKG system: Generating explanations from a non-discrete knowledge representation, in: *Proceedings AAAI-82*, Pittsburgh, PA (1982) 213–216.
3. E. Charniak and E. Santos, A connectionist context-free parser which is not context-free, but then it is not really connectionist either, in: *Proceedings Ninth Annual Conference of the Cognitive Science Society*, Seattle, WA (1987).
4. M. Derthick, Counterfactual reasoning with direct models, in: *Proceedings AAAI-87*, Seattle, WA (1987).
5. S.E. Fahlman, *NETL: A System for Representing and Using Real-world Knowledge* (MIT Press, Cambridge, MA, 1979).
6. J.A. Fodor and Z.W. Pylyshyn, Connectionism and cognitive architecture: A critical analysis, *Cognition* **28** (1988) 3–71.
7. G. Gazdar, Phrase structure grammar, in: P. Jacobson and G.K. Pullum, eds., *The Nature of Syntactic Representation* (Reidel, Dordrecht, 1982) 131–186.
8. W.D. Hillis, *The Connection Machine* (MIT Press, Cambridge, MA, 1985).
9. G.E. Hinton, Implementing semantic networks in parallel hardware, in: G.E. Hinton and J.A. Anderson, eds., *Parallel Models of Associative Memory* (Erlbaum, Hillsdale, NJ, 1981).
10. G.E. Hinton, Learning distributed representations of concepts, in: *Proceedings Eighth Annual Conference of the Cognitive Science Society*, Amherst, MA (1986).
11. G.E. Hinton, Deterministic Boltzmann learning performs steepest descent in weight-space, *Neural Comput.* **1** (1989) 143–150.
12. G.E. Hinton and K.J. Lang, Shape recognition and illusory conjunctions, in: *Proceedings IJCAI-85*, Los Angeles, CA (1985).
13. G.E. Hinton, J.L. McClelland and D.E. Rumelhart, Distributed representations, in: D.E. Rumelhart, J.L. McClelland and the PDP Research Group, eds., *Parallel Distributed Processing: Explorations in the Microstructure of Cognition* **1**: *Foundations* (MIT Press, Cambridge, MA, 1986).
14. G.E. Hinton and D.C. Plaut, Using fast weights to deblur old memories, in: *Proceedings Ninth Annual Conference of the Cognitive Science Society*, Seattle, WA (1987).

15. J.J. Hopfield, Neural networks and physical systems with emergent collective computational abilities, *Proc. Nat. Acad. Sci. USA* **79** (1982) 2554–2558.
16. M.I. Jordan and D.A. Rosenbaum, Action, in: M.I. Posner, ed., *Foundations of Cognitive Science* (MIT Press, Cambridge, MA, 1989) Chapter 19, 727–767.
17. T. Kohonen, *Associative Memory: A System-theoretical Approach* (Springer, Berlin, 1977).
18. J.E. Laird, P.S. Rosenbloom and A. Newell, Chunking in Soar: The anatomy of a general learning mechanism, *Mach. Learn.* **1** (1986) 11–46.
19. K. Lashley, In search of the engram, in: *Symposia of the Society for Experimental Biology* **4** (Academic Press, New York, 1950).
20. J.L. McClelland, The programmable blackboard model of reading, in: J.L. McClelland, D.E. Rumelhart and the PDP Research Group, eds., *Parallel Distributed Processing: Explorations in the Microstructure of Cognition* **2**: *Applications* (MIT Press, Cambridge, MA, 1986).
21. J.L. McClelland and D.E. Rumelhart, An interactive activation model of context effects in letter perception, Part 1: An account of basic findings, *Psychol. Rev.* **88** (1981) 375–407.
22. F.J. Pineda, Generalization of back propagation to recurrent and higher order neural networks, in: *Proceedings IEEE Conference on Neural Information Processing Systems*, Denver, CO (1987).
23. J.B. Pollack, Recursive distributed representations, *Artificial Intelligence* **46** (1990) 77–107, this issue.
24. D.E. Rumelhart, G.E. Hinton and R.J. Williams, Learning internal representations by back-propagating errors, *Nature* **323** (1986) 533–536.
25. A.L. Samuel, Some studies in machine learning using the game of checkers, in: E.A. Feigenbaum and J. Feldman, eds., *Computers and Thought* (McGraw-Hill, New York, 1963) 71–105.
26. L. Shastri, A connectionist system for rule based reasoning with multi-place predicates and variables, Tech. Rept. MS-CIS-89-06, Department of Computer and Information Science, School of Engineering and Applied Science, University of Pennsylvania, Philadelphia, PA (1989).
27. P. Smolensky, Schema selection and stochastic inference in modular environments, in: *Proceedings AAAI-83*, Washington, DC (1983) 109–113.
28. P. Smolensky, On the proper treatment of connectionism, *Behav. Brain Sci.* **11** (1988) 1–74.
29. P. Smolensky, Tensor product variable binding and the representation of symbolic structures in connectionist systems, *Artificial Intelligence* **46** (1990) 159–216, this issue.
30. D.S. Touretzky, Reconciling connectionism with the recursive nature of stacks and trees, in: *Proceedings Eighth Annual Conference of the Cognitive Science Society*, Amherst, MA (1986).
31. D.S. Touretzky, BoltzCONS: Dynamic symbol structures in a connectionist network, *Artificial Intelligence* **46** (1990) 5–46, this issue.
32. D.S. Touretzky and G.E. Hinton, Symbols among the neurons: Details of a connectionist inference architecture, in: *Proceedings IJCAI-85*, Los Angeles, CA (1985).
33. D.J. Willshaw, O.P. Buneman and H.C. Longuet-Higgins, Nonholographic associative memory, *Nature* **222** (1969) 960–962.

Recursive Distributed Representations

Jordan B. Pollack

*Laboratory for AI Research and Computer and
Information Science Department, The Ohio State University,
2036 Neil Avenue, Columbus, OH 43210, USA*

ABSTRACT

A longstanding difficulty for connectionist modeling has been how to represent variable-sized recursive data structures, such as trees and lists, in fixed-width patterns. This paper presents a connectionist architecture which automatically develops compact distributed representations for such compositional structures, as well as efficient accessing mechanisms for them. Patterns which stand for the internal nodes of fixed-valence trees are devised through the recursive use of backpropagation on three-layer auto-associative encoder networks. The resulting representations are novel, in that they combine apparently immiscible aspects of features, pointers, and symbol structures. They form a bridge between the data structures necessary for high-level cognitive tasks and the associative, pattern recognition machinery provided by neural networks.

1. Introduction

One of the major stumbling blocks in the application of connectionism to higher-level cognitive tasks, such as natural language processing, has been the inadequacy of its representations. Both local and distributed representations have, thus far, been unsuitable for capturing the dynamically-allocated variable-sized symbolic data structures traditionally used in AI. This limitation shows in the fact that pure connectionism has generated somewhat unsatisfying systems in this domain; for example, parsers for fixed length sentences [5, 8, 10, 37], without embedded structures [22].[1]

Indeed, some of the recent attacks on connectionism have been aimed precisely at the question of representational adequacy. According to Minsky and Papert [25], for example, work on neural network and other learning machines was stopped by the need for AI to focus on knowledge representation in the 1970s, because of the principle that "no machine can learn to recognize *X* unless it possesses, at least potentially, some scheme for *representing X* (p. xiii)." Fodor and Pylyshyn's [9] arguments against connectionism are

---

[1] Hybrid (connectionist–symbolic) models [3, 19, 31, 41] have the potential for more powerful representations, but do not insist on the neural plausibility constraints which create the limitations in the first place.

Artificial Intelligence **46** (1990) 77–105
0004-3702/90/$03.50 © 1990 — Elsevier Science Publishers B.V. (North-Holland)

based on their belief that connectionist machines do not even have the *potential* for representing X, where X is combinatorial (syntactic) constituent structure, and hence cannot exhibit (semantic) "systematicity" of thought processes.

Agreeing thoroughly that compositional symbolic structures are important, in this paper I show a connectionist architecture which can discover compact distributed representations for them. *Recursive auto-associative memory* (RAAM) uses backpropagation [33] on a nonstationary environment to devise patterns which stand for all of the internal nodes of fixed-valence trees. Further, the representations discovered are not merely connectionist implementations of classic concatenative data structures, but are in fact *new*, interesting, and potentially very useful.

The rest of this paper is organized as follows. After a background on connectionist representational schemes, the RAAM architecture is described, and several experiments presented. Finally, there is a discussion of the generative capacity of the architecture, and an analysis of the new representations and their potential applications.

1.1. Background: Connectionist representations

Normal computer programs have long used sequential data structures, such as arrays and lists, as primitives. Because of the built-in notion of "address", moreover, the contents of sequences can be the addresses of other sequences; hence it is also quite simple for computer programs to represent and manipulate tree and graph structures as well. Representing lists and trees is not a trivial problem for connectionist networks, however, which do not use adjacent or randomly addressed memory cells, or permit the real-time dynamic creation of new units.

Some of the earliest work in modern connectionism made an inappropriate analogy between semantic networks and neural networks. The links in the former represented logical relations between concepts. The links in the latter represented weighted paths along which "activation energy" flowed. Needless to say, these first connectionist networks, in which each concept was mapped onto a single neuron-like unit, did not have the representational capacity of their logically powerful cousins.

Furthermore, local representational schemes do not efficiently represent sequential information. The standard approach involves converting time into space by duplicating subnetworks into a fixed set of buffers for sequential input. Both early connectionist work, such as McClelland and Rumelhart's word recognition model [23], as well as more modern efforts [2, 10] use this approach, which is not able to represent or process sequences longer than a predetermined bound. One way to overcome this length limitation is by "sliding" the input across the buffer [4, 36]. While such systems are capable of processing sequences longer than the predetermined bound, they are not really representing them.

Distributed representations have been the focus of much research (including the work reported herein) since the circulation of Hinton's 1984 report [11] discussing the properties of representations in which "each entity is represented by a pattern of activity distributed over many computing elements, and each computed element is involved in representing many different entities."

The most obvious and natural distributed representation is a feature (or micro-feature) system, traditionally used in linguistics. A good example of a connectionist model using such a representation is Kawamoto's work on lexical access [17]. However, since the entire feature system is needed to represent a single concept, attempts at representing structures involving those concepts cannot be managed in the same system. For example, if all the features are needed to represent a NURSE, and all the features are needed to represent an ELEPHANT, then the attempt to represent NURSE RIDING ELEPHANT may come out either as a WHITE ELEPHANT or a rather LARGE NURSE WITH FOUR LEGS.

To solve the problem of feature superposition, one might use full-size constituent buffers, such as Agent, Action, and Object [22]. In each buffer would reside a feature pattern filling these roles such as NURSE, RIDING, and ELEPHANT. Unfortunately, because of the dichotomy between the representation of a structure (by concatenation) and the representation of an element of the structure (by features), this type of system cannot represent embedded structures such as "John saw the nurse riding an elephant." A solution to the feature-buffer dichotomy problem was anticipated and sketched out by Hinton [13], and involved having a "reduced description" for NURSE RIDING ELEPHANT which would fit into the constituent buffers along with patterns for JOHN and SAW.

However, it was not immediately obvious how to develop such reduced descriptions. Instead, avant-garde connectionist representations were based on coarse-coding [11], which allows multiple semi-independent representational elements to be simultaneously present, by superposition, in a feature vector. Once multiple elements can be present, conventional groupings of the elements can be interpreted as larger structures.

For example, Touretzky developed a coarse-coded memory system and used it in a production system [40], a primitive LISP data-structuring system called BoltzCONS [38], and a combination of the two for simple tree manipulations [39]. In his representation, the 15,625 triples of 25 symbols (A–Y) are elements to be represented, and using patterns over 2000 bits, small sets of such triples could be reliably represented. Interpreting the set of triples as pseudo-CONS cells, a limited representation of sequences and trees could be achieved.

Similarly, in their past-tense model, Rumelhart and McClelland [34] developed an *implicitly sequential representation*, where a set of well-formed overlapping triples could be interpreted as a sequence. It is instructive to view the basic idea of their representational scheme as the encoding of a sequence of tokens, $(i_1, \ldots, i_n)$ by an unordered set of overlapping subsequences (each of breadth k) of tokens:

$$\{(i_1, \ldots, i_k), (i_2, \ldots, i_{k+1}), \ldots, (i_{n-k+1}, \ldots, i_n)\} \ .$$

Thus, if a coarse-coded memory can simultaneously represent a set of such subsequences, then it can also represent a longer sequence.

The limits of this type of representation are that the cost of the representation goes up exponentially with its breadth, and, for any particular breadth, there may be sequences with too much internal duplication. Sets do not count multiple occurrences of their elements. So a system, for example, which represented the spellings of words as sets of letter-*pairs* would not be able to represent the word *yoyo*, and even if the breadth were increased to three, the system would still not be able to represent words with duplicate triples such as *banana.*[2]

Although both Touretzky's and Rumelhart and McClelland's coarse-coded representations were fairly successful for their circumscribed tasks, there remain some problems:

(1) A large amount of human effort was involved in the design, compression and tuning of these representations, and it is often not clear how to translate that effort across domains.

(2) Coarse-coding requires expensive and complex access mechanisms, such as pullout networks [26] or clause-spaces [40].

(3) Coarse-coded symbol memories can only simultaneously instantiate a small number of representational elements (like triples of 25 tokens) before spurious elements are introduced.[3] Furthermore, they assume that all possible tokens need to be combined.

(4) They utilize binary codes over a large set of units (hundreds or thousands).

(5) Their mode of aggregating larger structures out of basic elements is superpositional, the cause of problems (2) and (3).

In contrast, the distributed representations devised by the RAAM architecture demonstrate better properties:

(1) Encodings are developed mechanically by an adaptive network.

(2) The access mechanisms are simple and deterministic.

(3) A potentially very large number of primitive elements can *selectively* combine into constituent structures. Not all triples of symbols can, or need, be represented.

---

[2] To point out this "banana problem" with Rumelhart and McClelland's actual representation, which was phonological rather than orthographic, Pinker and Prince [27] discovered words with enough internal duplication in the Oykangand language.

[3] Rosenfeld and Touretzky [32] provide a nice analysis of coarse-coded symbol memories.

(4) The representations utilize real values over few units (tens).
(5) The aggregation mode is compositional.

2. Recursive Auto-Associative Memory

The problem under attack, then, is the representation of variable-sized symbolic sequences or trees in a numeric fixed-width form, suitable for use with
association, categorization, pattern recognition, and other neural-style processing mechanisms.

Consider two hypothetical mechanisms which could translate, in both directions, between symbolic trees and numeric vectors. The *compressor* should
encode small sets of fixed-width patterns into single patterns of the same size.
It could be recursively applied, from the bottom up, to a fixed-valence tree
with labeled terminals (leaves), resulting in a fixed-width pattern representing
the entire structure. For the binary tree $((A\ B)\ (C\ D))$, shown in Fig. 1, where
each of the terminals is a fixed-width pattern, this would take three steps. First
A and B would be compressed into a pattern, R_1. Then C and D would be
compressed into a pattern, R_2. Finally, R_1 and R_2 would be compressed into
R_3.

The *reconstructor* should decode these fixed-width patterns into facsimiles of
their parts, and determine when the parts should be further decoded. It could
be recursively applied, from the top down, resulting in a reconstruction of the
original tree. Thus, for this example, R_3 would be decoded into R_1' and R_2'. R_1'
would be decoded into A' and B', and R_2' into C' and D'.

These mechanisms are hypothetical, because it is not clear either how to
physically build or computationally simulate such devices, or what the R_i
patterns look like. In answer to the first question, I just assume that the
mechanism could be built out of the standard modern connectionist substrate
of layered fully-connected feed-forward networks of semilinear units.[4] For
binary trees with k-bit patterns as the leaves, the compressor could be a
single-layer network with $2k$ inputs and k outputs. The reconstructor could be
a single-layer network with k inputs and $2k$ outputs. Schematics for these are
shown in Fig. 2.

Fig. 1. Example of a binary tree.

[4] I also assume that the reader is, by now, familiar with this standard, as well as with the
backpropagation technique for adjusting weights [33], and will not attempt a re-presentation of the
mathematics. The work herein does not crucially depend on the default assumptions of semilineari-
ty and full-connectedness. By relying on these standard defaults, however, I hope to keep the focus
on issue of representation.

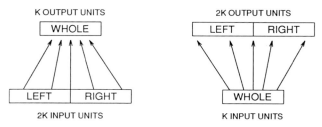

Fig. 2. Proposed feed-forward networks for the compressor and reconstructor working with binary trees.

In answer to the second, regarding what the patterns look like, we develop the strategy of letting a connectionist network devise its own representations. Consider simultaneously training these two mechanisms as a single $2k$-k-$2k$ network, as shown in Fig. 3.

This looks suspiciously like a network for the encoder problem [1]. Back-propagation has been quite successful at this problem,[5] when used in a self-supervised auto-associative mode on a three-layer network. The network is trained to reproduce a set of input patterns; i.e., the input patterns are also used as desired (or target) patterns. In learning to do so, the network develops a compressed code on the hidden units for each of the input patterns. For example, training an 8-3-8 network to reproduce the eight 1-bit-in-8 patterns usually results in a 3-bit binary code on the hidden units.

In order to find codes for trees, however, this auto-associative architecture

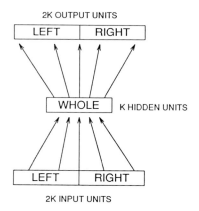

Fig. 3. Single network composed of both compressor and reconstructor.

[5] Rumelhart et al. [33] demonstrated only an 8-3-8 network, but other successful uses include a 64-16-64 network [6] and a 270-45-270 network [10]. The three numbers correspond to the number of units in the input, hidden, and output layers of a network.

must be used recursively (hence its name). Extending the simple example from above, if A, B, C, and D were k-bit patterns, the network could be trained to reproduce $(A\,B)$, (C, D), and $((A\,B)\,(C\,D))$ as follows:

input pattern	hidden pattern	output pattern
$(A\,B)$	$\rightarrow\quad R_1(t)$	$\rightarrow\quad (A'(t)\,B'(t))$
$(C\,D)$	$\rightarrow\quad R_2(t)$	$\rightarrow\quad (C'(t)\,D'(t))$
$(R_1(t)\,R_2(t))$	$\rightarrow\quad R_3(t)$	$\rightarrow\quad (R_1(t)'R_2(t)')$

where t represents the time, or epoch, of training. Assuming that backpropagation converges in the limit, the sum of the squares of the differences between the desired and actual outputs would go to 0, and:

$$A' = A, \quad C' = C, \quad R_1' = R_1,$$
$$B' = B, \quad D' = D, \quad R_2' = R_2.$$

   Therefore, R_3 would, in fact, be a representation for the tree $((A\,B)\,(C\,D))$, by virtue of the fact that the compressor would be a deterministic algorithm which transforms the tree to its representation, and the reconstructor a deterministic algorithm which transforms the representation back to the tree. Along the way, representations will also be devised for all subtrees, in this case, $(A\,B)$ and $(C\,D)$. Note that, as will be demonstrated later, this strategy works on a collection of trees just as it does on a single tree.

   There are a few details which form a bridge between theory and practice.

   (1) The (initially random) values of the hidden units, $R_i(t)$, are used as part of the training environment. Therefore, as the weights in the network evolve, so do some of the patterns that comprise the training environment. This form of nonstationary, or "moving target" learning has also been explored by others [7, 24]. The stability and convergence of the network are sensitive to the learning parameters. Following the explication of Rumelhart et al. [33, p. 330], there are two such parameters: the learning rate η, which controls the gradient descent step size, and the momentum α, which integrates the effects of previous steps. These parameters must be set low enough that the change in the hidden representations does not invalidate the decreasing error granted by the change in weights, and high enough that some change actually takes place. In the experiments described later in this paper, η was usually set to 0.1 (less for the larger experiments), and α to 0.3. As the learning curve flattens out, α is slowly increased up to 0.9, following [28].

   (2) The induction relied upon is outside the mechanical framework of learning. This induction, of global success arising from only local improvements, is similar to the bucket brigade principle used in classifier systems [14]. Since the training strategy never reconstructs the terminals

from R'_1 or R'_2, only the fact that they are equal, in the limit, to R_1 and R_2 allows this strategy to work.

But backpropagation cannot really run forever, and therefore, at least with use of the standard sigmoidal activation function, it is impossible to achieve the perfect encoding described above. So some practical way to decide when to stop training becomes necessary. When backpropagation is used to produce binary outputs, there is a tolerance, τ, conventionally set to 0.2, such that training can stop when every output value for every training pattern is within τ of the desired bit. For nonterminal patterns which may not be binary, however, 20% is far too permissive a tolerance. In order to successfully reconstruct A and B (to a tolerance of τ) from R'_1, for example, R'_1 must be *very* similar to R_1. Thus, a second tolerance, ν, is used for the real-valued non-terminals, which, for the experiments below, has been set at 0.05.

(3) The name for this architecture, recursive auto-associative memory (RAAM), accurately reflects that the codes developed by an auto-associative memory are being further compressed. It does not reflect that there are actually two separate mechanisms which happen to be simultaneously trained. These mechanisms also require some support in the form of control and memory, but nothing beyond the ability of simple neural networks using thresholds.

In order to encode a tree from the bottom up, the compressor needs a stack on which to store temporary results (such as R_1). In order to decode a tree from the top down, the reconstructor also needs an external stack on which to store intermediate patterns. Furthermore, it needs some mechanism to perform terminal testing. In the experiments presented below, it is assumed that this terminal test is merely a threshold test for "binary-ness", which checks that all the values of a pattern are above $1 - \tau$ or below τ. Alternatively, one could train a simple classifier, or use conventional computer programs which test for membership in a set, or perform error detection and correction.

2.1. Sequential RAAM

Since sequences, such as (X, Y, Z), can be represented as left-branching binary trees, i.e., $(((\text{NIL } X) \, Y) \, Z)$, an alternative version of the RAAM architecture works for developing representations and *last-in-first-out* access mechanisms for sequences.

This architecture is in fact simpler than the mechanism for trees. Compressed representations only have to be recirculated to one side, so they do have to be stored externally. There is less constraint on the size of the representations as well, and a higher dimension, M, can be assumed for the compressed patterns, than for the terminal symbols, L.

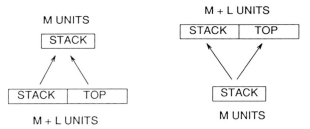

Fig. 4. Inverse sequencing mechanisms in single-layered networks. The compressor combines an *m*-dimensional representation for a sequence (STACK) with a new element (TOP), returning a new *m*-dimensional vector; the reconstructor decodes it back into its components.

Figure 4 shows the single-layer compressor and reconstructor networks for a sequential RAAM, which, when viewed as a single network has $M + L$ input and output units, and M hidden units. An M-vector of numbers, ε, is assumed to stand for NIL, the empty sequence. In the experiments below, vectors of all 0.5's are chosen, which are very unlikely ever to be generated as an intermediate state. Following the earlier logic, when this network is trained with the patterns:

input pattern		hidden pattern		output pattern
$(\varepsilon \ X)$	$\rightarrow$	$R_x(t)$	$\rightarrow$	$(\varepsilon'(t) \ X'(t))$
$(R_x(t) \ Y)$	$\rightarrow$	$R_{xy}(t)$	$\rightarrow$	$(R_x'(t) \ Y'(t))$
$(R_{xy}(t) \ Z)$	$\rightarrow$	$R_{xyz}(t)$	$\rightarrow$	$(R_{xy}(t)' \ Z'(t))$

it is expected that, after backpropagation converges, R_{xyz} will be a representation for the sequence $(X \ Y \ Z)$. Along the way, representations will also be developed for all prefixes to the sequence, in this case, (X) and $(X \ Y)$.

3. Experiments with Recursive Auto-Associative Memories

3.1. Proof of concept

To demonstrate that RAAM actually works under practical assumptions, and that it can discover compositional representations and simple access mechanisms, a small sequential RAAM is presented first.

The training set consisted of the eight possible sequences of three bits. Using a 4-3-4 network and an empty pattern of (0.5 0.5 0.5), the representations shown in Fig. 5 were developed. (The representations for all the prefixes are shown as well). The network has clearly developed into a tri-state shift register, where the first feature corresponds to the inverse of the last bit in, the second to the inverse of the next-to-last bit, and the third to the first bit encoded.

A shift register, which simply concatenates bits, is a classical means for

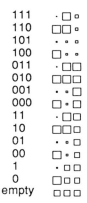

111	
110	
101	
100	
011	
010	
001	
000	
11	
10	
01	
00	
1	
0	
empty	

Fig. 5. Representations developed by a 4-3-4 RAAM for the complete set of bit patterns up to length 3. Each square represents a number between 0 and 1.

serially constructing and accessing an obviously compositional representation. But like any finite piece of hardware built to hold a certain number of bits, it degrades rather rapidly when over-filled. The more interesting area to explore involves pattern spaces which have underlying regularities, but do not depend on representing all possible combinations of subpatterns. It is under these conditions that an adaptive connectionist mechanism would be expected to display more desirable properties, such as content sensitivity and graceful degradation.

3.2. Letter sequences

Our second experiment involves learning to represent sequences of letters. Rather than trying to represent all possible sequences of letters, which would certainly give rise to another shift register, a limited subset of English words was chosen. Using an electronic spelling dictionary, those words containing only the 5 letters "B", "R", "A", "I", and "N" were selected, and then all prefixes (like "an" and "bar") were removed, resulting in the list below. Note that, in training, a representation is developed for every prefix:

AIR	ANA	ANI	BABAR	BANANA
BARBARIAN	BARN	BIBB	BIN	BRAIN
BRAN	BRIAR	INN	NAB	NIB
RABBI	RAIN	RAN	RIB	

Each terminal was coded as a 1-in-5 bit pattern, the empty vector, again, was all 0.5's, and a 30-25-30 RAAM was used to encode these words. Note that both BANANA and BARBARIAN would be troublesome for an implicit sequential representation of breadth three. Figure 6 shows the representations for these

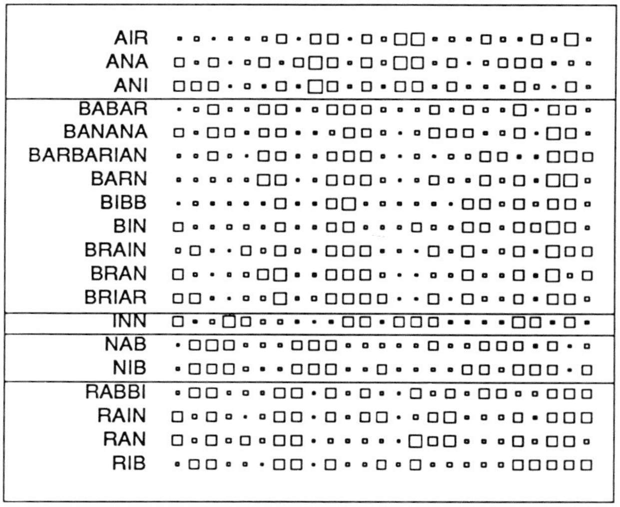

AIR
ANA
ANI
BABAR
BANANA
BARBARIAN
BARN
BIBB
BIN
BRAIN
BRAN
BRIAR
INN
NAB
NIB
RABBI
RAIN
RAN
RIB

Fig. 6. Representations developed by a 30-25-30 RAAM on letter sequences.

letter sequences, and the cluster diagram in Fig. 7 shows that, unlike a decaying sum representation in which information about older elements gets lost [16], this sequential representation is devoting the most resources to

INN
AIR
ANA
ANI
NAB
NIB
RAIN
RAN
RIB
RABBI
BIN
BIBB
BRIAR
BRAN
BRAIN
BARN
BARBARIAN
BABAR
BANANA

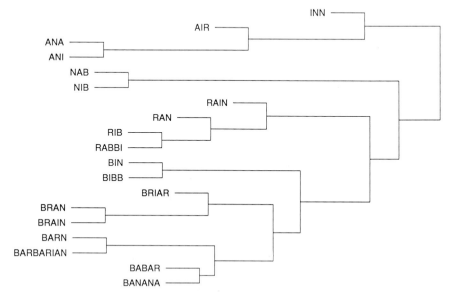

Fig. 7. Hierarchal clustering of the letter sequence representations.

keeping older elements alive. And even though there are enough resources to build a 5-letter shift register, the network cannot take this easy solution path because of its need to represent the 6- and 9-letter words.

3.2.1. *Learning well-formed syntactic trees*

The tree ((D (A N)) (V (P (D N)))) might be a syntactic parse tree for the sentence "The little boy ran up the street," given that the terminals D, A, N, V, and P stand respectively for *determiner, adjective, noun, verb,* and *preposition.* Consider a simple context-free grammar, where every rule expansion has exactly two constituents:

$$S \rightarrow NP\ VP\ |\ NP\ V$$
$$NP \rightarrow D\ AP\ |\ D\ N\ |\ NP\ PP$$
$$PP \rightarrow P\ NP$$
$$VP \rightarrow V\ NP\ |\ V\ PP$$
$$AP \rightarrow A\ AP\ |\ A\ N$$

Given a set of strings in the language defined by this grammar, it is easy to derive the bracketed binary trees which will make up a training set. With one such set of strings, a chart parser yielded the following set of trees:

$$(D\ (A\ (A\ (A\ N))))$$
$$((D\ N)\ (P\ (D\ N)))$$
$$(V\ (D\ N))$$
$$(P\ (D\ (A\ N)))$$
$$((D\ N)\ V)$$
$$((D\ N)\ (V\ (D\ (A\ N))))$$
$$((D\ (A\ N))\ (V\ (P\ (D\ N))))$$

Each terminal (D A N V & P) was then represented as a 1-bit-in-5 code padded with 5 zeros. A 20-10-20 RAAM devised the representations shown in Fig. 8.

Each tree and its representation have been labeled by the phrase type in the grammar, and then sorted by type. The RAAM has clearly developed a representation with similarity between members of the same type. For example, the third feature seems to be clearly distinguishing sentences from non-sentences, the fifth feature almost separates adjective phrases from others, while the tenth feature appears to distinguish prepositional and noun phrases from the rest.[6] Finally, a hierarchical cluster of these patterns in Fig. 9 reveals

---

[6] By these metrics, of course, ((D N) (P (D N))) is being classified as an S rather than an NP. This is not surprising since, like an S, it is not being further combined.

NP		
(D N)	□□□ □ · · • • □□	
(D (A (A (A N))))	□□□□ · · · · · □	
(D (A N))	□□□□ · · · · · □	
((D N) (P (D N)))	□ · □ · · · · □□ ·	

VP		
(V (P (D N)))	□ · □ · · • · □□ □	
(V (D (A N)))	· · □□ · □ · □□□	
(V (D N))	· · □□ · □ · □ · □	

PP		
(P (D N))	· · □ · · □ · □ □□	
(P (D (A N)))	· · □ · · □ · □□□	

AP		
(A N)	□ □□□□□ · □□ ·	
(A (A N))	· · □□□ · · □ □ ·	
(A (A (A N)))	· □ □□□ • · · □ ·	

S		
((D N) V)	□□ · □□ □ □□□ ·	
((D N) (V (D (A N))))	□ · □ · · · · □ □ ·	
((D (A N)) (V (P (D N))))	· □ □ □ · □ · □□ ·	

Fig. 8. Representations of all the binary trees in the training set, devised by a 20-10-20 RAAM, manually clustered by phrase type.

that the similarity between patterns generally follows the phrase type breakup, and also reflects the depths of the trees.

3.2.2. Learning to represent propositions

Tree representations are common data structures, used for semantic as well as syntactic structures. This final experiment sets up some propositional repre-

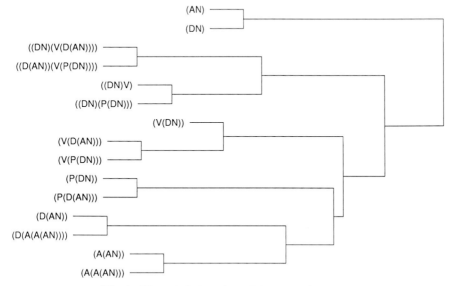

Fig. 9. Hierarchal clustering of the syntactic patterns.

sentations which will be exploited later in the paper, and merely demonstrates that the architecture is capable of working on more than just binary trees.[7]

Starting with a somewhat random collection of sentences, a RAAM was used to devise compact representations for corresponding propositional forms. The sentences used for training are shown in Table 1. The terminals for this RAAM are bit patterns for the symbols which appear in these sentences minus the determiners and pronouns, plus two new symbols: IS is used as a subject raiser in the representations for sentences 12 and 13, while MOD is used to specify adjectives in triples.

A similarity-based 16-bit binary representation was devised for the terminals, by first dividing them into five classes, THING, HUMAN, PREP, ADJ, and VERB, and then using one bit for each class along with a counter as shown in Table 2. Empty spots are all zeros. Each sentence was manually translated into a ternary tree (except sentence 10 which had two readings) as shown in Table 3. This representation is meant to capture the flavor of a recursive (Action Agent Object) case system. A 48-16-48 RAAM learned to construct representations and to recursively encode and decode these trees into their respective parts. These are again shown both pictorially (Fig. 10) and clustered (Fig. 11).

4. Discussion

4.1. Studies of generalization

Perhaps the most important question about recursive auto-associative memories is whether or not they are capable of any productive forms of

Table 1
Collection of sentences for propositional experiment

1	Pat loved Mary
2	John loved Pat
3	John saw a man on the hill with a telescope
4	Mary ate spaghetti with chopsticks
5	Mary ate spaghetti with meat
6	Pat ate meat
7	Pat knew John loved Mary
8	Pat thought John knew Mary loved John
9	Pat hoped John thought Mary ate spaghetti
10	John hit the man with a long telescope
11	Pat hoped the man with a telescope saw her
12	Pat hit the man who thought Mary loved John
13	The short man who thought he saw John saw Pat

[7] Of course, binary trees of symbols (along with a distinguished NIL element) are sufficient for arbitrary tree representations.

Table 2
16-bit patterns for the terminal symbols

WORD	THING 4 Bits	HUMAN 3 Bits	PREP 3 Bits	ADJ 2 Bits	VERB 4 Bits
HILL	1000				
STREET	1001				
TELESCOPE	1010				
CHOPSTICKS	1011				
MEAT	1100				
SPAGHETTI	1101				
MAN		100			
JOHN		101			
MARY		110			
PAT		111			
MOD			100		
WITH			101		
ON			110		
LONG				10	
SHORT				11	
IS					1000
KNEW					1001
HOPED					1010
THOUGHT					1011
LOVED					1100
HIT					1101
ATE					1110
SAW					1111

Table 3
Ternary trees for propositional experiment

1	(LOVED PAT MARY)
2	(LOVED JOHN PAT)
3	((WITH SAW TELESCOPE)JOHN (ON MAN HILL))
4	((WITH ATE CHOPSTICKS) MARY SPAGHETTI)
5	(ATE MARY (WITH SPAGHETTI MEAT))
6	(ATE PAT MEAT)
7	(KNEW PAT (LOVED JOHN MARY))
8	(THOUGHT PAT (KNEW JOHN (LOVED MARY JOHN)))
9	(HOPED PAT (THOUGHT JOHN (ATE MARY SPAGHETTI)))
10a	((WITH HIT (MOD TELESCOPE LONG)) JOHN MAN)
10b	(HIT JOHN (WITH MAN (MOD TELESCOPE LONG)))
11	(HOPED PAT (SAW (WITH MAN TELESCOPE) PAT))
12	(HIT PAT (IS MAN (THOUGHT MAN (LOVED MARY JOHN))))
13	(SAW (IS (MOD MAN SHORT) (THOUGHT MAN (SAW MAN JOHN))) PAT)

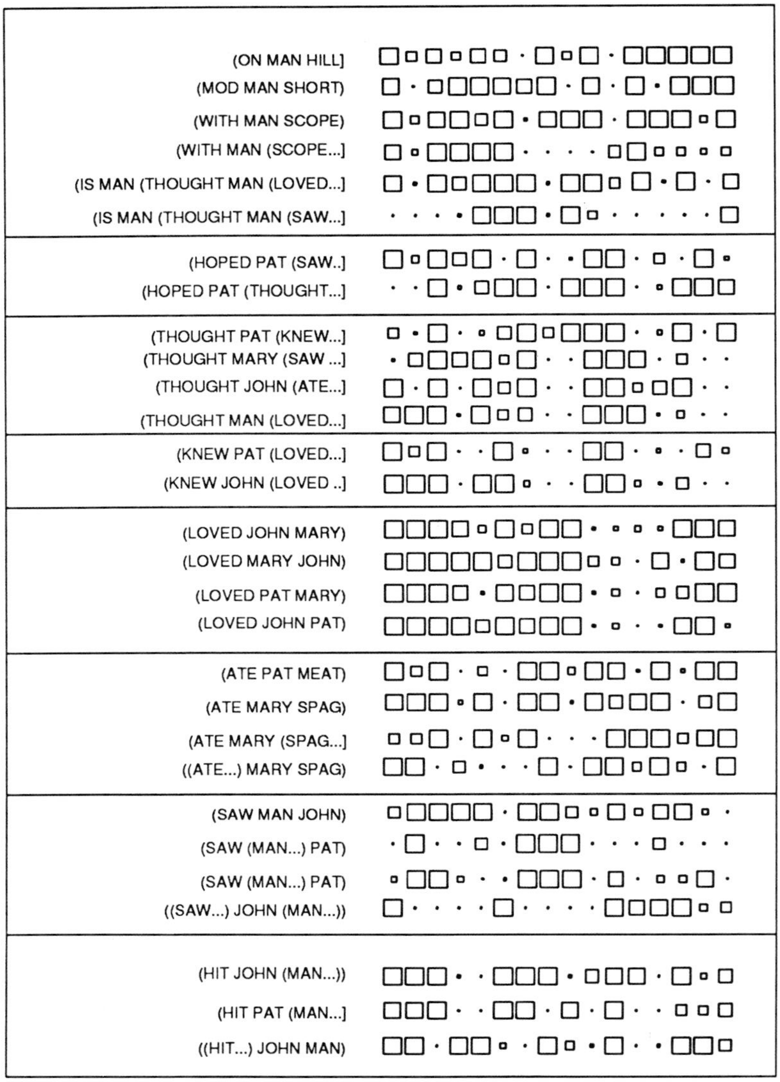

Fig. 10. Representations of the ternary semantic trees in the training set, devised by a 48-16-48 RAAM, manually clustered. The symbolic trees have been abbreviated to fit.

generalization. If it turned out that, as in the shift register example, they were just *memorizing* the training set, finding a convenient mapping from given structures to unassigned vertices in a high dimensional hypercube, then this work would ultimately be uninteresting. Luckily, this turns out not to be the case.

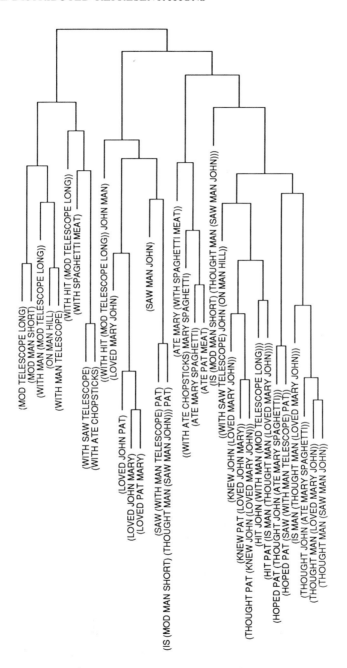

Fig. 11. Hierarchal clustering of the semantic patterns

It is a straightforward matter to enumerate the set of sequences or trees that a RAAM is capable of representing beyond the training set. Taken together, the encoder and decoder networks form a recursive well-formedness test as follows: Take two patterns for trees, encode them into a pattern for the new, higher-level, tree, and decode that back into the patterns for the two subtrees. If the reconstructed subtrees are within tolerance, then that tree can be considered well-formed.[8]

Using this procedure for tree RAAMs, a program can start with the set of terminals as the pool of well-formed patterns, and then exhaustively (or randomly) combine all pairs, adding new well-formed patterns to the pool. For sequential RAAMs, the pool is begun with just the pattern for the empty sequence, and a program merely attempts to compose each terminal with each pattern in the pool, adding new prefixes to the pool as they are found.

Running this generator over the network formed from the syntactic tree experiment yielded 31 well-formed trees, which are shown in Table 4. Of these, the first 12 are not really grammatical, although 8 of these seem to be based on a rule which allows two NPs to combine. There are three new instances of NPs, four new VPs, and twelve new Ss. Clearly some sort of generativity, beyond memorization, is going on here, though not yet in an infinite manner. At the least, new instances of the syntactic classes are being formed by recombination of parts.

The sequential RAAM for letter sequences is quite a bit more productive. It is able to represent about 300 new sequences of letters, of which approximately one-third are word-like, including names not in the electronic spelling dictionary like BRIAN, RINA, and BARBARA. Mostly, however, the novel sequences reflect low-order letter-transition statistics, indicating, again, that some recollective process more powerful than rote (list) memorization but less powerful than arbitrary random-access sequential storage is taking place.

There is also a tendency, especially by the 48-16-48 RAAM, to decode novel trees back to existing members of the training set. For example, the pattern encoded for

(THOUGHT JOHN (KNEW PAT (LOVED MARY JOHN)))

is reconstructed to

(THOUGHT PAT (KNEW JOHN (LOVED MARY JOHN))) ,

one of the original trees.

This lack of productivity is probably attributable to the problem that the input patterns are *too* similar; i.e., the Hamming distance between JOHN and

---

[8] Actually, this is a bit of a simplification, since the well-formedness test does not actually guarantee that the pattern for new tree can be fully decoded. If the tolerance is kept low enough, however, the full tree will be recoverable.

Table 4
Additional trees that can be represented by the 20-10-20 RAAM

(D A)
(V A)
(V N)
(V V)
(((D N) (P (D N))) N)
(((D N) (P (D N))) (D (A N)))
((D N) (((D N) (P (D N))) (D (A N))))
(((D N) (P (D N))) ((D N) (P (D N))))
(((D N) (P (D N))) ((D (A N)) (P (D N))))
((D N) (((D N) (P (D N))) ((D (A N)) (P (D N)))))
(((D N) (P (D N))) ((D N) (P (D N))) (D (A N))))
(((D N) (P (D N))) (((D N) (P (D N))) ((D (A N)) (P (D N)))))

((D (A N)) (P (D N)))
((D N) (P (D (A N))))
((D (A N)) (P (D (A N))))

(V ((D N) (P (D N))))
(V ((D (A N)) (P (D N))))
(V ((D N) (P (D (A N)))))
(V ((D (A N)) (P (D (A N)))))

((D N) (V (D N)))
(((D N) (P (D N))) V)
((D N) (V ((D N) (P (D N)))))
(((D N) (P (D N))) (V (D N)))
((D N) (V ((D (A N)) (P (D N)))))
((D N) (V ((D N) (P (D (A N))))))
(((D N) (P (D N))) (V (D (A N))))
((D N) (V ((D (A N)) (P (D (A N))))))
(((D N) (P (D N))) (V ((D N) (P (D N)))))
(((D N) (P (D N))) (V ((D N) (P (D (A N))))))
(((D N) (P (D N))) (V ((D (A N)) (P (D N)))))
(((D N) (P (D N))) (V ((D (A N)) (P (D (A N))))))

PAT is only one bit. But, while this RAAM was not as productive as hoped for, it was still quite systematic, according to Fodor and Pylyshyn's [9, p. 39] own definition:

> What does it mean to say that thought is systematic? Well, just as you don't find people who can understand the sentence "John loves the girl" but not the sentence "the girl loves John," so too you don't find people who can think the thought that John loves the girl but can't think the thought that the girl loves John.

All 16 cases of (LOVED X Y), with X and Y chosen from the set {JOHN, MARY, PAT, MAN}, were able to be reliably represented, even though only four of them were in the training set.

4.1.1. *Improving generalization capacity*

The productive capacity of these systems is not yet what it should be. There ought to be some way to acquire, at least theoretically, the ability to represent infinite numbers of similar structures in such recursive distributed representations.

Given that the simplest formulation (i.e., a three layer fully-connected semilinear network) using rather arbitrary training sets has shown some limited capacity in the form of a small number of new useful representations composed out of existing constituents, it seems likely that (1) better training environments and (2) different mathematical assumptions will be needed.

First, the similarity and difference relationships between terminal patterns affects the productivity of a RAAM. In the case of the semantic triples, the fact that terminals in the same class, like JOHN and MARY, were assigned very similar patterns, lead both to their ability to be used systematically, and to the problem that single-bit errors in reconstruction were damaging. On the other hand, one would expect fully random patterns to not generalize very well either. This brings up the question of how to design compressible representations. It seems very likely that the same sort of representations devised by a RAAM for the nonterminal patterns would lead to the best possible compression and generalization properties if adopted for terminals.

Secondly, to achieve truly infinite representational capacity in fixed-width patterns, it will be necessary, at least theoretically, to consider the underlying mathematical basis for connectionist networks, freed from the default implementational assumptions of back-propagation, i.e., floating-point calculations of linear combinations and sigmoids. On the one hand, it must be considered whether or not to use real numbers at all since they seem biologically and computationally problematic. An unbounded number of bits can be trivially compressed into a real number, leading to unbounded storage and communication costs. A simulated connectionist system using real numbers might be able to use these bits, (i.e. in very precise output values) without properly paying for them. By using only a binary code, a system must be able to exploit the redundancy (i.e. sparseness or regularity) in the environment. On the other hand, it is certainly reasonable, however unbiological, to assume rational numbers for a competence theory. The question to answer is whether there is a similarity-preserving mapping from complex structured representations to high-dimensional spatial representations.

4.2. Analysis of the representations

I do not yet have a prescription for engineering recursive distributed representations, but have a few insights into how they work. Top-down and bottom-up constraints work together to forge the representations. The bottom-up constraint is that each pattern is completely determined by its constituents and the knowledge eventually fixed in the network weights: *Trees with similar constituents must be similar*. The top-down constraint is that redundant information must be compressed out of similar structures (such as two NPs which both can combine with the same VP): *The possible siblings of a pattern must be similar*. Working against this drive towards similarity is the system-wide goal of minimizing error, which serves to "constrain apart" the patterns for different trees in the environment. The result of these pressures is that these representations consist of at least two types of features: *categorical* features, such as those identified earlier as being able to separate classes, and *distinctive* features, which vary across, and discriminate between, the members of each class.

The categorical features developed by the syntactic tree experiment become clear in examination of a small classifier. The patterns for each tree in the training set were used as input to a 10-input 5-output network which was trained to discriminate the classes NP, VP, PP, AP, and S.

Table 5 shows all the weights in this network, rounded to integers. The columns correspond to the categories, and the rows correspond to the features. The bias inputs to the category units are also shown as the first row, as are the sums of the absolute values of the weights in each row. Looking at the column labeled NP, for example, it is clear that the first, ninth, and tenth features strongly code for NP, while the eighth and fifth features code against NP. Looking at the column labeled VP, the third and eight features code for it, and the second and tenth against.

The "strength" of each row indicates how categorical or distinctive a feature is. The tenth feature, for example, strongly codes for NP and PP and against VP, AP, and S. The features which do not connect strongly everywhere, like the seventh and ninth, are used for discriminations within the categories. With regard to the binary-versus-real question raised earlier, it seems that RAAM may build a hybrid code. Strong binary distinctions are used for categorical

Table 5
Weights of single-layer classifier network rounded to integers

	NP	VP	PP	AP	S	Strength
Bias	−2	−8	−3	−4	6	
1	8	0	−2	−5	−4	19
2	2	−8	−3	−1	5	19
3	0	7	−2	3	−9	21
4	−1		−5	5	−1	14
5	−5	−6	−1	3	−1	16
6	−3		4	0	−4	14
7	−2	−1	0	−5	3	11
8	−10	10	−4	−5	2	31
9	3	0	2	2	−4	11
10	4	−9	7	−6	−3	29

judgements, while weaker analog distinctions are used for discriminating (and labeling) members within the categories.

4.2.1. *Geometric interpretation*

An alternative means of understanding these representations may come from geometry. The terminal patterns are vertices of a k-dimensional hypercube which contains all of the nonterminal patterns.

For binary trees, a RAAM is finding a consistent invertible mapping which works the same way on composable pairs of vertices, as it does on the internal points that are also composed. To view an image of this, a 6-3-6 RAAM was trained on the two trees $((A\ B)\ (C\ D))$ and $((A\ C)\ (B\ D))$, with $A = (0, 0, 0)$, $B = (1\ 0\ 0)$, $C = (0\ 1\ 0)$, and $D = (1\ 1\ 0)$; i.e. with A, B, C, and D the four points on the "floor" of a three-dimensional cube.

Figure 12 shows a perspective plot of the three-dimensional hypercube for the codes developed for these two trees. If one stares long enough, taking each pair of composable points in one's mental left and right hands, one can see triangles falling forward as they reduce in scale.

Saund [35] has investigated (nonrecursive) auto-association as a method of *dimensionality reduction*, and asserted that, in order to work, the map must be constrained to form a small-dimensional parametric surface in the larger-dimensional space. Consider just a 2-1-2 auto-associator. It is really an invertible mapping from certain points on the unit square to points on the unit line. In order to work, the network might develop a parametric one dimension-

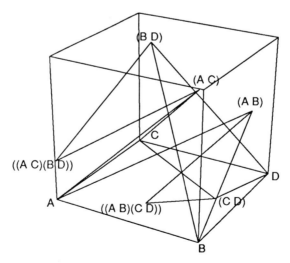

Fig. 12. Perspective diagram for the three-dimensional codes developed for the trees (A B) (C D)) and ((A C) (B D)).

al curve in two space, perhaps a set of connected splines. As more and more points need to be encoded, this parametric curve must get "curvier" to cover them. In the limit, especially if there are any dense "patches" of two-space which need to be covered, it can no longer be a one-dimensional curve, but must become a space-filling curve with a fractal dimension [21]. The notions of associative and reconstructive memories with fractal dimensions are further discussed elsewhere [30].

4.3. Applications

4.3.1. *Associative inference*

Since RAAM can devise representations of trees as numeric vectors which then can be attacked with the fixed-width techniques of neural networks, this work might lead to very fast inference and structural transformation engines. The question, of course, is whether the patterns for trees can be operated on, in a systematic fashion, without being decoded first. Below is a very simple demonstration of this possibility.

Since the RAAM for the propositional triples was able to represent all 16 cases of (LOVED $X\,Y$), it should be possible to build an associative network which could perform the simple implication: "If (LOVED $X\,Y$) then (LOVED $Y\,X$)." This would be a trivial shifting task if performed on an explicit concatenative representation. However, since the (48-bit) triples are compressed into 16-dimensional pattern vectors, it is not quite as simple a job.

The task is to find an associator which can transform the compressed representation for each antecedent (e.g. (LOVED MARY JOHN)) into the compressed representation for its consequent (e.g. (LOVED JOHN MARY)). Using backpropagation, a 16-8-16 feed-forward network was trained on 12 of the 16 pairs of patterns (to within 5% tolerance) and was then able to successfully transform the remaining 4 pairs.

What about a system which would need to follow long chains of such implications? There has recently been some work showing that under certain conditions, feed-forward networks with hidden layers can compute arbitrary nonlinear mappings [15, 18, 20]. Therefore, I anticipate that the sequential application of associative inference will be able to be compiled, at least by slow training, into fast networks of few layers.

Consider homogenous coordinate transformations (in computer graphics), where the linear nature of the primitive operations (scaling, rotation, and translation) allows any sequence of them to be "compiled" into a single matrix multiplication. The field of AI has not, to date, produced any compiling methods which can rival this speedup, because most interesting AI problems are nonlinear and most interesting AI representations are not numeric. The point is that given suitable representations, efficient nonlinear mapping engines could generate significant speed improvements for inferential processing.

4.3.2. *Massively parallel parsing revisited*

I introduced this paper by noting that natural language processing posed some problems for connectionism, precisely because of the representational adequacy problem. One cannot build either a parser or a generator without first having good "internal" representations. RAAMs can devise these compositional representations, as shown by the experiment on semantic triples, which can then be used as the target patterns for recurrent networks which accept sequences of words as input.

A feasibility study of this concept has been performed as well, using a sequential cascaded network [29], a higher-order network with a more restricted topology than Sigma-Pi [42]. Basically, a cascaded network consists of two subnetworks: The *function network* is an ordinary feed-forward network, but its weights are dynamically computed by the purely linear *context network*, whose outputs determine each weight of the function net. In a sequential cascaded network, the outputs of the function network are directly fed back to the inputs of the context network. This network is trained with presentations of initial context, input sequences, and desired final state.

A new 10-bit similarity-based encoding was created for the words appearing in the sentences, making HE and HER identical. The first 5 bits define the class, and the second 5 bits distinguish the members. The patterns are displayed in Table 6. A sequential cascaded network consisting of a 10-10-16 function network and a 16-286 context network was trained using sequences of these bit patterns corresponding to the sentences in Table 1. The initial context vectors were all zeroes, and the desired final states were the compressed 16-dimensional representations devised by the 48-16-48 RAAM for the trees in Table 3 (not including 10b).

This system is the closest thing yet to a barely adequate connectionist system for processing language: Given a variable-length sequence of words, the network, in linear time, returns a 16-dimensional vector which can be decoded into a "meaning" by a RAAM, and can perhaps be operated upon by associative inference engines.

On the one hand, this system has extreme deficiencies if it is evaluated as a cognitive model. It can only produce a single tree for a sentence, and only handles a very small corpus of sentences. The simplifying assumption, that internal representations can first be devised and then used as target patterns, is questionable. On the other hand, the system has some very interesting aspects. Besides the fact that it runs in linear time and outputs a compositional representation for the sentences, it automatically performs prepositional phrase attachment (i.e., correctly parses the "MARY ATE SPAGHETTI WITH MEAT/ CHOPSTICKS" examples) and pronoun resolution (i.e., automatically replaces HE or HER with the proper filler). Finally, it is the first connectionist parser which can deal with embedded structures without resorting to external symbolic computational power.

Table 6
10-bit input patterns for sequential cascaded parser

WORD	CLASS	IDENTITY
JOHN	1 0 0 0 0	1 1 0 0 0
MAN	1 0 0 0 0	0 1 0 0 0
PAT	1 0 0 0 0	1 1 1 0 0
MARY	1 0 0 0 0	1 0 1 0 0
HE/HER	1 0 0 0 0	0 1 0 1 0
TELESCOPE	0 1 0 0 0	0 0 1 0 1
SPAGHETTI	0 1 0 0 0	1 0 0 1 0
CHOPSTICKS	0 1 0 0 0	0 0 1 1 0
HILL	0 1 0 0 0	0 1 0 0 0
MEAT	0 1 0 0 0	1 0 0 0 1
ON	0 0 1 0 0	1 0 0 0 0
WITH	0 0 1 0 0	0 1 0 0 0
WHO	0 0 1 0 0	0 0 1 0 0
BY	0 0 1 0 0	0 0 0 1 0
ATE	0 0 0 1 0	0 0 1 0 0
HIT	0 0 0 1 0	0 0 0 1 0
SAW	0 0 0 1 0	0 0 0 0 1
LOVED	0 0 0 1 0	0 1 1 0 0
HOPED	0 0 0 1 0	0 1 1 0 0
THOUGHT	0 0 0 1 0	0 1 0 1 0
KNEW	0 0 0 1 0	0 1 0 0 1
LONG	0 0 0 0 1	0 0 0 1 0
SHORT	0 0 0 0 1	0 0 0 0 1

4.4. Further work

There is a great deal of research still to be conducted in this area, besides the conversion of the small feasibility studies into both falsifiable cognitive models and reliably engineered artifacts. Immediate concerns include:

- Understanding the convergence and stability properties of the "moving target" learning strategy; both empirical and analytical studies are called for. Similarly, the relationship between the termination condition (using τ an ν) and the depth capacity of RAAM needs to be better understood.
- Developing a complete understanding of the representations and mechanisms which are developed. A good outcome would be a general representational scheme which could be analytically derived for a particular representational task without relying on slow, gradient-descent learning.

5. Conclusion

Here is a conundrum for theories of human and machine learning: *Which came first*, the mental procedure or the mental representation? Minsky and Papert claimed that the representational egg must come before the procedural chicken, while Fodor and Pylyshyn claimed to intimately know the egg and, by extension, the exclusive class of fertile chickens. The flip side, of course, is that this perfect egg may only be layable by an impossible chicken: A formal representational theory, specified without consideration of its own genesis, may not be learnable by any mechanism in principle.

This work points to a biologically certified way out of the dilemma: Co-Evolution. The representations and their associated procedures develop slowly, responding to each other's constraints through a changing environment. The constraint that the representations fit into fixed-width patterns interacts with the constraint that the patterns must compose in certain well-formed ways, giving rise to fixed-width patterns which capture structural similarity in spatial distance.

The RAAM architecture has been inspired by two powerful ideas. The first is due to Hinton [12], who showed that, when properly constrained, a connectionist network can develop semantically interpretable representations on its hidden units. The second is an old idea, that given a sufficiently powerful form of learning, a machine can learn to efficiently perform a task by example, rather than by design. Taken together, these ideas suggest that, given a task, specified by example, which *requires* embedded representations, a network might be able to develop these representations itself.

It turns out that there is no *single* task which requires such representations. There have to be at least two tasks; one to construct the representations, and another to access them. On address-based machines, these tasks, such as string concatenation and array indexing, are so computationally primitive and natural that they fall far below notice. They are not natural to neural networks and thus need to be examined anew. Here, the resulting task-specific mechanisms, the compressor and reconstructor, together form a *reconstructive* memory system, in which only traces of the actual memory contents are stored, and reliable facsimiles are created with the use of domain knowledge.

The systematic patterns developed by RAAM are a very new kind of representation, a recursive, distributed representation, which seems to instantiate Hinton's notion of the "reduced description" mentioned earlier [13]. They combine apparently immiscible aspects of well-understood representations: They act both like feature vectors with their fixed width and simple measures of similarity, and like pointers, so that, with simple efficient procedures their contents can be "fetched". Even further, they act like compositional symbol structures: Simple associative procedures, such as the reconstructor, pattern classifiers, and pattern transformers, are clearly sensitive to their internal structure.

However, unlike feature vectors, these representations recursively combine into constituent structures, according to statistically inferred well-formedness constraints. Unlike pointers (or symbols like G0007), they contain information suitable for similarity measurements and, thus, nearest-neighbor judgements. And, unlike symbol structures, they can be easily compared, and do not have to be taken apart in order to be worked on. Recursive distributed representations may thus lead to a reintegration of the syntax and semantics at a very low level.

Currently, symbolic systems use information-free "atoms" which physically combine (through bit or pointer concatenation) in a completely unrestricted fashion. Thus, for any domain, a syntax is required to restrict those "molecules" *after the fact*, to the set of semantically interpretable ones. With further work, recursive distributed representations might undergo a metamorphism into symbols which contain their own meanings and physically combine *only* in a systematic fashion. After all, real atoms and molecules do so all the time.

ACKNOWLEDGEMENT

This work has been partially supported by the State Legislatures of New Mexico and Ohio and by the Office of Naval Research, under grant N00014-89-J-1200. Thanks to Tony Plate, who implemented back-propagation in C, and to Yoshiro Miyata for a copy of his hierarchical cluster program. Comments from B. Chandrasekaran, G. Hinton, J. McClelland, D. Touretzky, T. VanGelder, and many, many others helped to improve this presentation.

REFERENCES

1. D.H. Ackley, G.E. Hinton and T.J. Sejnowski, A learning algorithm for Boltzmann Machines, *Cognitive Sci.* **9** (1985) 147–169.
2. R. Allen, Several studies on natural language and back propagation, in: *Proceedings First International Conference on Neural Networks*, San Diego, CA (1987) II-335-342.
3. G. Berg, A parallel natural language processing architecture with distributed control, in: *Proceedings Ninth Annual Conference of the Cognitive Science Society*, Seattle, WA (1987) 487–495.
4. E. Charniak and E. Santos, A context-free connectionist parser which is not connectionist, but then it is not really context-free either, in: J. Barnden and J. Pollack, eds., *Advances in Connectionist and Neural Computation Theory* (Ablex, Norwood, NJ, 1990).
5. G.W. Cottrell, Connectionist parsing, in: *Proceedings Seventh Annual Conference of the Cognitive Science Society*, Irvine, CA (1985).
6. G. Cottrell, P. Munro and D. Zipser, Learning internal representations from gray-scale images: An example of extensional programming, in: *Proceedings Ninth Annual Conference of the Cognitive Science Society*, Seattle, WA (1987) 461–473.
7. J.L. Elman, Finding structure in time, *Cognitive Sci.* **14** (2) (1990) 179–212.
8. M. Fanty, Context-free parsing in connectionist networks, Tech. Rept. 174, University of Rochester, Computer Science Department, Rochester, NY (1985).
9. J. Fodor and Z. Pylyshyn, Connectionism and cognitive architecture: A critical analysis, *Cognition* **28** (1988) 3–71.
10. S.J. Hanson and J. Kegl, PARSNIP: A connectionist network that learns natural language grammar from exposure to natural language sentences, in: *Proceedings Ninth Annual Conference of the Cognitive Science Society*, Seattle, WA (1987) 106–119.

11. G.E. Hinton, Distributed representation, Tech. Rept. CMU-CS-84-157, Carnegie-Mellon University, Computer Science Department, Pittsburgh, PA (1984).

12. G.E. Hinton, Learning distributed representations of concepts, in: *Proceedings Eighth Annual Conference of the Cognitive Science Society*, Amherst, MA (1986) 1–12.

13. G.E. Hinton, Representing part–whole hierarchies in connectionist networks, in: *Proceedings Tenth Annual Conference of the Cognitive Science Society*, Montreal, Que. (1988) 48–54.

14. J.H. Holland, K.J. Holyoak, R.E. Nisbett and P.R. Thagard, *Induction: Processes of Inference, Learning, and Discovery* (MIT Press, Cambridge, MA, 1986).

15. K. Hornik, M. Stinchcombe and H. White, Multi-layer feedforward networks are universal approximators, *Neural Networks* (to appear).

16. M.I. Jordan, Serial order: A parallel distributed processing approach, Tech. Rept. ICS 8608, Institute for Cognitive Science, University of California, San Diego, La Jolla, CA (1986).

17. A.H. Kawamoto, Dynamic processes in the (re)solution of lexical ambiguity, Doctoral Dissertation, Department of Psychology, Brown University, Providence, RI (1985).

18. A.S. Lapedes and R.M. Farber, How neural nets work, Tech. Rept. LAUR-88-418, Los Alamos, NM (1988).

19. W.G. Lehnert, Case-based problem-solving with a large knowledge base of learned cases, in: *Proceedings AAAI-87*, Seattle, WA (1987) 301–306.

20. R.P. Lippman, An introduction to computing with neural networks, *IEEE ASSP Mag.* **4** (2) (1987) 4–22.

21. B. Mandelbrot, *The Fractal Geometry of Nature* (Freeman, San Francisco, CA, 1982).

22. J. McClelland and A. Kawamoto, Mechanisms of sentence processing: Assigning roles to constituents, in: J.L. McClelland, D.E. Rumelhart and the PDP Research Group, eds., *Parallel Distributed Processing: Experiments in the Microstructure of Cognition* **2**: *Applications* (MIT Press, Cambridge, MA, 1986).

23. J.L. McClelland and D.E. Rumelhart, An interactive activation model of the effect of context in perception, Part 1: An account of basic findings, *Psychol. Rev.* **88** (1981) 375–407.

24. R. Miikkulainen and D.G. Dyer, Forming global representations with back propagation, in: *Proceedings Second Annual International Conference on Neural Networks*, San Diego, CA (1988).

25. M. Minsky and S. Papert, *Perceptrons* (MIT Press, Cambridge, MA, 1988).

26. M. Mozer, Inductive information retrieval using parallel distributed computation, Tech. Rept., Institute for Cognitive Science, University of California, San Diego, La Jolla, CA (1984).

27. S. Pinker and A. Prince, On language and connectionism: Analysis of a parallel distributed processing model of language acquisition, *Cognition* **28** (1988) 73–193.

28. D.C. Plaut, S. Nowlan and G.E. Hinton, Experiments on learning by backpropagation, Tech. Rept. CMU-CS-86-126, Computer Science Department, Carnegie-Mellon University, Pittsburgh, PA (1986).

29. J.B. Pollack, Cascaded back propagation on dynamic connectionist networks, in: *Proceedings Ninth Annual Conference of the Cognitive Science Society*, Seattle, WA (1987) 391–404.

30. J.B. Pollack, Implications of recursive distributed representations, in: D. Touretzky, ed., *Advances in Neural Information Processing Systems* (Morgan Kaufman, Los Altos, CA, 1989).

31. J.B. Pollack and D.L. Waltz, Natural language processing using spreading activation and lateral inhibition, in: *Proceedings Fourth Annual Conference of the Cognitive Science Society*, Ann Arbor, MI (1982) 50–53.

32. R. Rosenfeld and D. Touretzky, Four capacity models for coarse-coded symbol memories, *Complex Syst.* **2** (1988) 463–484.

33. D.E. Rumelhart, G. Hinton and R. Williams, Learning internal representations through error propagation, in: D.E. Rumelhart, J.L. McClelland and the PDP Research Group, eds., *Parallel Distributed Processing: Experiments in the Microstructure of Cognition* **1**: *Foundations* (MIT Press, Cambridge, MA, 1986) 25–40.

34. D.E. Rumelhart and J.L. McClelland, On learning the past tenses of English verbs, in: J.L. McClelland, D.E. Rumelhart and the PDP Reseach Group, eds., *Parallel Distributed Processing*: *Experiments in the Microstructure of Cognition* **2**: *Applications* (MIT Press, Cambridge, MA, 1986) 216–217.
35. E. Saund, Dimensionality reduction and constraint in laser vision, in: *Proceedings Ninth Annual Conference of the Cognitive Science Society*, Seattle, WA (1987) 908–915.
36. T.J. Sejnowski and C.R. Rosenberg, Parallel networks that learn to pronounce English text, *Complex Syst.* **1** (1987) 145–168.
37. B. Selman, Rule-based processing in a connectionist system for natural language understanding Tech. Rept. CSRI-168, University of Toronto, Computer Systems Research Institute, Toronto, Ont. (1985).
38. D.S. Touretzky, BoltzCONS: Reconciling connectionism with the recursive nature of stacks and trees, in: *Proceedings Eighth Annual Conference of the Cognitive Science Society*, Amherst, MA (1986) 522–530.
39. D.S. Touretzky, Representing and transforming recursive objects in a neural network, or "trees do grow on Boltzmann machines", in: *Proceedings International Conference on Systems, Man, and Cybernetics*, Atlanta, GA (1986).
40. D.S. Touretzky and G.E. Hinton, Symbols among the neurons: Details of a connectionist inference architecture, in: *Proceedings IJCAI-85*, Los Angeles, CA (1985).
41. D.L. Waltz and J.B. Pollack: Massively parallel parsing: A strongly interactive model of natural language interpretation, *Cognitive Sci.* **9** (1) (1985) 51–74.
42. R. Williams, The logic of activation functions, in: D.E. Rumelhart, J.L. McClelland and the PDP Research Group, eds., *Parallel Distributed Processing*: *Experiments in the Microstructure of Cognition* **1**: *Foundations* (MIT Press, Cambridge, MA, 1986) 423–443.

Mundane Reasoning by Settling on a Plausible Model

Mark Derthick

MCC, 3500 West Balcones Center Drive, Austin, TX 78759, USA

ABSTRACT

Connectionist networks are well suited to everyday common sense reasoning. Their ability to simultaneously satisfy multiple soft constraints allows them to select from conflicting information in finding a plausible interpretation of a situation. However these networks are poor at reasoning using the standard semantics of classical logic, based on truth in all possible models. This article shows that using an alternate semantics, based on truth in a single most plausible model, there is an elegant mapping from theories expressed using the syntax of propositional logic onto connectionist networks. An extension of this mapping to allow for limited use of quantifiers suffices to build a network from knowledge bases expressed in a frame language similar to KL-ONE. Although finding optimal models of these theories is intractable, the networks admit a hill climbing search algorithm that can be tuned to give satisfactory answers in familiar situations. The article concludes with an example of retrieval involving incomplete and inconsistent information. Although this example works well, much remains before realistic domains are feasible.

1. Introduction

1.1. Mundane reasoning

Mundane reasoning is the process of making the kind of unconscious decisions people constantly make every day: which chair to sit in, what a word means, how to categorize an object given its properties. It constitutes what others have called "the micro-structure of cognition" [48] or "subcognition" [26]. Categorization may require recalling earlier instances and consideration of the current context, in addition to general knowledge about the category. Yet people perform this task automatically and quickly. This ability must at least reflect expertise in retrieving relevant accumulated experience from a vastly larger store. Schank [49] calls this *reminding*, and considers it to be a fundamental ingredient of intelligence. Other mundane tasks appear to have this same characteristic. Acquiring the ability to interpret complex stimuli quickly requires extensive familiarity with the domain. The term "mundane reasoning"

Artificial Intelligence **46** (1990) 107–157

indicates both that it is commonplace and that it must be grounded in experience of the world.

1.2. Theories of reasoning

A competence theory describes a class of problems and their solutions. Such theories are also called "knowledge level" [39] or normative theories. In contrast are theories that take into account practical limitations on rationality and computability, and explain how a real agent will carry out a task. These are called performance or "symbol level" [39] theories. The field of artificial intelligence subsumes both the explanation of intelligence and the building of agents, and thus it needs both kinds of theories.

Because they idealize away from practical problems, competence theories are likely to be more perspicuous. Often a performance theory is derived from a competence theory by adding a process model that would implement the competence theory correctly, except for some resource limitations that must be imposed. Although it is difficult to characterize the performance of the resource-limited system independently of the process model, the loose relationship to the competence theory is still an important source of intuition. This article uses a combination of a competence theory and a resource-limited process model in just this way. The rest of this section reviews the background of the competence theory used, and discusses psychological evidence for a kind of process model that allows an effective implementation.

1.2.1. *Frames as competence theories*

One of the goals of knowledge representation (KR) is to find formal languages for writing down facts that are powerful enough that the desired consequences of those facts may be derived automatically. If the system can take care of manipulating the facts in appropriate ways, the facts play a more important role than those in a simple database; they constitute *knowledge*. There can certainly be programs that perform difficult tasks and have no separation between knowledge and rules for manipulating it, but in AI terminology such a program does not *represent* the knowledge it embodies. It is often the case that a system composed of a few inference rules and a lot of declarative knowledge makes intuitively good sense. Such a system can also be very powerful because of the combinatorial number of ways that facts can be combined using rules. An equally powerful system in which the facts are not separated from how they are used is likely to be inpenetrably complex.

There is also a question of space efficiency. In the limit of context dependence, where a fact only is used in a single situation, the system is a lookup table. For real-world problems this just is not an alternative—there are many more possible situations than can possibly be stored. Any mundane reasoning system must make some use of rules, at least in the weak sense of combining some kind of data.

Many artificial intelligence application programs organize the knowledge they contain as frames [38]. A frame describes a single concept and its properties. The properties are expressed in terms of restrictions on conceptual constituents, with each constituent thought of as filling a *slot* of the frame. The BIRTHDAY-PARTY frame may, for example, contain a slot for the kind of food served, which is filled by CAKE. The HOST slot may be filled by the name of the person whose birthday it is, and the PARTICIPANTS slot is filled by a small number of children, who must be friends of the host. Restrictions on slot fillers can represent knowledge of various sorts. For example, they can specify a particular item, as in the case of the cake, or a type restriction as in the case of the host being a person. There can also be relations imposed among fillers of various slots, as in the case of the friendship requirement between host and participants. CAKE and PERSON in turn name other frames, so a knowledge base (KB) is a network of connected frames. There is also a special relationship, ISA, between frames indicating that one is more specific than the other. For instance a BIRTHDAY-PARTY ISA kind of PARTY, so knowledge about parties in general applies to birthday parties. The fact that the participants must be friends of the host applies to all parties, and this knowledge does not have to be repeated for birthday parties. In this case, BIRTHDAY-PARTY would be said to *inherit* that knowledge.

The expressive power of frame systems is the result of the abstract nature of frames. The fact that the participants at a party must be friends of the host is a concise statement that applies to all parties, including all birthday parties, including the birthday parties of all individuals the system knows about, and all the friends of all those individuals. This is an example of a rule, which can apply to innumerable specific situations. Some frame languages, including the one used in this article, can specify sufficiently powerful rules that deciding whether a conclusion is a necessary consequence of a KB is NP-hard. NP-hard problems are termed *intractable*, because it is unlikely that any polynomial-time algorithm exists for deciding them [17].

1.2.2. *Semantically based performance theories*

Psychological experiments indicate that the inference rules people use are not very general. Even in domains where simple rules suffice to exactly capture the structure, people make errors. For instance Tversky and Kahneman [57] have shown that in some contexts people assign higher probability to a statement of the form $a \wedge b$ than to a alone. They hypothesize that this may be due to making judgements based on representativeness rather than probability: people seem to reason by judging how well an exemplar fits a category, and by retrieving exemplars of a category, rather than by using abstract rules. Johnson-Laird [28] has shown that people tend to draw false conclusions from syllogisms. Given the statements that "All of the bankers are athletes," and

"None of the councillors are bankers" they are more likely to conclude, incorrectly, that "None of the councillors are athletes" than the correct answer, "Some of the athletes are not councillors."

Whether people perform correctly in these kinds of experiments is highly dependent on the semantics of the terms used in the problems. It seems that people cannot help but draw upon world knowledge even when the task is explicitly formal. Johnson-Laird's theory of how people reason is that they construct mental models of the situation and draw conclusions based on what is true in the model. For instance they may build a model of the first premise in which there are two bankers (both of whom are athletes), and one other athlete who is not a banker. The second premise suggests adding some councillors, say two. The resulting model is then examined and a conclusion drawn. If the two councillors are disjoint from all the athletes, the subject may respond that "none of the councillors are athletes," even though this is not true in all possible models. For instance the athlete who is not a banker could have been a councillor.

These tasks are examples in which there seems to be a plausible theory, yet people's actual performance is not explained by it. I maintain that it would be much better to follow the competence theory, but that for mundane reasoning any competence theory will be intractable. Model-based reasoning is a technique for doing mundane reasoning that admits tractable heuristic algorithms. Similarly, Levesque has suggested simplifying the knowledge representation problem by using "vivid knowledge bases," which are essentially models [31]. A vivid KB is complete, which means it has a unique model. To guarantee that the unique model is easy to compute, two constraints are imposed [50]:

(1) There is a one-to-one correspondence between a subset of the symbols in the KB and the objects of interest in the world.
(2) For every relationship of interest in the world, there is an easily computable relationship among symbols in the KB.

"Easily computable" means something like locally computable, or computable in constant time. Given an ordinary KB, it is first put in vivid form. In that form, answering queries will be simple. Unfortunately, putting an incomplete KB in vivid form requires assumptions to be made, with the result that unsound inferences may result. There are three reasons that failing to correctly follow the competence theory may not be too bad.

In the usual semantics for KR systems, a proposition is believed only if it holds in all possible models. If the system does not have enough knowledge to eliminate models with conflicting conclusions, it would report that no conclusion is certain. In mundane domains it may be better to guess and occasionally be wrong than to believe nothing. Decision theory is a widely used framework for making good guesses in economics. Although it requires examining all possible models to make optimal guesses, one commonly used heuristic in decision theory, Maximum Likelihood estimation,[1] has the same motivation as the one used here: to guess based on the most likely model.

Second, if the system has built up a large KB, the facts may rule out all but a handful of possible models, in which case basing conclusions on a single model will often give the same result as checking all models. If this is not the case for some particular query, and the error that results is detected, new facts can be added to the KB to cover this situation. Eventually enough facts will have been added so that in the familiar kinds of situations that have been encountered many times before, the system will almost always find the correct answer. It would be nice to have an automatic training algorithm to do this, but there currently is none (see Section 5.6).

A final justification for using an error-prone, but fast, retrieval system is if there is a supervisory reasoner to catch errors. For instance in a system for parsing natural language, Charniak [9] uses a fast spreading activation algorithm to find related sets of concepts. Candidate sets are then evaluated by a slower reasoner that checks to see if the concepts are related in an appropriate way. In people, this conception may apply to mathematicians at work. While theorem verification must be done carefully, hypothesizing is often errorful, and seems to be beyond introspection. This is in keeping with my intuitive notion that mundane reasoning is what people do subconsciously.

Using a reasoner that has difficulty in chaining inferences and relies on redundant assertions to make up for these deficiencies, makes this approach more like ones used in low-level perceptual reasoning than most common sense reasoning (CSR) systems. Like mundane reasoning, CSR covers domains in which the rules used to describe the world are at a higher level of abstraction than the numerical laws of physics, and are general enough in scope to admit exceptions. However, CSR theories are usually concerned only with competence, and do not propose approximate algorithms (for instance [11, 34]). In CSR, "model-based reasoning" usually means reasoning using a causal model of the domain [15]. In this article, the term indicates that conclusions are drawn by searching over model theory models of the domain, rather than by using logical rules of inference. In the terminology of this article, causal models are actually theories since they specify constraints over possible domain states rather than the states themselves.

1.3. Overview of μKLONE

In this article I describe a system functionally similar to conventional frame-based KR systems, yet implemented as a model-based reasoner for efficiency. The name, μKLONE (pronounced micro-klone), indicates that it is functionally similar to KL-ONE [7], a widely used frame system, yet is implemented in a

---

[1] Maximum Likelihood estimation is explained in decision theory textbooks, for instance [10].

connectionist system using *micro*-features [24]. μKLONE is not intended to be a psychological theory. I do not assert that people approximate a frame-based competence theory of retrieval, nor that the model-based implementation is the kind of implementation people are. The psychological results cited in the previous section are meant only to provide evidence that an intelligent system need not perform according to any concise formal theory.

The goal of combining frames with models is to produce an expressively powerful system with robust performance in mundane domains, in spite of incomplete and inconsistent KBs and in spite of the probable intractability of any adequate competence theory. The existing expressively powerful frame systems that have a formal semantics and complete implementation are not robust with respect to either problem. Their knowledge bases must be logically consistent, no guesses are made to remedy incomplete KBs, and they fail to return answers in a reasonable time, even for many seemingly easy queries.

Another interesting class of KR systems are based on connectionist networks. Connectionist networks were originally inspired by what is known of the structure of neural networks in the brain, and consist of many simple processors (called units), each of which communicates with many other units [14, 48]. They are more robust in that they can be made to always return an answer quickly, knowledge is combined evidentially, and there is no concept of inconsistency or incompleteness. However no previous connectionist implementation has had the expressive power of symbolic frame-based systems. Many connectionist systems also lack any means of specifying the KB in a high level language, independent of the mechanism ([51] is a notable exception).

Implementing model-based reasoning in a connectionist network is conceptually simple and elegant. The models themselves are strict model theory models, in that they specify a domain and a truth assignment for all the predicates over that domain. (μKLONE theories have no function symbols, except for constants.)

μKLONE theories always have finite models, which can therefore be specified by a finite set of ground atomic formulas. In the network, there is one unit to represent each possible such formula, so each assignment of binary states to units represents a model. Every assertion corresponds to a constraint among a subset of the units. For instance the theory $\{a, a \rightarrow b\}$ has a corresponding network with two units and two constraints. The unit representing the proposition a is constrained to be on, and the unit representing b is constrained to be on if unit a is on.

Unfortunately, these models are exponentially large, so a heuristic is used to determine a search space of partial models containing the information most likely to be relevant to the current query. Even searching this reduced space is intractable, so a fast hill climbing algorithm is used which is not guaranteed to find the best partial model. The motivation for these heuristic approximations is the hope that allowing the system the freedom to guess and be wrong in

some cases, rather than not return an answer, will result in a closer correspondence between what is hard for the system and what looks hard to a human.
Some of the advantage of having a formal competence theory is lost if the
actual system does not follow it. However, by thinking of the tractable system
as an approximation to the larger provably correct one, the relation to a formal
theory of reasoning is much more clear than it has been for related connectionist KR systems, such as [21, 22, 36, 47, 55]. More of the ability to reason about
structured knowledge has been retained than for any previous connectionist
KR system.

This article makes two principal contributions: it uses probability theory to
extend the conventional logic-based semantics of frame-based KR languages to
enhance their usefulness in mundane domains, and it describes an implementation made tractable by using heuristics that, although not formally correct, are
intuitively plausible and that work well in an example domain that includes
incomplete and inconsistent knowledge. Within logic, the problem of discarding beliefs in the face of conflicting evidence is called nonmonotonic reasoning,
and the problem of assuming knowledge to explain beliefs is called abductive
reasoning. Using probability, both types of reasoning are subsumed by the
problem of finding the most probable model.

1.4. Outline

Section 2 describes methods for specifying a set of plausible models, and brave
and cautious strategies for making belief commitments given a set of plausible
models. Finally, it describes the Hopfield and Tank search method for finding a
plausible model using a connectionist network.

Section 3 describes μKLONE's frame language and uses it to express the
example "role shift" problem, in which counterfactual information causes
beliefs about one role to slip to another, similar role. Section 4 describes the
μKLONE architecture, including the heuristic simplifications, and how the
system solves the role shift problem.

The conclusion assesses the significance of μKLONE, in terms of contributions to model based reasoning and approximate reasoning. The need for
embedding in a sequential reasoner, recursive representations, reasoning with
prototypes, and the prospects for practical application are discussed.

2. Reasoning with Inconsistent Information

2.1. Brave and cautious reasoning

A μKLONE knowledge base is a theory, which determines a set of most
plausible models. This set can be compared to the set of classical logic models
of a theory, or the models of the extensions of a theory expressed in Reiter's
default logic [45]. This section defines all three methods, and considers them as

an orderly progression in which the most plausible models are the maximal elements of ever more discriminating partial orders.

In classical logic a theory is a set of sentences, called axioms. An interpretation of a theory is a $\langle D, I \rangle$ tuple, where D is a set of individuals, or *domain*, and I is a function that specifies for each n-place predicate letter which n-tuples of individuals it is true of, and for each function symbol which individual is denoted when it is applied to each n-tuple. An interpretation satisfies a theory if all the axioms are true when the quantifiers range over D and the predicates and functions are given the interpretation I. Normally the term "model" is reserved for satisficing interpretations, but this article uses it interchangeably with "interpretation," which allows even inconsistent theories to have models. For classical theories, the partial order defining the most plausible models is a trivial one: model A is more plausible than model B if and only if A satisfies the theory and B doesn't.

In Reiter's default logic, a KB consists of both axioms and default rules. Axioms are the same as in classical logic. An example of a default rule is:

$$\frac{bird(Tweety) : M \, fly(Tweety)}{fly(Tweety)}$$

Reading left-to-right and top-to-bottom, the three parts of a default rule are called the *prerequisite*, the *justification*, and the *consequent*. This rule means "if Tweety is a bird, and it is consistent to believe that Tweety flies, then conclude that Tweety flies." In the absence of any other information, if Tweety is a bird, then the system will believe that Tweety flies But if there are axioms stating that Tweety is a penguin, and that penguins do not fly, then the system will believe that Tweety is a bird, but does not fly.

In default logic, determining the most plausible models requires an intermediate step. First a set of *extensions* is found. An extension is a minimal superset of the axioms closed under the standard rules of inference, and containing in addition the consequent of each default rule whose prerequisite is contained in that set and whose justification is not inconsistent with that set.

The models of a default theory are usually said to be all the models of all the extensions. In this article, though, the models include all interpretations. In keeping with the desire to equate "most plausible model" with what are normally called simply models, a partial order over interpretations for default logic can be defined. A default rule whose prerequisite is true but whose consequent is false will be called "defeated." Model A is more plausible than model B if its set of defeated defaults is properly contained in that of B. The most plausible models under this ordering are those that satisfy an extension. If we pretend assertions in classical logic are the consequents of default rules whose prerequisite and justification are empty, then this partial order becomes a refinement of the one above for classical logic.

In classical logic, a proposition is believed true if it is valid, that is, true in all plausible models. It is believed false if its negation is valid, and no commitment is made otherwise. Since adding more axioms can only reduce the set of satisficing models, finding out more about the world will never invalidate any beliefs. In default logic, however, the set of most plausible models is not so special. One is never sure that new information won't introduce new extensions, so checking all models which are currently most plausible doesn't carry with it the same guarantees that it does in classical logic. And if neither the proposition nor its negation holds in all these models, the system is in a quandary in common sense domains where a guess is better than no answer at all. For these reasons, a different strategy is used in Reiter's default logic [45]. A proposition is believed if it is valid in *one* extension. McDermott [37] calls this *brave reasoning*, as opposed to the cautious strategy of only believing a proposition if it is valid in all extensions. Even in brave reasoning, it may be that neither a proposition nor its negation is valid in any extension.

In mundane reasoning, there is no time to gather more information if these strategies do not lead to a belief commitment. A third strategy can be used, however. In contrast to brave reasoning, which believes a proposition that is true in all models of one extension, μKLONE might be said to do foolhardy reasoning in believing a propositon that is true in *one* model of one extension. Given that a single model is to be chosen, it is only reasonable that as much knowledge should be brought to bear on the choice as possible. If the partial order is not very discriminating, the behavior of the system will be largely unconstrained by the semantics, and will depend greatly on how the program is implemented. It is desirable, therefore, that the partial order be as specific as possible.

For instance if the rule that penguins do not fly is made a default rule instead of an axiom, there are two different extensions. In one Tweety flies, and in the other Tweety does not fly. Given only this much information, the fact that the system includes two alternatives in its set of most plausible models is quite reasonable. The problem is that information about preferences cannot be expressed concisely in unadorned default logic. Each default rule must explicitly mention situations in which it is to be overridden [54].

To illustrate the inefficiency that may result, consider the sets of default rules in the first two lines of Table 1. If any of the P's hold, we want to conclude R, but if any of the Q's hold we want to conclude $\neg R$. In the case where both some P and some Q hold, we want to conclude R if more P's hold and $\neg R$ if more Q's hold. In default logic the only way to express this is to write $O(2^n)$ separate rules.

A more concise way to express preferences is to refine the partial order defined above based on properties of the models. Ginsberg [19] calls this ordering predicate *better-world*. If it is specified by enumeration, the resulting KB will be as verbose as if exceptions are mentioned explicitly in the default

Table 1

Illustration of the unwieldiness of default logic for expressing preference for the conclusion supported by the largest number of rules. The independent rules are given on the first two lines. To express the desired preference, an exponential number of rules similar to that on the third line are required. For simplicity of illustration, the number of P's and Q's is assumed to be the same, n. For every number k up to n, a separate rule must be added for all the ways to choose k of n P's, and $n - k$ Q's with the conclusion R, and another set of rules with k Q's and $n - k$ P's with the conclusion $\neg R$.

$$\frac{P_1 : MR}{R} \quad \cdots \quad \frac{P_n : MR}{R}$$

$$\frac{Q_1 : M\neg R}{\neg R} \quad \cdots \quad \frac{Q_n : M\neg R}{\neg R}$$

$$\frac{P_1 \wedge P_2 \wedge \cdots \wedge P_k : MR \wedge \neg Q_1 \wedge \neg Q_2 \wedge \cdots \wedge \neg Q_{n-k}}{R}$$

rules. If $better\text{-}world(E_1, E_2)$ can be specified in terms of a simple predicate and a function defined over extensions,

$$better\text{-}world(E_1, E_2) \equiv p(f(E_1), f(E_2)) ,$$

then the augmented theory may be much more compact. For instance the partial order defined above for default logic results when f computes the defeated defaults and p is subset. In μKLONE, f is a cost function called the *energy function* and p is arithmetic $<$. f counts up the (weighted) number of assertions that fail to hold. For the example in Table 1, the energy function gives the desired ordering without requiring the exceptions to be explicitly mentioned in the rules. Of course, this example is a setup. Not all orderings can be expressed by a weighted sum of defeated defaults. Still, for orderings that can be expressed, the space required is only linear in the size of the unaugmented theory and the ordering that results is total.

This total order is a refinement of the partial order defined above for default logic. μKLONE assertions have no prerequisite, so any assertion that fails to hold is a defeated default. If the defeated defaults of model A are a subset of those of B, and all defaults have a positive certainty, then the energy assigned to A, which is the sum of the certainties of the defeated defaults, must be less than the energy assigned to B.

μKLONE uses one further refinement of the plausibility ordering to effect a "closed-world assumption" [44]. This is done by adding weak (NOT p) assertions for every propositional variable. As long as the certainty of these assertions is much smaller than that of the other assertions, adding them will only prune the set of most plausible models, and never introduce new models into the set. This numerical notion of minimality is stronger than the subset notion usually used in defining minimal models, in that $\{p\ q\}$ is smaller than $\{q\ r\ s\}$ rather than incomparable.

Since μKLONE's partial order is a refinement of the ones which pick out the most plausible models of classical and default logic, μKLONE's most plausible models are a subset of the models of classical or default theories when those theories have models. For classical logic this requires the axioms to be consistent; for default logic this requires in addition that there be a stable extension.

In discussing these partial orders, the differences between axioms, default rules, and μKLONE assertions were ignored. μKLONE assertions behave like default rules with no prerequisite and with identical justification and consequent. Theories consisting entirely of rules of this form always have a stable consistent extension.[2] In μKLONE, the way to approximate axioms is to assign a very high certainty to an assertion. Still, the distinctions that can be made in logic using axioms or default rules of more general forms cannot be fully captured.

It is a desirable consequence that μKLONE theories always have the equivalent of a stable consistent extension. However this property is not due to the numerical aspect of the semantics nor the connectionist implementation, and could be achieved in default logic by using only default rules of the restricted form. Although logic is not usually considered as providing a framework for counterfactual reasoning, if some manner of ensuring that the counterfactual premise has priority over other default rules, counterfactuals can be handled just as they are in μKLONE

2.2. Plausible models in μKLONE

2.2.1. *Certainties*

The numbers attached to assertions are called *certainties* because their function is analogous to the numbers attached to rules in MYCIN [52], PROSPECTOR [13], and other expert systems. "Certainty" is a generic term, since different systems have different calculi for deriving the certainty of a conclusion from the certainties of its justifications. MYCIN's combination rules are based on confirmation theory [8] and PROSPECTOR's are based on probability theory. μKLONE's certainty calculus is particularly simple. Meaningful interpretations of certainties in terms of probability can only be derived in the context of all the other certainties in the KB. This frees the (local) evidence combination functions from the difficulties associated with estimating (global) conditional dependencies.

To a first approximation, the energy of a model is the number of assertions violated, weighted by their certainty. The precise translation is a structural

---

[2] This is a property of all normal default rules [45].

mapping from logical formulas to arithmetic ones. μKLONE translates AND as
+, OR as min, and NOT as $f(x) = 1 - x$. A number of similar schemes have been
used to capture the meaning of propositional formulas in arithmetic expressions. In Boolean algebra with positive logic, where 1 represents true and 0
false, AND corresponds to min, OR to max, and NOT to $1 - x$. In fuzzy logic,
the same functions are used, but the domain is expanded to the continuous
interval between zero and one, rather than only the endpoints [60]. The truth
value of an expression is meant to capture the likelihood of the whole as a
function of the likelihoods of its parts.

The goal of μKLONE is very different. It does not need the exact likelihood
of a formula being true, but only an ordering over models. This gives it the
flexibility to use numbers outside the range [0, 1]. These numbers are proportional to log probabilities, so they do in fact determine the probability of
formulas. However a normalization step is required to find the proportionality
constant, so it is impossible to compute the probability of a formula strictly
from the probabilities of its constituents. Therefore this scheme is unsuitable
for syntactic reasoning, as is usually done in fuzzy logic and expert systems.
The ability to use numbers in the interval $(0, \infty)$ in model-based reasoning gives
it more power to discriminate between models, as the following example
shows. In Boolean algebra or fuzzy logic, the sentences "Lincoln was buried in
Grant's tomb" and "Lincoln was buried in Grant's tomb and violets are green"
have the same likelihood, yet they impose different orderings on possible
models. A KB containing the second sentence will rank the actual world lower
than a world like ours except that violets *are* green. A KB containing only the
first sentence would make no distinction.

A second difference between μKLONE and most other schemes is the
polarity of the mapping between truth values and numbers. In Boolean
algebra, positive logic is conventional, but negative logic could equally well be
used. In this case, true is zero, false is one, AND is max, and OR is min. For
μKLONE, which counts constraint violation, it is crucial that zero constraint
violation correspond to true. If the KB contains the single assertion that the
atomic proposition p holds, the energy of models in which p fails to hold
should be increased. The constraint expressing this is (ON p). The energy
assigned to model α by the assertion p is $E_p^\alpha = s_p^\alpha$ where s_p^α, the state of the unit
representing the proposition p in model α, is zero if p is true in model α and
one otherwise. For convenience, the distinction between the propositional
variable p and the state, s_p^α, of the unit representing the variable is dropped, as
is the superscript indicating the model. The constraint (ON p) is also usually
written simply p.

Like the negative logic version of Boolean algebra, μKLONE translates OR
as min and NOT as $1 - x$. However, to be able to distinguish pairs of sentences
like the ones about Lincoln, it translates AND as + rather than max. The
correct way to think about this is that models that violate multiple conjuncts of

an assertion have a higher constraint violation. Being sloppy, it is also possible to think of the propositions themselves as having truth values that range from true to false to extra false. On this view, ANDing two false propositions results in a proposition that is even more false. A problem now arises with NOT when it is applied to these extra false propositions. If proposition p has energy 2, then (NOT p) has energy $1 - 2 = -1$, which is outside the domain of plausibilities. Therefore a syntactic restriction is imposed on the language that NOT can never be applied to a proposition whose plausibility can be greater than one. In logic, it is always possible to use De Morgan's laws to push in negation signs so they only apply to atoms, and this can at most double the size of the formula.

However, using De Morgan's laws changes the meaning of a formula under the above translation. The energy contribution of the assertion $A \wedge B$ is $A + B$, while that of $\neg(\neg A \vee \neg B)$ is $1 - \min(1 - A, 1 - B) \equiv \max(A, B)$. In the model where both a and b are false, the energy contribution of the first assertion is two, while that of the second is one. The two forms correspond to different beliefs about the independence of a and b. In the first, they are statistically independent, while in the second they are positively correlated. The expert system PROSPECTOR [13] uses a similar mapping of logic onto logarithms of probabilities, and explicitly has two forms of AND available for the user, one corresponding to adding the log probabilities, and one corresponding to taking their maximum.

2.2.2. Probabilities

Probabilities can be derived from certainties using the Boltzmann distribution, which relates the energy of possible states in a physical system to their

Table 2
The constraint types described in Section 2.2 enable any propositional theory to be expressed as an energy function. Here each assertion in the Tweety domain is given a certainty, and produces one term in the energy equation. With this equation the energies of each of the 2^3 models can be calculated. For instance the energy of the model $\{penguin(Tweety), bird(Tweety)\}$ is $50 \times \min((1 - 0), 1) + 100 \times \min((1 - 0), 0) + 80 \times \min((1 - 0), (1 - 1)) + 80 \times 0 = 50$. This is the most plausible model.

Certainty	Assertion	Energy function
50	$bird(Tweety) \rightarrow flier(Tweety)$	$\min((1 - bird(Tweety)), flier(Tweety)) +$
100	$penguin(Tweety) \rightarrow bird(Tweety)$	$\min((1 - penguin(Tweety)), bird(Tweety)) +$
80	$penguin(Tweety) \rightarrow \neg flier(Tweety)$	$\min((1 - penguin(Tweety))(1 - flier(Tweety)) +$
80	$penguin(Tweety)$	$penguin(Tweety)$

probability:

$$\frac{P(\alpha)}{P(\beta)} = \exp\{-(E_{KB}^{\alpha} - E_{KB}^{\beta})/T\} \, . \tag{1}$$

Here α and β are any two states of the system, $P(\alpha)$ is the probability of state α, and T is temperature. E_{KB}^{α} is the energy of model α due to all the constraints in the KB. The log of the probability ratio between any two states is proportional to the energy difference between the states. Temperature is the constant of proportionality, and provides a degree of freedom in the mapping from energies to probabilities. At high temperatures the ratio is close to one, meaning that the probabilities are relatively insensitive to energy differences. But as the temperature approaches zero only the lowest energy models will have an appreciable probability. Given the probability ratios between all pairs of models, the probability of each model is uniquely determined.

The main difference between PROSPECTOR's semantics and μKLONE's is that PROSPECTOR uses absolute log probabilities, rather than unnormalized ones. This enables it to determine real probabilities while doing syntactic inference, but only by making conditional independence assumptions at each step. These assumptions may not be globally consistent, so the reasoning algorithm does not necessarily respect the semantics. This is put forward as a feature, because it means the algorithm works even when the knowledge engineer specifies an inconsistent probability distribution, a case that seems hard to avoid in practice. By using the Boltzmann distribution, any set of certainties specified by the μKLONE knowledge engineer results in a consistent probability distribution, the one that minimizes free energy. This is related to the maximum entropy distribution, which Konolige suggests as an improvement to the PROSPECTOR method [30]. Free energy equals energy minus temperature times entropy. Temperature is a free parameter that can be used to adjust the relative importances of maximizing entropy and minimizing energy. Using free energy, the distribution is the one that maximizes entropy subject to soft constraints, which can be inconsistent. Using maximum entropy, the distribution is the one that maximizes entropy subject to hard constraints, which must be consistent.

2.2.3. Differentiable approximation to MIN

The search algorithm described next, which is the one μKLONE actually uses, requires computing the derivative of the energy function in order to do hill climbing. Since min has discontinuous derivatives it is less than ideal for this search technique. Its derivative is zero for all arguments except the smallest, for which the derivative is one. If the two smallest arguments are close to one another, the derivative changes discontinuously for small changes in the state of each unit. It would be much better if the derivative could be divided among all the arguments, with the biggest share going to the lowest ones. Generalized mean values [46] have the desired effect. One way to define the generalized mean value of a vector of positive numbers a is with its p-*norm*, $M_p(a)$, where p is an arbitrary parameter:

$$M_p(a) = \left(\frac{1}{n} \sum_{i=1}^{n} a_i^p \right)^{1/p} , \tag{2}$$

where n is the length of the vector a. For $p = 1$ this is just the ordinary arithmetic mean, and as $p \to -\infty$ it becomes the min function. As $p \to \infty$ it becomes the max function. The restriction to positive numbers is unfortunate, since the energy of component propositions may be zero. However, if $p > 0$, the generalized mean value behaves appropriately for arguments of zero. Hence $\min(a, b, c)$ is rewritten

$$1 - \max((1 - a), (1 - b), (1 - c)) .$$

The arguments to OR, like those to NOT, may only take on energies between zero and one.

Table 3 lists the value of the approximate max function for various p. Currently μKLONE uses $p = 16$. For values closer to zero, the system would regard an OR constraint with one argument true, and the rest false, as partially unsatisfied. It would waste too much effort trying to satisfy more of the arguments. For larger values of p, the energy barriers between states with different arguments satisfied would be too large, and the system would commit itself too soon. For simplicity, the theoretical analysis in this article treats energy functions as if OR were translated as min. Keep in mind that the running system uses the generalized mean value approximation.

Table 3
How the approximate max function behaves for the vector $a = (0.80, 0.75, 0.60, 0.10)$, as p approaches ∞, and how much of the derivative is attributable to the largest argument.

p	$M_p(a)$	$\dfrac{\partial M_p(a)}{\partial a_1} \Big/ \sum_i \dfrac{\partial M_p(a)}{\partial a_i}$
1	0.56	0.25
2	0.63	0.36
4	0.68	0.44
8	0.72	0.56
16	0.75	0.72
32	0.77	0.88
64	0.78	0.98
128	0.79	0.999

2.3. Gradient descent in μKLONE energy space

Energy-based connectionist networks are usually drawn as undirected labeled graphs, where each vertex represents a unit and each edge represents a symmetric connection. The label is a signed connection weight, w_{ij}, indicating the magnitude of the influence of the state of unit i on that of unit j and vice versa. Positive weights are excitatory and negative weights inhibitory. The energy function is:

$$E^{\alpha}_{KB} = -\sum_{i<j} w_{ij} s^{\alpha}_i s^{\alpha}_j .$$

The partial derivative of the energy function with respect to each unit is dependent only on the states of its neighbors in the graph, so gradient descent search can be done on a parallel architecture with the topology of the graph. If we insist that the energy must monotonically decrease, no two neighboring units may update their state simultaneously, so the amount of parallelism attainable is dependent on the sparseness of the graph. Simulations suggest that synchronous updates do not usually cause problems, however [29].

In μKLONE, where the terms in the energy function can involve arbitrarily many units, a unit's neighbors include all the other units that occur in terms where it does. For instance, the energy function for the theory $\{\neg a \vee b \vee c, d\}$ is

$$E = \min(1 - a, b, c) + d .$$

$a, b,$ and c are all neighbors and cannot update simultaneously, but no synchronization is required of d. If the theory consists of many relatively short assertions, a high degree of parallelism is possible.

Large neighborhoods would have a double impact if the time to calculate the derivative of the energy contribution of each term with respect to the state of a unit grew with the size of a term. However, by saving some state information about each AND and OR constraint, the derivative with respect to a single conjunct or disjunct can be found in constant time. To find the energy derivative with respect to a single unit state using the chain rule, the derivative for the all conjunctions and disjunctions it is nested inside must also be known. Therefore the total time complexity for finding the derivative of the energy with respect to a unit state is proportional to the sum of the nesting depths of all occurences of that unit in the energy function.

Constraints in μKLONE are significantly more complicated than connections in normal connectionist networks, being defined recursively and maintaining state information. Hence it may be less misleading to call it a parallel constraint satisfaction system and not label it "connectionist." To the extent that the energy function can be regarded as composed of independent contributions from many individual constraints, each involving only a small fraction of the units, the term "connectionist network" conveys the spirit of the approach.

2.4. Hopfield and Tank search algorithm

Section 2.2 described how to assign energies to models, given a set of assertions in propositional logic. Even with logically incomplete or inconsistent information, the Boltzmann distribution can be used to specify a complete probability distribution from this energy function. Then the probability of any proposition can be determined by summing the probabilities of the models in which it holds. In cases where classical logic would find the proposition true, it will have a probability of one using the zero temperature Boltzmann distribution. In cases where logic makes no decision, the numerical probability can still be used as the basis of a decision.

This process is computationally intensive, requiring a summation over an exponential number of models. One often used heuristic is Maximum Likelihood estimation. The most probable model is found, and the truth of the proposition in that model is used to make the decision. Model-based reasoning, as used in this article, is in fact Maximum Likelihood estimation.[3]

Finding even a single most plausible model is still a hard problem. It reduces the problem of determining whether a Boolean formula has a model, which is well known to be NP-complete by Cook's theorem [17]. Still, model-based approaches seem to be better suited to mundane problems than approaches based on finding derivations of an answer.

One heuristic for finding reasonably good solutions to intractable problems quickly is hill climbing. The space of models is discrete, consisting of the corners of a hypercube in which each propositional variable occupies one dimension, and can take on the value of zero or one. Hill climbing requires a smooth search space, so the search takes place in an expanded space that includes the interior of the hypercube, and variables can take on continuous values between zero and one. The search begins in the center of the space, where all states are $\frac{1}{2}$, and must end up at a corner, which will correspond to a model. If all terms in the energy function are at most linear in the state of any given unit, no interior point will be a local minimum, and the search will terminate at a corner.

To the extent that the energy space is smooth, there will be broad basins of attraction in the direction of the corners with the lowest energy. If the deepest basins are the broadest, then the basin for the best model will extend the

---

[3] μKLONE queries have presuppositions, which are combined with the prior information contained in the KB to produce a posterior distribution, and the most plausible model is a mode of this distribution. When Maximum Likelihood estimation is applied to posterior distributions, it is sometimes called Maximum a Posteriori estimation [18].

farthest toward the center of the search space. This is the rationale for starting the search at the point where all states are $\frac{1}{2}$.

The energy function as defined above is less than ideal for searching because the "continental divides" of the various basins of attraction encroach far into the center of the search space, forcing the system to make decisions early. In a Hopfield and Tank network [27], a second term is added to the energy equation to smooth the space further:[4]

$$E = E_{\text{constraints}} + \sum_i \int_0^{s_i} g^{-1}(s) \, ds \qquad (3)$$

where

$$g(u) = \frac{1}{1 + e^{-u/T}} ,$$

and so

$$g^{-1}(s) = T \cdot \log \frac{s}{1 - s} .$$

T stands for temperature, which has the same meaning here as in the Boltzmann equation and the free energy equation.

At high temperatures the second term dominates, but it goes to zero as T does. It is minimized at $s_i = \frac{1}{2}$, so early in the search, units whose state is relatively unimportant in determining the global energy take on states near $\frac{1}{2}$. As T is gradually lowered, the search proceeds by choosing states for the most important propositions first. By deferring commitments on less important ones, shallow local minima resulting from their interactions are avoided.

3. μKLONE Language

μKLONE inherits its view of what a knowledge representation system should provide from its intellectual ancestors, the KL-ONE [7] family of knowledge representation systems. The current generation, including LOOM [32], KRYPTON [5], and KANDOR [40], provide a reasoning service to a higher level reasoning system. The KR component is intended to be a fast black box, and is not intended to be powerful enough to solve all the problems the reasoner as a whole is capable of. In a hybrid reasoner there may be many black boxes specialized for particular kinds of reasoning [32].

The KL-ONE family of KR systems uses a frame-style language for defining knowledge bases. The frame language is typically given a formal semantics in

---

[4] This description leaves out some parameters of the Hopfield and Tank Model that will not be used in this article, and changes the notation to use temperature instead of gain.

terms of a translation to first-order logic; however the frame-based syntax is important. It seems to reflect the way users think about domains, and it results in languages less powerful than full first-order logic, so more efficient reasoning algorithms can be used.

μKLONE differs from other KL-ONE-style systems in that there is a special purpose query language, which is quite limited in expressive power, and retrieves frames. The other systems typically include a general-purpose theorem prover which attempts to determine the validity of arbitrary sentences.

3.1. Definition language

3.1.1. Overview

The frame language (henceforth KB language) contains three ontological categories: concepts, roles, and individuals. Individuals are objects or actions in the domain. Concepts are classes of individuals, like PERSON. Roles are relationships between pairs of individuals, like HAS-MOTHER. If *has-mother* (*John,Sue*), then Sue is said to be a *role filler* of the HAS-MOTHER role for John. Concepts and roles are both *terms*.[5]

Ideally, terms are defined intensionally using a language the system itself can understand. This way the system can decide for itself what terms a new individual, or pair of individuals, instantiates. This process is called *realization* [33]. More abstract than realization is the process of *classification*, which involves relationships between terms, and is completely independent of anything in the world. One term is said to *subsume* another if an instance of the latter must be an instance of the former, no matter what the world turns out to be like. For instance, UNICORN subsumes RED-UNICORN even if in our world there are none. Being model-based, μKLONE must always have particular individuals in mind, and cannot find abstract subsumption relations between terms. Since users are presumably most interested in facts about the world, purely terminological reasoning seems to have little functional importance. By caching subsumption relations, however, systems like KRYPTON are able to significantly speed up reasoning about the world.

Terminological reasoning sets KL-ONE-style KR systems apart from those in which concept definitions can include arbitrary LISP code. These systems cannot understand the definitions, and therefore cannot use them in perform-

---

[5] In this article, term names are usually printed in SMALL CAPITALS, individual names are in the normal font and Capitalized, propositions are *italicized*, and pieces of μKLONE syntax are in sanserif font. Sometimes the normal font is used when the distinction between English and μKLONE is unimportant. To emphasize that "individual" is used in its technical sense to mean an element of the domain over which logical quantifiers range, rather than the ordinary sense in which it applies only to humans, I often use "it" to refer to individuals, even when they are known to be human. Appendix A summarizes all the typographical conventions used.

ing realization or classification [2, 3, 59]. Unfortunately, it is impossible for *all* definitions to be in terms a system can understand. There must be some base terms that an unanalyzed. In μKLONE these terms are called *primitive*, and their extensions must be explicitly enumerated.

(DEFCONCEPT Person (PRIMITIVE))

introduces PERSON as a primitive concept.

Nonprimitive concepts can be defined in terms of other concepts using DEFCONCEPT as well. However, the only use for nonprimitive defined terms is as a notational convenience, similar to macros in programming languages. If a domain contains many facts about squares, it is more concise to avoid repeating "equilateral rectangle." There is a front end to μKLONE which immediately expands out all definitions, so that the actual reasoning system only sees assertions, and these refer only to primitive terms.

There are many ways to express logically equivalent information in μKLONE. The following two fragments are converted by the front end into exactly the same set of assertions:

(DEFCONCEPT Parent (SOME Has-Child))
(DEFCONCEPT Father (And Parent Male))
(INSTANTIATE-CONCEPT Father Bob)

and

(INSTANTIATE-CONCEPT (AND (SOME Has-Child) Male) Bob)

3.1.2. *Language constructs*

There are eight concept-forming constructs: DISJOINT, AND, OR, ALL, SOME (two types), FILLS, and RVM (see Fig. 1). Circular definitions are not allowed. A (DISJOINT c) clause means that the extension of the concept being defined is disjoint from that of c. For instance the definition of MAN may include (DISJOINT Woman). This makes WOMAN disjoint from MAN as well. WOMAN would have to be defined without reference to MAN to avoid circularity. (AND $c_1 c_2 \ldots c_n$) defines a concept whose extension is the intersection of the extensions of the c_i. Similarly, for OR clauses the result is the union of the extensions of the arguments. An (ALL $r c$) clause requires that all fillers of the role r must be instances of the concept c. For instance someone's definition of SUCCESSFUL-PARENT might include (ALL Has-Child Professional). A (SOME r) clause specifies that there must be at least one filler of r. The definition of PARENT is (SOME Has-Child). With two arguments, as in (SOME Has-Child Male), there must be at least one filler of a given type. A (FILLS $r i$) clause specifies that an individual i fills the role r. For instance the definition of CANADIAN includes (FILLS Has-Homeland Canada). Role value maps (RVMs) specify set inclusion relations between fillers of different roles. For example,

```
                    〈KB〉 ::= (〈S〉*)
                     〈S〉 ::= (DEFCONCEPT〈concept〉(PRIMITIVE))
                          |   (DEFCONCEPT〈concept〉
                                 〈concept form〉)
                          |   (ASSERT-CONCEPT〈certainty〉
                                 〈concept form〉〈concept form〉)
                          |   (DEFROLE〈role〉(PRIMITIVE))
                          |   (DEFROLE〈role〉〈role form〉)
                          |   (ASSERT-ROLE〈certainty〉〈role form〉
                                 〈role form〉)
                          |   (INSTANTIATE-CONCEPT〈certainty〉
                                 〈concept form〉〈individual〉)
                          |   (INSTANTIATE-ROLE〈certainty〉
                                 〈individual〉〈role form〉〈individual〉)
       〈concept form〉 ::= 〈concept〉
                          |   (DISJOINT〈concept form〉)
                          |   (AND〈concept form〉*)
                          |   (OR〈concept form〉*)
                          |   (ALL〈role form〉〈concept form〉)
                          |   (SOME〈role form〉)
                          |   (SOME〈role form〉〈concept form〉)
                          |   (FILLS〈role form〉〈individual〉)
                          |   (RVM〈role form〉〈role form〉)
           〈role form〉 ::= 〈role〉
                          |   (DISJOINT〈role form〉)
                          |   (AND 〈role form〉*)
                          |   (OR〈role form〉*)
                          |   (DOMAIN〈concept form〉)
                          |   (RANGE〈concept form〉)
             〈concept〉 ::= 〈symbol〉
                〈role〉 ::= 〈symbol〉
          〈individual〉 ::= 〈symbol〉
           〈certainty〉 ::= 〈positive real number〉
```

Fig. 1. KB language syntax. OR, RVM and the two-argument SOME do not add to the expressive power of the language. They are macros that are expanded into the remaining constructs. Having both ALL and SOME is redundant, too, but both are implemented directly. μKLONE provides all the constructs common to KL-ONE-style frame languages except number restrictions, role chains, inverse roles, and structural descriptions.

(DEFCONCEPT Deadbeat (RVM Has-Friend Has-Creditor))

means that a deadbeat is something all of whose friends are also its creditors. This is equivalent to:

```
(DEFCONCEPT Deadbeat
  (DISJOINT (SOME (AND Has-Friend
  (DISJOINT Has-Creditor)))))
```

There are five role-forming constructs: DISJOINT, AND, OR, DOMAIN, and RANGE. The first three have the same meaning as for concepts. A (DOMAIN c) clause specifies that the domain of the relation is subsumed by c.[6] A (RANGE c) clause specifies that the range of the relation is subsumed by c. For instance, the definition of HAS-EXPENSIVE-HOBBY includes (RANGE Expensive-Activity). Role-forming constructs induce a taxonomy over roles; for instance R1 subsumes (AND R1 R2).

3.2. Assertion language

In addition to their use for defining what is meant by various terms, these same constructs are used for making assertions about the world. In this respect μKLONE differs from other members of the KL-ONE family, where totally different languages are used for definitions and assertions. If an assertion is made about a term, it does not affect the recognition of instances of the term, but it does affect the beliefs about individuals, or pairs of individuals, that are recognized. For instance if it is *asserted* of SELF-MADE-MILLIONAIRE-PLAYBOYs that (SOME Has-Job), then it is not necessary to know that an individual has a job in order to conclude that it is a SELF-MADE-MILLIONAIRE-PLAYBOY, as it would be if this were part of the definition. However, anything that meets the definition of SELF-MADE-MILLIONAIRE-PLAYBOY will be believed to have a job.

There are two additional constructs that can only be used to make assertions, INSTANTIATE-CONCEPT and INSTANTIATE-ROLE. They assert that an individual instantiates a given concept, and that a pair of individuals instantiates a given role.

Assertions have certainties, which determine probabilities of the associated proposition as described in Section 2.2. Formally, a certainty can be any positive real number. By convention, values in (0, 100] are used. Figure 1 gives the full KB language syntax, including both definitions and assertions.

The distinction between criteria for recognizing instances of a term, and facts necessarily true of instances of a term can be quite subtle. This is most acute in relation to primitive terms. Is a PERSON an ANIMAL by definition, or is this a necessary, but *a posteriori* truth? The domain specifications used in this article are open to debate; the important point is that either philosophical position can be expressed. In NIKL and KRYPTON, the difference in expressive power between definition language and assertion language tempts users to express

---

[6] In KL-ONE, specifying the domain of a role was done by "attaching" the role to a concept, and it was considered to affect the meaning of the concept. In μKLONE roles have equal status with concepts, and can be defined independently. Role definitions never have any effect on the meaning of concepts.

sentences in whichever one it is expressible in, or in whichever one leads to most efficient reasoning, rather than the one that carries the correct epistemological import [20].

3.3. Query language

After a knowledge base has been defined using the KB language, it is compiled into a connectionist network. Further interaction with the system takes place using a separate query language. Answering the queries involves a hill climbing search, but the (patient) user need not be aware of the underlying connectionist implementation.

The query language is a pattern matching language for matching frames. The query itself is a partially instantiated frame, and the answer is a fully instantiated version that matches some individual in the system's internal model of its environment. For instance the query,

```
((SUBJECT ?)
 (SUBJECT-TYPE Professional-Sailor)
 (WITH (ROLE Has-Hobby) (FILLERS Flying)))
```

tells the system to match some individual who is a professional sailor and whose hobby is flying. The answer would be in the same format, but the ? would be filled in with some particular individual.

Internally, the system extracts the instantiated parts of the frame to be matched, which are called the *presuppositions* of the query. In this case the presuppositions are that there exists some individual that is a professional sailor and whose hobby is flying. The presuppositions are combined with the permanent information in the KB, and a model is constructed that is the most likely interpretation of all this information. A subject is also selected to serve as the focus of attention within the model. The unspecified parts of the query are instantiated based on the part of the model within the focus of attention.

The reason an internal model is used, rather than matching directly on a representation of the KB, is that the KB may be incomplete and inconsistent. In order to retrieve coherent answers, some processing must be done to clean up and complete the KB. In traditional KL-ONE-style systems, this reasoning is accomplished syntactically using a theorem prover or a special purpose deduction system. In a model-based approach, construction of a model serves this purpose. It would be computationally cheaper to construct a model once and for all from the KB, and then do matching. But by finding a new model for every query, hypothetical or counterfactual presuppositions may be incorporated. In addition, by building the model starting from the subject of the query and working out toward indirectly-related knowledge, local consistency can be maintained around the focus of attention even when the KB as a whole is inconsistent.

There are two constructs to specify the subject of a query, and four to restrict the role fillers. A query may contain a SUBJECT clause, which specifies the individual the query is about. It may contain an arbitrary number of SUBJECT-TYPE clauses, and the subject of the query must instantiate the argument of each of these clauses.

Constructs restricting the fillers of a role are grouped together, with one set of constructs for each role the query concerns. The query can have an arbitrary number of WITH clauses, each of which can have up to four subclauses relating to one role. The ROLE subclause specifies the role that the current WITH clause is about. A FILLERS subclause specifies particular individuals that must fill the role. A VR (value restriction) subclause specifies a type restriction that all role fillers must meet. A MINIMUM-FILLERS subclause specifies that there must be a minimum number of fillers of a role. The syntax of the query language is shown in Fig. 2. The syntax of answers is exactly the same, except without ?'s.

There are some limitations on the syntax imposed by the size of a particular network. A query is translated directly into a pattern of activity over a set of input/output units in the connectionist network. There must be a separate group of units for every clause that appears in the query. Rarely would more than half a dozen clauses appear in a query, so this architectural limitation does not seem to be important in practice. Second, a unary representation is used to represent the argument to MINIMUM-FILLERS subclauses. There is no need for arguments to MINIMUM-FILLERS to be larger than the number of individuals represented in the network. Even building this many units seems wasteful, because arguments to MINIMUM-FILLERS are usually very small integers. Therefore, the user must specify all possible integers that are allowed to appear as MINIMUM-FILLERS arguments at the time the network is built.

$$\begin{aligned}
\langle\text{query}\rangle &::= (\{(\text{SUBJECT}\langle i\rangle)\} \\
&\quad (\text{SUBJECT-TYPE}\langle c\rangle))^*\langle\text{with form}\rangle^*) \\
\langle\text{with form}\rangle &::= (\text{WITH}\{(\text{ROLE}\langle r\rangle)\}\{(\text{VR}\langle c\rangle)\} \\
&\quad \{(\text{FILLERS}\langle i\text{-list}\rangle)\} \\
&\quad \{(\text{MINIMUM-FILLERS}\langle n\rangle)\}\}) \\
\langle c\rangle &::= \langle\text{concept}\rangle\,|? \\
\langle r\rangle &::= \langle\text{role}\rangle\,|? \\
\langle i\rangle &::= \langle\text{individual}\rangle\,|? \\
\langle n\rangle &::= \langle\text{whole number}\rangle\,|? \\
\langle i\text{-list}\rangle &::= \langle i\rangle\,|\,(\langle\text{individual}\rangle^*)
\end{aligned}$$

Fig. 2. Query language syntax. Query arguments and arguments to WITH forms may appear in any order. The number of SUBJECT-TYPE and WITH forms is limited by the implementation; four or five seems sufficient.

3.4. The role shift problem

The domain for the role shift problem is well suited for reasoning by satisfying multiple soft constraints. The KB is incomplete not only with respect to beliefs about individuals, but also with respect to what individuals there are. The set of beliefs about single individuals is complex enough that interesting reasoning can be done within μKLONE's architectural limitation of representing only a single frame at a time.

3.4.1. Informal description

Imagine walking along a pier and meeting Ted, who is dressed as a sailor. Ted launches into an excited monolog on the influence of independent television stations on TV programming. It seems reasonable to conclude that Ted is a professional sailor, and that he is interested in television. If later it is discovered that Ted is a self-made millionaire playboy, the previous conclusions about Ted would probably be changed. While self-made millionaire playboys generally have jobs, they are unlikely to be involved in manual labor. Millionaire playboys often have ostentatious pastimes, so perhaps sailing is Ted's hobby rather than his job. Given that he has some job, the fact that he is interested in television suggests that that field may be his profession.

The domain description in Appendix B is an attempt to encode the original beliefs about Ted. The primary query considered in this article asks counterfactually, "If Ted were a self-made millionaire playboy, what would his job and hobby be?" The exact query is:

```
((SUBJECT Ted)
 (SUBJECT-TYPE Self-Made-Millionaire-Playboy)
 (WITH (ROLE Has-Hobby) (FILLERS ?))
 (WITH (ROLE Has-Job) (FILLERS ?)))
```

The important KB definitions are: A PROFESSIONAL-SAILOR is a PERSON among whose HAS-JOBs is Sailing. A SELF-MADE-MIILLIONAIRE-PLAYBOY is a PERSON with some HAS-HOBBY that is an EXPENSIVE-ACTIVITY, all of whose HAS-JOBs must be ARMCHAIR-ACTIVITYs. A TV-BUFF is something with some HAS-INTEREST that is a TELEVISION-RELATED-ACTIVITY. The critical assertion is that SELF-MADE-MILLIONAIRE-PLAYBOYs must have at least one HAS-JOB. Both HAS-JOBs and HAS-HOBBYs are HAS-INTERESTs.

When the μKLONE network constructed from the knowledge base is asked "If Ted were a self-made millionaire playboy, what would his job and hobby be?" the system must try to reconcile being a millionaire playboy with its previous knowledge about Ted, that he is a professional sailor and is interested in TV. The counterfactual premise conflicts with the knowledge base because sailing is asserted to be a vigorous activity, and the jobs of millionaire playboys must be armchair activities. The initial impact of this conflict on the selection of a model is that sailing is likely to still be one of Ted's interests, but perhaps not his job. Since millionaire playboys must have expensive hobbies and only two activities known to require expensive equipment are in the KB, flying and sailing are the most likely candidates. Sailing is chosen because it is already thought to be an interest. The plausible substitution that sailing is Ted's job rather than his hobby is made because HAS-JOB and HAS-HOBBY are both subsumed by HAS-INTEREST, making it relatively easy to slip between them.

A millionaire playboy must have a job that is an armchair activity and a profitable activity. Both TV-Network-Management and Corporate-Raiding fit this category, but the former is chosen because it is known that Ted is interested in television. TV-Acting is rejected because it is not an Armchair-Activity, and TV-Watching is rejected because it is not a Profitable-Activity.

If the knowledge base did not specify that millionaire playboys had expensive hobbies, the bias towards having sailing as an interest would not be sufficient for its being picked out as a hobby. Similarly, if millionaire playboys did not have to have jobs none would be picked out. And if the query had been simply "What are Ted's job and hobby?" no contradictory information would have been introduced. The answer, that sailing is Ted's job and he has no hobbies, would be constructed from knowledge in the KB alone. Although no constraints are violated in this last case if Ted does have a hobby, the system prefers minimal models.

An alternative to disbelieving that Ted is a professional sailor is disbelieving the rule that millionaire playboy's jobs must be armchair activities. However, the solution in that case is not very interesting. To illustrate the way conflicting rules cause a "role shift" it must be particular facts that are rejected. Thus the certainties of the general rules about this domain are set higher (100) than the certainties of individual facts (50). In retrospect this is not realistic. In most real-world situations particular information about a person's profession would override stereotypes. However the point of the role shift problem is not that the system has an adequate representation to conclude that the owner of Turner Broadcasting in fact races sailboats for a hobby, but is rather the demonstration that nontrivial inferences can be done in a connectionist system. By setting up the example as it is, a several step propagation results.

The problem is difficult for two reasons:

(1) The search is for an optimal model, rather than a satisficing one, so even if an oracle were abailable for suggesting a model, it is still hard to verify that it is the best model.
(2) The best solution cannot be found by considering the constraints strictly in order of importance, a technique used in prioritized default logic.

A model in which Ted's job is corporate raiding and his hobby is TV watching is just as good when only domain constraints are considered. It is the influence of the much weaker minimal model constraints that argues against this model, so constraints of all strengths must be considered at once.

3.5. A straightforward connectionist architecture

This section describes how to build an impractibly large and slow network which would correctly implement μKLONE. The purpose of this section is to push the formal theory as far as possible toward a connectionist architecture, in order to make the relationship of the actual system to conventional systems clearer. The model-based aspect of the reasoning is apparent, for the models over which the system searches are possible models in the model theory sense. The input and output of queries and answers is not described. Section 4.2 outlines how input/output is done in the actual implementation; for a full description see [12].

Any theory expressed in the μKLONE frame language is finitely controllable, and a bound, Ω, can be calculated such that if the theory has a consistent model, it has one with a domain of size Ω [12]. Therefore, the quantifiers which result from ALL and SOME clauses in the KB can be expanded into conjunctions or disjunctions over this domain, producing a propositional theory amenable to translation into an energy function as described in Section 2.2. Global minima correspond to most plausible models, so a search procedure guaranteed to find global minima would constitute a correct implementation of μKLONE. Although the Hopfield and Tank search algorithm is only guaranteed to find local minima, the Boltzmann machine search algorithm [25] has such a guarantee if run for exponential time. In addition, Ω is an exponential function of the size of the KB, so this construction is not of practical value. Still, it provides a foundation from which the tractable architecture described in the next section is derived.

Using the mapping of Section 2.2, the resulting propositional theory can be translated into a connectionist network with one unit for each atomic proposition. If n is the number of symbols in the KB, there will be $O(n)$ predicates, both one-place and two-place. The former have Ω possible arguments, and the latter Ω^2. Thus the number of connectionist units required is $O(n \cdot \Omega^2)$.

In a KB of size n, ALLs and SOMEs can be nested to a depth of $O(n)$, so recursively expanding the quantifiers over a domain of size Ω results in a propositional formula of size $O(\Omega^n)$. Since the constraints built for the complete implementation are structured like the assertions, the total space to represent all the constraints is also this ridiculously large number.

4. μKLONE Architecture

This section describes an alternative architecture in which searching for a model is faster, but global energy minima of the search space are no longer guaranteed to correspond to most plausible models. Just as attempts have been made in syntactic systems to limit the form of the KB or the inferences that can be made in order to achieve tractability, in a semantic system the model space may be limited. It will be impractical to formally characterize the answers such a system will give, just as it is for syntactically limited KR systems. The usefulness of the approach can only be decided by empirical testing.

4.1. Modifications to straightforward implementation

4.1.1. *Caching intermediate results*

The most important modification is the introduction of nonprimitive predicates that eliminate the need for deeply nested constraints. Quantifiers are only introduced in μKLONE by concept-forming constructs, which are one-place predicates. Therefore quantifiers can have only one free variable in their scope, and that free variable is always the one introduced by the quantifier nested immediately outside (see Fig. 3). Therefore deeply nested constructs, although replicated many times when the outermost quantifiers are expanded, do not refer to the outermost variables. Their value can be calculated once, and cached in the state of extra units added for this purpose.

The disadvantage is that some units in the network will now represent nonatomic propositions like (*All Has-Job Armchair-Activity*)(*Ted*), whose states are definitionally dependent on that of other units. The complex predicates which form these propositions will be written in notation borrowed from the KB language. Thus (ALL Has-Job Armchair-Activity) is a one-place predicate whose extension includes individuals all of whose jobs are armchair activities.

(ASSERT-CONCEPT Millionaire
   (SOME Has-Hobby
     (SOME Has-Expensive-Equipment)))

$$\forall x[M(x) \rightarrow \exists y[H(x, y) \wedge \exists z[E(y, z)]]] \qquad (1)$$

$$[E(y, A) \vee E(y, B) \vee \cdots] \qquad (2)$$

$$\begin{aligned}
&(\{H(A, A) \wedge [E(A, A) \vee E(A, B) \vee \cdots]\} \vee \qquad (3)\\
&\ \ \{H(A, B) \wedge [E(B, A) \vee E(B, B) \vee \cdots]\} \vee\\
&\ \ \cdots) \qquad\qquad\qquad\qquad\qquad\qquad\qquad \wedge\\
&(\{H(B, A) \wedge [E(A, A) \vee E(A, B) \vee \cdots]\} \vee\\
&\ \ \{H(B, B) \wedge [E(B, A) \vee E(B, B) \vee \cdots]\} \vee\\
&\ \ \cdots) \qquad\qquad\qquad\qquad\qquad\qquad\qquad \wedge\\
&\cdots
\end{aligned}$$

Fig. 3. Illustration of the constraint explosion resulting from nested quantifiers, and how it can be avoided by computing common subexpressions only once. The KB language fragment at the top is equivalent to the logic formula (1). When the quantifiers are expanded to produce a propositional theory, the subexpression derived from the last existential quantifier (2) is seen to recur many times for each value of y in (3). The network complexity is reduced by building units like (*SOME Has-Expensive-Equipment*)(*A*) to cache these intermediate results.

The predicates from which the nonatomic propositions are formed include four types of one-place predicates: (DISJOINT c), (FILLS r i), (SOME r), and (ALL r c); and three types of two-place predicates: (DISJOINT r), (DOMAIN c), and (RANGE c). In the previous architecture, the representation was completely vivid [31, 50], with no possibility for meaningless representations. Now, with explicit derived information the search space contains self-contradictory states. These states are given a very high energy by defining new constraints, termed *structural constraints*, with weights much higher than domain constraints (300 for the role shift problem). For example, there would be strong inhibition between the units Person(Ted) and (DISJOINT PERSON)(Ted).

The computational efficiency gained by explicitly representing as unit states, accessible to many different constraints, what would be recomputed by each of these constraints in the vivid architecture outweighs this overhead. The number of units in the network is still $O(n \cdot \Omega^2)$, just as it was in the complete architecture. The constraint complexity, however, has been reduced from $O(\Omega^n)$ to $O(n^2\Omega^2)$.

Another disadvantage of not expanding the KB into its full clausal form is that the semantics are no longer fully respected. In particular, embedded conjunctions can contribute a maximum of one to the energy because no matter how many conjuncts are unsatisfied, the effect on the state of the unit that caches the value of the conjunction is the same.

4.1.2. *Eliminating most made-up individuals*

The second most important architectural modification is that the domain includes individuals mentioned in the KB plus a handful, rather than Ω of them. It is expected that in reasoning about an individual, it may be necessary to consider related but unfamiliar individuals, for instance a mother, a job, or a favorite novel, but that mundane reasoning will rarely require simultaneous consideration of more than a handful of these made-up individuals. This reduces the number of units to $O(n^3)$ and the time and space complexity to $O(n^4)$.

4.1.3. *Representing a single subject*

The architecture described above may be practical as it stands. However by restricting the problems it can solve to those in which all relevant information is attached to a single individual, the unit complexity can be reduced from $O(n^3)$ to $O(n^2)$ and the constraint complexity from $O(n^4)$ to $O(n^3)$. This factor of n comes from eliminating the information about each individual's role fillers. Instead, complete information is only represented about a single individual, the subject, which can map to a different individual for every query. With this restriction no problem requiring chaining through knowledge about multiple individuals, can be answered. If the KB is viewed as a semantic network, the system considers only individuals within a radius of one from the focus of attention, the subject, as well as their type information (see Fig. 4).

The limited knowledge still represented about all individuals is used to constrain the knowledge about the subject; the units standing for the identity of the subject in the Subject group gate the type information about the individual who is the subject into the Subject-Type group (see Figs. 5 and 6). This is another source of redundant representations, and two more types of structural constraints are required to maintain a self-consistent model. These constraints force exactly one Subject group unit to be on, and force the subject's type to be the same as the type of the individual who is the subject.

4.2. Input and output

When the user types a query, the LISP front end converts each concept, role, or individual into a pattern of activation over additional groups of units, which pass the presuppositions to the four central groups of units. These groups are conceptually unimportant, and are not discussed in this article (see [12]). For the example query, the presuppositions are that the subject is Ted, and that the

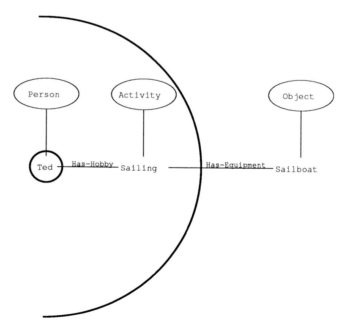

Fig. 4. Illustration of the effect of representing a single subject on the knowledge accessible to the network. If Ted is the subject of the query, his type, his role fillers, and the type of his role fillers are accessible. The role fillers of his role fillers, such as Sailboat, are not available. The focus of attention is a circle of radius one, centered on Ted.

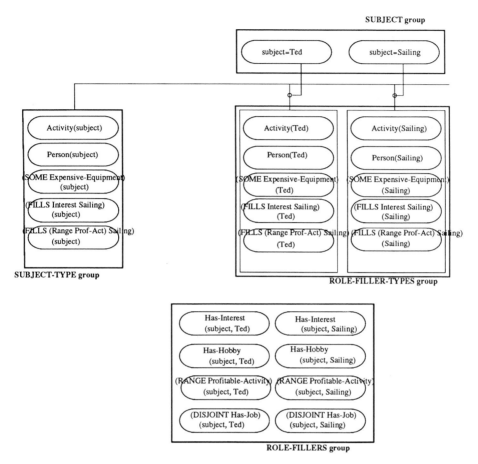

Fig. 5. The four groups of units of the tractable μKLONE architecture. Each group represents one kind of information within the focus of attention in Fig. 1. In the sample query, the Subject group would represent Ted by turning on the unit *subject = Ted*, and turning off all other units in the group. The Subject-Type group would represent millionaire playboy by turning on units like *Person(subject)*. The Role-Fillers group has a unit for every combination of a role feature with an individual, and can represent any combination of roles and fillers. To represent that sailing is the subject's hobby and that TV network management is the subject's job, the units *Has-Hobby(sub-ject, Sailing)*, *Has-Interest(subject, TV-Network-Management)*, and *(RANGE Profitable-Activity)(subject, TV-Network-Management)* are turned on. The Role-Filler-Types group repre-sents the type of all potential role fillers.

subject has the features of self-made millionaire playboys. In this particular case, the presuppositions can be enforced by clamping the *subject = Ted* unit on in the Subject group and all other units in this group off, and by clamping the features for millionaire playboys on in the Subject-Type group (and not

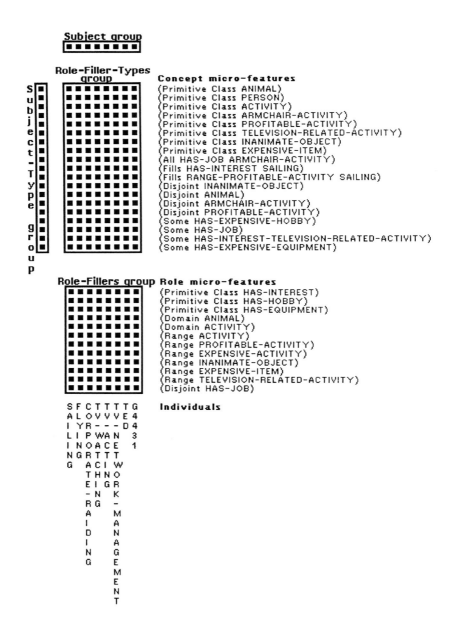

Subject group

Role-Filler-Types group

Concept micro-features

(Primitive Class ANIMAL)
(Primitive Class PERSON)
(Primitive Class ACTIVITY)
(Primitive Class ARMCHAIR-ACTIVITY)
(Primitive Class PROFITABLE-ACTIVITY)
(Primitive Class TELEVISION-RELATED-ACTIVITY)
(Primitive Class INANIMATE-OBJECT)
(Primitive Class EXPENSIVE-ITEM)
(All HAS-JOB ARMCHAIR-ACTIVITY)
(Fills HAS-INTEREST SAILING)
(Fills RANGE-PROFITABLE-ACTIVITY SAILING)
(Disjoint INANIMATE-OBJECT)
(Disjoint ANIMAL)
(Disjoint ARMCHAIR-ACTIVITY)
(Disjoint PROFITABLE-ACTIVITY)
(Some HAS-EXPENSIVE-HOBBY)
(Some HAS-JOB)
(Some HAS-INTEREST-TELEVISION-RELATED-ACTIVITY)
(Some HAS-EXPENSIVE-EQUIPMENT)

Role-Fillers group   **Role micro-features**

(Primitive Class HAS-INTEREST)
(Primitive Class HAS-HOBBY)
(Primitive Class HAS-EQUIPMENT)
(Domain ANIMAL)
(Domain ACTIVITY)
(Range ACTIVITY)
(Range PROFITABLE-ACTIVITY)
(Range EXPENSIVE-ACTIVITY)
(Range INANIMATE-OBJECT)
(Range EXPENSIVE-ITEM)
(Range TELEVISION-RELATED-ACTIVITY)
(Disjoint HAS-JOB)

Individuals

Fig. 6. The four central groups in full detail. One made-up individual (G4431) is included. There is no room to explicitly label each unit, but the labels can be inferred from the row and column labels, and by comparison with the previous figure.

clamping other units in this group). Therefore the data reported here were taken using clamping in the central groups, rather than using extra groups. For some queries, for instance those involving a MINIMUM-FILLERS clause, the query cannot be posed by clamping the central groups, and extra groups must be used.

4.3. Constraint types

4.3.1. *Domain constraints*

These constraints result from assertions about the domain, and are unidirectional implications. There are four kinds of domain constraints, corresponding to the four assertion forms in the KB language: ASSERT-CONCEPT, ASSERT-ROLE, INSTANTIATE-CONCEPT, and INSTANTIATE-ROLE. For instance, the fact that people are animals is enforced by an implication from the *person* feature to the *animal* feature in every column of the Role-Filler-Types group. The strengths of these constraints are determined by the certainties of the assertions, and by convention are expected to have a maximum value of 100.

4.3.2. *Structural constraints*

To the extent that the tractable architecture is not a direct model of the domain, there are units whose states are definitionally dependent on the states of other units. The structural constraints ensure that these dependencies are enforced. For instance, the unit (*DOMAIN Animal*)(*subject, Flying*) should be true if and only if the unit *Animal*(*subject*) is true. To ensure that self-consistent answers are found, even at the cost of violating some domain constraints, structural constraints are given much higher weights—300 in the role shift problem. Higher values result in high energy barriers between alternative models and worsen the performance of the hill climbing search algorithm.

4.3.3. *Minimal model constraints*

These constraints are used to make sure that the model chosen is minimal over the set of models that best meet the domain constraints. They are made much weaker than the other two types of constraints, so that small counterfactual models are not preferred over large factual ones. For the role shift problem, a value of 10 was used.

All units in the Role-Filler-Types and Role-Fillers groups that represent *primitive* predicates are given a weak (NOT (ON x)) constraint. The values of nonprimitive predicates are determined by the values of primitive predicates, and are not distinct assumptions. However, the primitive predicates on which SOME, ALL, and FILLS predicates depend are determined by each individual's role fillers, and these are not represented in the tractable implementation. Hence, it is not possible to determine exactly how many assumptions would be required to fill out a complete model. Still, it is a reasonable heuristic to treat SOME, ALL, and FILLS predicates as if they were primitive for the purposes of counting assumptions, and so they are also given a weak constraint to turn off in the Role-Filler-Types group.

This approximation makes the energy of a model sensitive to which individual is the subject. That is, even if the implicit complete model remains the same, some views of it will be preferred because the subject has fewer role fillers. Ideally, an extra penalty would be added proportional to the number of primitive role propositions true of all individuals other than the subject. While this number cannot be determined exactly, the number explicitly mentioned in INSTANTIATE-ROLE clauses is used as an estimate. Each Subject group unit is given a (NOT (ON x)) constraint whose strength is proportional to this estimate.

4.4. Details of reasoning process

When the LISP interface to the Hopfield and Tank network processes the query, the pattern for Ted is clamped into the Subject group, and the active features of SELF-MADE-MILLIONAIRE-PLAYBOY are clamped on in the Subject-Type group (see Fig. 7). The pattern for HAS-HOBBY and HAS-JOB would be clamped into some of the I/O groups, so that the fillers of these roles are properly read out. The I/O groups are not discussed here, however.

Since, Ted is asserted to be a professional sailor in the KB, there are domain constraints built into the Role-Filler-Types group that excite the units

> (*FILLS Has-Interest Sailing*)(*Ted*)

and

> (*FILLS (RANGE Profitable-Activity) Sailing*)(*Ted*) .

Since the *subject* = *Ted* unit is on in the Subject group, Ted's features are copied into the Subject-Type group, where these two features will be excited. Similarly, the

> (*SOME Has-Interest-TV-Related-Activity*)(*Subject*)

unit will be excited because of the assertion that Ted is a TV-BUFF. Simultaneously, the states of the units

> (*SOME Has-Expensive-Hobby*)(*subject*) ,

> (*ALL Has-Job Armchair-Activity*)(*subject*) ,

and

> *person*(*subject*)

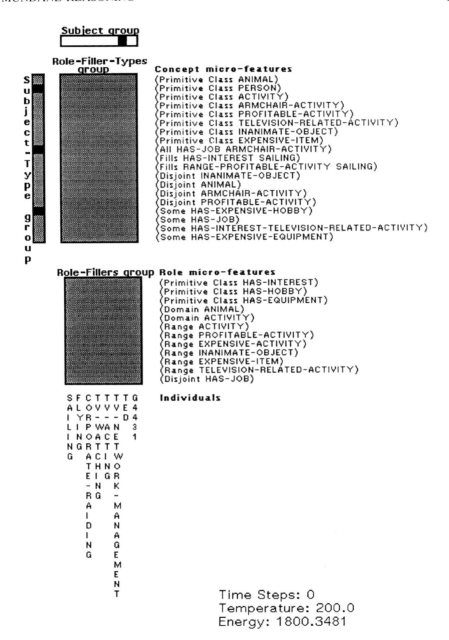

Subject group

Role-Filler-Types group

S
u
b
j
e
c
t
-
T
y
p
e

g
r
o
u
p

Concept micro-features
(Primitive Class ANIMAL)
(Primitive Class PERSON)
(Primitive Class ACTIVITY)
(Primitive Class ARMCHAIR-ACTIVITY)
(Primitive Class PROFITABLE-ACTIVITY)
(Primitive Class TELEVISION-RELATED-ACTIVITY)
(Primitive Class INANIMATE-OBJECT)
(Primitive Class EXPENSIVE-ITEM)
(All HAS-JOB ARMCHAIR-ACTIVITY)
(Fills HAS-INTEREST SAILING)
(Fills RANGE-PROFITABLE-ACTIVITY SAILING)
(Disjoint INANIMATE-OBJECT)
(Disjoint ANIMAL)
(Disjoint ARMCHAIR-ACTIVITY)
(Disjoint PROFITABLE-ACTIVITY)
(Some HAS-EXPENSIVE-HOBBY)
(Some HAS-JOB)
(Some HAS-INTEREST-TELEVISION-RELATED-ACTIVITY)
(Some HAS-EXPENSIVE-EQUIPMENT)

Role-Fillers group **Role micro-features**
(Primitive Class HAS-INTEREST)
(Primitive Class HAS-HOBBY)
(Primitive Class HAS-EQUIPMENT)
(Domain ANIMAL)
(Domain ACTIVITY)
(Range ACTIVITY)
(Range PROFITABLE-ACTIVITY)
(Range EXPENSIVE-ACTIVITY)
(Range INANIMATE-OBJECT)
(Range EXPENSIVE-ITEM)
(Range TELEVISION-RELATED-ACTIVITY)
(Disjoint HAS-JOB)

```
S F C T T T T G        Individuals
A L O V V V E 4
I Y R - - - D 4
L I P WA N   3
I N O A C E   1
N G R T T T
G   A C I   W
    T H N   O
    E I G   R
    - N     K
    R G     -
    A       M
    I       A
    D       N
    I       A
    N       G
    G       E
            M
            E
            N
            T
```

Time Steps: 0
Temperature: 200.0
Energy: 1800.3481

Fig. 7. Initial state of the network for the example query. Ted is clamped to be the subject, and the features for millionaire playboy are clamped on in the Subject-Type group. Other units in this group are unclamped, as are the units in all other groups, and their state is initialized to $\frac{1}{2}$.

in the Subject-Type group, which have been clamped on, are copied into the Ted column of the Role-Filler-Types group. Here the combination of these features, which together define SELF-MADE-MILLIONAIRE-PLAYBOY, excite the (*SOME Has-Job*)(*Ted*) unit. This feature is in turn copied back into the Subject-Type group, where it will exert its influence on Ted's particular role fillers, represented in the Role-Fillers group. Figure 8 shows the states of the units at an intermediate stage in the search, when the assertion that Ted's job is sailing is just being overwhelmed by the presupposition that he is a millionaire playboy.

The two units

$$(FILLS\ Has\text{-}Interest\ Sailing)(subject)$$

and

$$(FILLS\ (RANGE\ Profitable\text{-}Activity)\ Sailing)(subject)$$

excite the pattern for HAS-JOB in the Sailing column of the Role-Fillers group, that is, the units

$$has\text{-}interest(subject,\ Sailing)$$

and

$$(RANGE\ Profitable\text{-}Activity)(subject,\ Sailing)\ .$$

Simultaneously, the

$$(ALL\ Has\text{-}Job\ Armchair\text{-}Activity)(subject)$$

unit activates a constraint that recognizes that Sailing is filling the HAS-JOB role, yet is not an ARMCHAIR-ACTIVITY. This constraint tends to inhibit the pattern for HAS-JOB in the Sailing column. That is, it tries to turn off one of the two units representing HAS-JOB.

The (*SOME Has-Expensive-Hobby*)(*subject*) unit tries to excite the HAS-EXPENSIVE-HOBBY pattern over some column in the Role-Fillers group. This pattern includes the features (*RANGE Expensive-Activity*) and *has-hobby*. The former feature will already have an activity greater than $\frac{1}{2}$ for the individuals Sailing and Flying due to the explicit KB assertions, so it will be easier to assert the pattern for HAS-EXPENSIVE-HOBBY in one of these columns. The other feature of this pattern, *has-hobby* tries to excite the *has-interest* feature because hobbies are asserted to be interests. But this feature is already somewhat active for Sailing because it is part of the pattern for HAS-JOB. Thus Sailing gets a small head start over Flying, and the system chooses it as Ted's hobby.

It is important that the role HAS-JOB is not atomic. If it were, when the

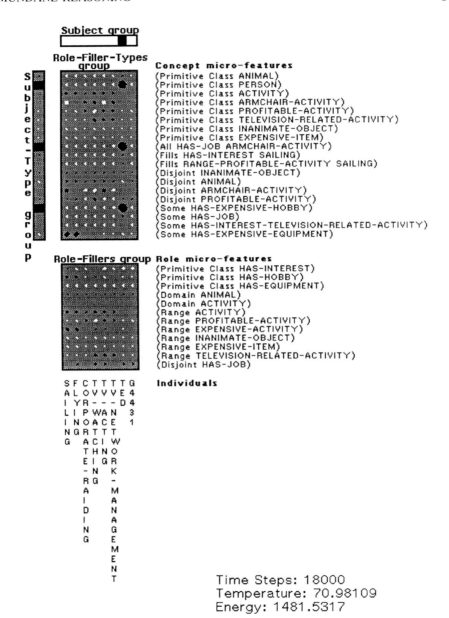

Time Steps: 18000
Temperature: 70.98109
Energy: 1481.5317

Fig. 8. Intermediate state of the network for the example query, after searching for 18,000 time steps. In the Subject-Type group, the feature (*All Has-Job Armchair-Activity*) prevents the feature (*FILLS (RANGE Profitable-Activity) Sailing*) from being asserted, enabling sailing to be Ted's hobby rather than his job.

presupposition that Ted is a millionaire playboy results in the system discarding the belief that his job is sailing, there would be no more reason to believe that sailing is any kind of interest. HAS-JOB is in fact defined as an interest that is a profitable activity, so when the system decides it is not profitable in Ted's case, the semantics still prefers models in which Ted is interested in sailing. However the decision to represent only partial models prevents knowledge about role fillers from being represented directly. Instead such information is represented via the creation of complex predicates, such as (*FILLS Has-Job Sailing*). Representing this predicate atomically results in the loss of the ability to represent its being only half true; when the system retracts its belief that sailing is a profitable activity, this predicate becomes false of the subject, and hence there is no more reason to believe the subject has any interest in sailing. To force the system to build two complex predicates,

(*FILLS Has-Interest Sailing*)

and

(*FILLS (RANGE Profitable-Activity) Sailing*) ,

the definition of SAILOR explicitly mentions both of these features (see Appendix B). This kind of shortcoming of the tractable architecture is one of the reasons µKLONE is intended to be used in familiar domains where the form of the KB can be adjusted until uniformly good performance results.

   Choosing Ted's job is the result of three constraints: that all his jobs must be armchair activities, that he must have some television related interest, and that any job must be a profitable activity. There are two profitable armchair activities, Corporate-Raiding and TV-Network-Management. The constraints on jobs alone do not distinguish between these alternatives. Similarly, Ted's television-related interest could be TV-Watching, TV-Acting, or TV-Network-Management. The constraints that make the system prefer small models lead the system to choosing the single activity in the intersection of these sets, TV-Network-Management, so that only one relationship must be postulated rather than two. Figure 9 shows the final state of the network.

4.5. Performance

The Ted Turner domain includes seven explicitly mentioned individuals, and one more made-up individual is added in case some frame requires an individual whose properties do not match any of the seven. There are eight primitive concept micro-features and ten non-primitive ones. There are three primitive role micro-features and nine nonprimitive ones. The network has 266 units in the central groups, and the size of the constraint tree is 2817.

   The procedure for finding an annealing schedule involves trial and error, but

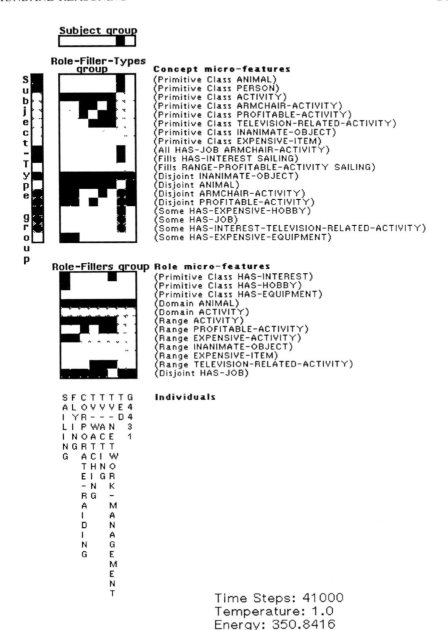

Subject group

Role-Filler-Types group

Concept micro-features
(Primitive Class ANIMAL)
(Primitive Class PERSON)
(Primitive Class ACTIVITY)
(Primitive Class ARMCHAIR-ACTIVITY)
(Primitive Class PROFITABLE-ACTIVITY)
(Primitive Class TELEVISION-RELATED-ACTIVITY)
(Primitive Class INANIMATE-OBJECT)
(Primitive Class EXPENSIVE-ITEM)
(All HAS-JOB ARMCHAIR-ACTIVITY)
(Fills HAS-INTEREST SAILING)
(Fills RANGE-PROFITABLE-ACTIVITY SAILING)
(Disjoint INANIMATE-OBJECT)
(Disjoint ANIMAL)
(Disjoint ARMCHAIR-ACTIVITY)
(Disjoint PROFITABLE-ACTIVITY)
(Some HAS-EXPENSIVE-HOBBY)
(Some HAS-JOB)
(Some HAS-INTEREST-TELEVISION-RELATED-ACTIVITY)
(Some HAS-EXPENSIVE-EQUIPMENT)

Role-Fillers group **Role micro-features**
(Primitive Class HAS-INTEREST)
(Primitive Class HAS-HOBBY)
(Primitive Class HAS-EQUIPMENT)
(Domain ANIMAL)
(Domain ACTIVITY)
(Range ACTIVITY)
(Range PROFITABLE-ACTIVITY)
(Range EXPENSIVE-ACTIVITY)
(Range INANIMATE-OBJECT)
(Range EXPENSIVE-ITEM)
(Range TELEVISION-RELATED-ACTIVITY)
(Disjoint HAS-JOB)

Individuals

```
Time Steps: 41000
Temperature: 1.0
Energy: 350.8416
```

Fig. 9. Final state of the network for the example query. After the 40,000 steps of the annealing schedule gradually cooling from $T = 200$ to $T = 20$, the temperature was lowered to 1 and the network was run at constant temperature for 1000 time steps.

is straightforward. First the starting and ending temperatures are found. A good starting temperature is the lowest one for which all the unit states are close to $\frac{1}{2}$, and a good ending temperature is the highest one for which they are all near zero or one. Next a value for the step size is found. The network is most susceptible to oscillation at low temperatures, so a good value is the largest step size that does not cause oscillation at the ending temperature. Finally, the best number of steps to take is the smallest number such that the network stays close to equilibrium during search. As the temperature is lowered during annealing, the component of the energy function due to constraints (see equation (3)) of the energy monotonically decreases. If the system is close to equilibrium, the energy will not change while the system is run at constant temperature. Thus the number of steps is adjusted until pausing the annealing and running at constant temperature does not change the energy much.

For the Ted Turner problem, a schedule of 40,000 time steps to decrease the temperature from 200 to 20 with a step size of 0.001 was used. This takes a day on a Symbolics 3600. While it is easy to predict how the size of the network will scale with the domain, there is as yet little basis for making such a prediction about the number of time steps. In one comparison using an earlier version of μKLONE, some unnecessary information was deleted from the Ted Turner domain. The resulting KB was 34% smaller, yet the annealing schedule could only be shortened by 16%. I am hopeful that for KBs that grow in number of facts faster than in the number of ways the facts interact, a sublinear relation between KB size and annealing schedule length will continue to hold.[7]

4.6. Significance of Ted Turner problem

The common sense answers to the queries discussed above are given primarily because the representations of roles are distributed across atomic propositions: HAS-JOB generates a pattern of activity similar to that generated by HAS-HOBBY. Since constraints operate over individual units rather than whole roles, roles which share many units have similar properties. Viewed from the level of units, this is not remarkable at all, but symbolic systems that represent roles atomically must have externally specified rules for judging similarity, and such systems must explicitly perform similarity reasoning to get the sort of inexact match achieved here.

The particular answer found is also not critical. There are other reasonable answers that also reflect reasoning by similarity over meaningful patterns. For instance the system could have decided that sailing is not a VIGOROUS-ACTIVITY, in which case Ted's job could be sailing. This answer is slightly

---

[7] Recall that the total search time on a sequential machine is the product of the network size and the number of time steps.

worse in terms of energy because two more minimal model constraints must be violated.

The Ted Turner domain demonstrates that in spite of the small fraction of a complete model that can be explicitly represented by μKLONE, the system can still do interesting mundane reasoning. There is no limit on the number of factors that can be taken into account in answering a query. In choosing Ted's job, assertions about jobs in general, about millionaire playboy's jobs in particular, and even assertions about Ted's other interests were considered.

The single severe limitation is that contradictions that can only be detected by knowing the role fillers of the subject's role fillers will not be found. For instance if Jaqueline-Kennedy was asserted to be a

> (SOME Has-Spouse (AND Professional-Sailor
> Self-Made-Millionaire-Playboy)) ,

the system would happily pick an individual as a filler of the spouse role. Since the contradiction between PROFESSIONAL-SAILOR and SELF-MADE-MILLIONAIRE-PLAYBOY is only apparent upon consideration of the spouse's role fillers, μKLONE does not detect it. The limitations imposed by the query language guide the user to ask questions that are likely to be appropriate. All clauses in a query must be about one individual, which may be previously known by the system or dynamically created by recruiting a generic made-up individual.

5. Conclusion

5.1. Provides unifying framework

μKLONE neatly combines Johnson-Laird's ideas about model-based reasoning, Levesque's ideas about vivid representations, and Hinton's ideas about distributed representations, none of which have been implemented in anything but a rudimentary way. Whereas connectionists have generally thought of their systems as diametrically opposed to logic-based systems, I have argued that the difference is not whether a formal logical semantics can be usefully applied, but whether the system uses sequential syntactic inference in which only information contained in a single rule is considered at one time, or parallel model-based inference in which all information simultaneously constrains the search.

Connectionist architectures provide the foundation for this unifying framework. They seem ideally suited for approximating probabilistic reasoning in complex domains. Using probability theory for describing mundane domains rather than defaults offers a concise way to reduce the number of anomalous extensions. By defining a family of probability distributions from weighted assertions via the Boltzmann distribution, and considering the zero temperature limit, the μKLONE semantics specifies a set of models contained in the set resulting from applying Reiter's default logic to the same (unweighted) assertions. This provides a way to relate probability theory and default logic.

Connectionist architectures have the drawback that the meaning of a unit is essentially fixed by the architecture, so it is difficult to have variables without simulating a higher-level machine. But model-based reasoning does not require variables. Given the particular nonlogical constants of a theory, the space of possible models is well defined, and for finitely controllable languages only a finite subspace needs to be searched.

Connectionist systems using deterministic energy minimization have the drawback that only one model is found, even when others may be equally good. But this is what Levesque suggests on more general grounds. Having a model allows the system to reason about the truth of each assertion independently, which is much simpler than detecting the inconsistency or arbitrary subsets of assertions. From the perspective of complete and correct inference this is just pushing the problem down one level, since finding such a model is in general as hard as theorem proving. However for best-guess inference the difference is important if better heuristics are available for quickly finding plausible models.

The notion of similarity between models arises directly out of the architecture, and the system naturally finds reasonable approximate answers. In model-based reasoning there is no place for abstractions like SELF-MADE-MILLIONAIRE-PLAYBOY, but only for primitive predicates. This is the essence of distributed representations, where these abstractions are strictly emergent properties of the unit-level representation. No inheritance algorithm is required to find the properties of a term, because they are explicit in the term's representation. No previous connectionist system has had a principled way to find appropriate primitives from which abstract concepts would emerge, nor performed any kind of emergent inheritance among roles.

5.2. Automatic generation of prototypes

In the example query about Ted, the model found by the system is the only one with minimal energy. Yet there are some situations where several models have minimal energy, yet the dynamics of the search process ensure that the one which is most prototypical is chosen. Units representing alternative ways to meet the constraints are partially active during the search, so the global state is the superposition of many models. To the extent that distinct models share propositions, they reinforce one another.

For instance if the query ((SUBJECT-TYPE Activity)) is asked, without any other context, then each known activity is an equally good answer in terms of energy. In this domain, three of the six known activities are asserted to be profitable activities, and only one is asserted not to be. As the system searches over activities, everything else being equal, half the time the *profitable-activity* unit in the Subject-Type group will receive net excitation, and only a sixth of the time will it be inhibited. Once the unit becomes active, there is a process of positive feedback. TV-Watching is less likely to be selected, because of the activity of the *profitable-activity*(*subject*) unit, which becomes even less likely to receive inhibition. Once *profitable-activity*(*subject*) is firmly on, activities that are known to have the feature become more likely than those than merely may have it. In order to match the pattern in the Subject-Type group, the latter activities must activate the feature in their column of the Role-Filler-Types group, increasing the size of the model. The former activities, however, would already have this feature active. The system tends to pick activities that are prototypical of all the activities it knows about. McClelland [35] has previously described prototype extraction from knowledge about particular individuals due to positive feedback from a feature set to the individuals having the features.

5.3. Sequential reasoning

In spite of the power to combine sources of evidence and to find plausible interpretations of incomplete and inconsistent information, there are hard limits to what a system like this can do. In many ways its reasoning is like perceptual reasoning, being fast, nondecomposable, inflexible, and only useful after lots of training (or tuning) in familiar situations. An intelligent agent must respond in unfamiliar situations as well. Since by definition these situations are unpredictable, it seems to require symbols with arbitrary referents. It is also impossible to predict the logical relations among individuals in a novel situation, so an analog parallel architecture will not in general be available. Even in familiar domains a problem involving chains of role fillers cannot be solved in parallel when the architecture is limited to representing only one frame at a time. It seems that sequential reasoning will be required, and concomitantly control structures and interpreters.

A hybrid production system in which the match is done by a connectionist KR module seems like a natural way to get both common sense behavior and sequential control. In such a system, the inner loop would be much more powerful than in current production systems, and many familiar problems could be solved in one match step. In other situations that require sequential reasoning and introspection, the full mundane KB would still play a part.

5.4. Reduced descriptions

μKLONE represents concepts and roles as sets of features, so that assertions can be tied directly to relevant aspects of the model. This reduces the computational overhead that would be involved if terms were represented as atomic symbols, only used to access data structures containing the features. In particular, there need be no "inheritance" algorithm to look up the ISA hierarchy and find features. But conventional implementations of knowledge representation systems can and do use sets to represent terms internally [41, 58]. And since μKLONE's features are the same as those consulted in conventional implementations, there is no knowledge level advantage to its use of distributed representations.

Yet connectionists seem to believe that distributed representations have the potential, at least, to be functionally different from symbolic representations [24]. By symbolic representations, or "local representations," is meant that each unit can be given a reasonably concise meaning in the same terms that the user uses to describe the domain. In μKLONE the meaning of each unit is an atomic proposition in which the predicates are taken directly from the user's domain description. In contrast, DCPS [56] stores triples of letters using units that stand for unnatural predicates, such as "a triple in which the first element is one of {b j m t v y}, the second element is one of {c f o r u w} and the third is one of {a e g m q x}."

One interpretation of the significance of μKLONE is that there is no fundamental difference between local representations and distributed, uninterpretable representations. μKLONE's architecture is similar to previous connectionist systems that have used distributed representations or coarse coding, with the major difference being that their features were chosen randomly, and μKLONE's are created algorithmically from a high level domain description. What could possibly be the advantage of having no basis for the choice of features? Indeed, DCPS and BoltzCONS [53] get no advantage from their unnatural representations. DUCS [55] has demonstrated the ability to slip between roles in answering questions involving contradictory knowledge, but the same kind of capability was demonstrated for μKLONE.

Although no knowledge representation system to date has demonstrated functionality beyond that achieved by μKLONE by virtue of using non-symbolic representations, I think this will not remain true for long. Access to complex structures from small fixed-size objects is of fundamental importance in computer science. Symbols are the most common way to accomplish this, but they have only an arbitrary relation to the structures they designate. Hash codes are a way to form finite objects from complex structures in a well-defined way, but the goal has generally been to make the relationship as obscure as possible, so that similar structures will have *different* representations. In document retrieval, signature files are composed of hash functions from segments of text to a set of features, and the goal is to make similar documents have similar encodings. Then good guesses can be made as to which documents are appropriate to a query without having to examine the document itself. As with μKLONE's term features, the signature features have a natural description at the level of the user's domain description, and the representations are guaranteed to preserve certain properties.

μKLONEs features only preserve properties that are explicitly mentioned in the KB. For instance the Ted Turner KB uses the clause (SOME Has-Job), so this indirect property is made a concept feature. But there is no feature (SOME Has-Hobby). It would be nice if all the information that could be looked up about an individual was directly represented in its type, but in general this is impractical. One particular kind of information that would be especially useful was pointed out by Ron Brachman [4]. The part-of relation is semi-transitive, so some information about parts of parts would be useful. The top level parts of a car are things like engines and wheels. But if the query is "What part of a car is a valve?" a valve of the engine of the car makes a good guess in the absence of any top level component valves.

Hinton [23] suggests that a term representation should include features of all the role-fillers at a reduced level of detail. Hence he calls these representations "reduced descriptions." Since the role filler's properties will in turn include properties of their role fillers, the result is conceptually an infinite tree of frames at ever lower levels of detail, stored in a finite object. And since role chains can be cyclic, somewhere down in the tree will be another copy of the whole structure. Jordan Pollack [42] has suggested using fractal functions to generate representations. Less far-fetched, David Ackley [1] and Jordan Pollack [43] have used connectionist networks to learn flat representations from which trees can be reconstructed.

5.5. Reducing space complexity

One of μKLONE's disadvantages is that the number of units grows as the square of the KB size. However most of these units represent propositions with "type errors," such as *activity(Ted)*. Thinking of the KB concept hierarchy in graphical terms, it is a rooted directed acyclic graph. Each frame in the graph can be expected to be associated with a constant number of new features, so the number of features can be expected to grow linearly with the KB. Yet the number of features an instance of one of these concepts has would grow with the height of the tree, $O(\log n)$. The number of units grows with the square of the number of features, but the number of active units will only grow as $O(\log^2 n)$. Thus there is a great waste of processing power using the straightforward encoding in terms of the cross product of all the knowledge-level features. Perhaps by learning sets of features appropriate to a particular domain, this potential complexity reduction can be realized. Unfortunately, in the resulting network there might be no neat rows and columns, but rather a coarse coded jumble of unintelligible units. Also, eliminating units standing for propositions with type errors would prevent some kinds of counterfactual reasoning. One would not want the knowledge that sailing is a vigorous activity to result in the elimination of the unit *armchair-activity(Sailing)*. The KB language could be augmented with a construct like DON'T-EVEN-CONSIDER, analogous to DISJOINT except with the side effect that units which would falsify statements made with it aren't built.

5.6. Prospects for practical application

The expressive power of μKLONE's KB language seems adequate for some real-world applications. KL-ONE-style KR systems are being widely used, and the features that μKLONE lacks do not seem to be critical. The adequacy of the query language, and its semantics based on possibility rather than validity, is less certain, as are the effects of considering only information directly connected to the subject. In database applications, these restrictions pose no problem. Database queries normally relate only to a single subject, and there is little interaction between facts in the KB. A modified version of μKLONE, called CRUCS [6], has been used as a database system using a domain twice as large as the Ted Turner domain. CRUCS is primarily designed to fill in the SUBJECT clause of queries, and it is able to retrieve the best-fitting individual on the first query, followed by successively poorer matches for each additional query.

The most spectacular possibility for applicaiton of μKLONE is as a learning expert system. Present successful expert systems incorporate KBs that are painstakingly constructed by hand. There are proposals for connectionist expert systems that would learn automatically, but it is difficult to give them initial domain-specific knowledge ([16] is an exception). With μKLONE, experts could program an initial KB using a high-level language, followed by automatic learning using the Boltzmann learning algorithm [25]. The hard part of automatic learning, forming the right concepts, would already be done. The system could do the fine tuning that seems harder for humans. Such a system would be ideal for domains like oil well-log interpretation, in which the relevant parameters are known, but a good set of rules is elusive.

The outlook for learning is uncertain. The network created from the Ted Turner KB is larger than any in which successful learning has been carried out before. Having several scales of constraint strengths is sure to be a problem, because it makes equilibrium distributions much harder to estimate. On the other hand, if learning is restricted to fine tuning the assertion strengths and the relation between the strengths of the five types of constraints, there are far fewer parameters to adjust than in other connectionist networks.

Using a connectionist architecture to support approximate, model-based mundane reasoning is a promising technique. There are a number of variations on μKLONE's architecture that optimize its behavior for certain applications, such as DUCS and CRUCS, which are just beginning to be explored. Already, μKLONE has provided a new way to view the relationship between logic, probability, and connectionist networks.

Appendix A. Notation

Category	Examples
Concept	PERSON
	(ALL HAS-JOB ARMCHAIR-ACTIVITY)
Role	HAS-JOB
Individual	Corporate-Raiding
μKLONE language fragment	(ASSERT-CONCEPT 100 Person Animal)
	WITH
Constraint	IMPLIES
Group	Role-Filler-Types group
Proposition	*has-hobby(Ted, Sailing)*
	(ALL Has-Job Armchair-Activity)(Ted)
Unit	*has-hobby(subject, Sailing)*
	subject = Sailing

Item	Meaning
E_C^α	Energy contribution of constraint C in model α
s_u^α	State of unit u in model α

Appendix B. Ted Turner Domain Definition

```
(DEFCONCEPT Animal (PRIMITIVE))
(DEFCONCEPT Person (PRIMITIVE))
(ASSERT-CONCEPT 100 Person Animal)
(DEFCONCEPT Self-Made-Millionaire-Playboy (AND Person
  (SOME Has-Expensive-Hobby)
  (ALL Has-Job Armchair-Activity))
(ASSERT-CONCEPT 100
  Self-Made-Millionaire-Playboy (SOME Has-Job))
(DEFCONCEPT Professional-Sailor (AND Person
  (FILLS Has-Interest Sailing)
  (FILLS (RANGE Profitable-Activity) Sailing)))
;; The two FILLS clauses above are together logically equivalent to
;; (FILLS Has-Job Sailing), however the latter won't work
;; in the actual implementation. See Section 4.4.
(DEFCONCEPT TV-Buff (SOME Has-Interest
  Television-Related-Activity))
(ASSERT-CONCEPT 100 TV-Buff Person)
(DEFCONCEPT Activity (PRIMITIVE))
```

```
(ASSERT-CONCEPT 100 Activity (AND (DISJOINT Inanimate-Object)
   (DISJOINT Animal)))
(DEFCONCEPT Expensive-Activity (AND Activity
   (SOME Has-Expensive-Equipment)))
(DEFCONCEPT Armchair-Activity (PRIMITIVE))
(ASSERT-CONCEPT 100 Armchair-Activity Activity)
(DEFCONCEPT Vigorous-Activity (AND Activity
   (DISJOINT Armchair-Activity)))
(DEFCONCEPT Profitable-Activity (PRIMITIVE))
(ASSERT-CONCEPT 100 Profitable-Activity Activity)
(DEFCONCEPT UnProfitable-Activity (AND Activity
   (DISJOINT Profitable-Activity)))
(DEFCONCEPT Television-Related-Activity (PRIMITIVE))
(ASSERT-CONCEPT 100 Television-Related-Activity Activity)
(DEFCONCEPT Inanimate-Object (PRIMITIVE))
(ASSERT-CONCEPT 100 Inanimate-Object (DISJOINT Animal))
(DEFCONCEPT Expensive-Item (PRIMITIVE))
(ASSERT-CONCEPT 100 Expensive-Item Inanimate-Object)
(DEFROLE Has-Interest (PRIMITIVE))
(ASSERT-ROLE 100 Has-Interest (AND (DOMAIN Animal)
   (RANGE Activity)))
(DEFROLE Has-Job (AND Has-Interest
   (RANGE Profitable-Activity)))
(DEFROLE Has-Hobby (PRIMITIVE))
(ASSERT-ROLE 100 Has-Hobby (AND Has-Interest
   (DISJOINT Has-Job)))
(DEFROLE Has-Expensive-Hobby (AND Has-Hobby
   (RANGE Expensive-Activity)))
(DEFROLE Has-Equipment (PRIMITIVE))
(ASSERT-ROLE 100 Has-Equipment (AND (DOMAIN Activity)
   (RANGE Inanimate-Object)))
(DEFROLE Has-Expensive-Equipment
   (AND Has-Equipment (RANGE Expensive-Item)))

(INSTANTIATE-CONCEPT 50 (AND Vigorous-Activity
   Expensive-Activity) Sailing)
(INSTANTIATE-CONCEPT 50 Expensive-Activity Flying)
(INSTANTIATE-CONCEPT 50 (AND Profitable-Activity
   Armchair-Activity) Corporate-Raiding)
(INSTANTIATE-CONCEPT 50 (AND Television-Related-Activity
   Armchair-Activity UnProfitable-Activity) TV-Watching)
(INSTANTIATE-CONCEPT 50 (AND Television-Related-Activity
   Vigorous-Activity Profitable-Activity) TV-Acting)
```

(INSTANTIATE-CONCEPT 50 (AND Television-Related-Activity
  Armchair-Activity Profitable-Activity)
  TV-Network-Management)
(INSTANTIATE-CONCEPT 50 (AND Professional-Sailor
  TV-Buff) Ted)

ACKNOWLEDGEMENT

This research was conducted while I was a happy graduate student at Carnegie-Mellon University, sponsored in part by an Office of Naval Research Graduate Research Fellowship, and in part by the National Science Foundation under Contract Number EET-8716324. I thank Geoff Hinton and Dave Touretzky for their patient supervision.

REFERENCES

1. D.H. Ackley, Personal communication (1984).
2. R.J. Brachman, On the epistemological status of semantic networks, in: N.V. Findler, ed, *Associative Networks*: *Representation and Use of Knowledge by Computers* (Academic Press, New York, 1979) 3–50.
3. R.J. Brachman, "I lied about the trees" (or, defaults and definitions in knowledge representation), *AI Mag.* **6** (3) (1985) 80–93.
4. R.J. Brachman, Personal communication (1987).
5. R.J. Brachman, R.E. Fikes and H.J. Levesque, Krypton: A functional approach to knowledge representation, *IEEE Comput.* **16** (10) (1983) 67–73.
6. R.J. Brachman and D.L. McGuinness, Knowledge representation, connectionism, and conceptual retrieval, in: *Proceedings 11th International Conference on Research and Development in Information Retrieval*, Grenoble, France (Presses UniPresses Universitaires de Grenoble, Grenoble, 1988) 161–174.
7. R.J. Brachman and J.G. Schmolze, An overview of the KL-ONE knowledge representation system., *Cognitive Sci.* **9** (2) (1985) 171–216.
8. R. Carnap, *Logical Foundations of Probability* (University of Chicago Press, Chicago, IL, 1950) 19–51.
9. E. Charniak, A neat theory of marker passing, in: *Proceedings AAAI-86*, Philadelphia, PA (1986) 584–588.
10. H. Chernoff and L.E. Moses, *Elementary Decision Theory* (Wiley, New York, 1959).
11. J. de Kleer and J.S. Brown, A qualitative physics based on confluences, *Artificial Intelligence* **24** (1984) 7–83.
12. M. Derthick, *Mundane Reasoning by Parallel Constraint Satisfaction* (Morgan Kaufmann, Los Altos, CA/Pitman, London, 1990).
13. R.O. Duda, J. Gaschnig and P.E. Hart, Model design in the Prospector consultant system for mineral exploration, in: D. Michie, ed., *Expert Systems in the Micro-Electronic Age* (Edinburgh University Press, Edinburgh, 1979) 153–167.
14. J.A. Feldman and D.H. Ballard, Connectionist models and their properties, *Cognitive Sci.* **6** (1982) 205–254.
15. K.D. Forbus, Qualitative process theory, *Artificial Intelligence* **24** (1984) 85–168.
16. S.I. Gallant, Connectionist expert systems, Unpublished manuscript, Northeastern University, Boston, MA (1987).
17. M.R. Garey and D.S. Johnson, *Computers and Intractability*: *A Guide to the Theory of NP-Completeness* (Freeman, San Francisco, CA, 1979).
18. S. Geman and D. Geman, Stochastic relaxation, Gibbs distributions, and the Bayesian restoration of images, *IEEE Trans. Pattern Anal. Mach. Intell.* **6** (1984) 721–741.

19. M.L. Ginsberg, Counterfactuals, *Artificial Intelligence* **30** (1986) 35–79.
20. I.J. Haimowitz, Using NIKL in a large medical knowledge base, Tech. Rept., MIT/LCS/TM-348, MIT, Cambridge, MA (1988).
21. G.E. Hinton, Implementing semantic networks in parallel hardware, in: G.E. Hinton and J.A. Anderson, eds., *Parallel Models of Associative Memory* (Erlbaum, Hillsdale, NJ, 1981) 161–188.
22. G.E. Hinton, Learning distributed representations of concepts, in: *Proceedings Eighth Annual Conference of the Cognitive Science Society*, Amherst, MA (1986) 1–12.
23. G.E. Hinton, Representing part-whole hierarchies in connectionist networks, in: *Proceedings Tenth Annual Conference of the Cognitive Science Society*, Montreal, Que. (1988).
24. G.E. Hinton, J.L. McClelland and D.E. Rumelhart, Distributed representations, in: D.E. Rumelhart, J.L. McClelland, and the PDP Research Group, eds., *Parallel Distributed Processing*: *Explorations in the Microstructure of Cognition* **1**: *Foundations* (Bradford Books/MIT Press, Cambridge, MA, 1986) 77–109.
25. G.E. Hinton and T.J. Sejnowski, Learning and relearning in Boltzmann Machines, in: D.E. Rumelhart, J.L. McClelland and the PDP Research Group, eds., *Parallel Distributed Processing*: *Explorations in the Microstructure of Cognition* **1**: *Foundations* (Bradford Books/MIT Press, Cambridge, MA, 1986) 282–317.
26. D.R. Hofstadter, *Metamagical Themas* (Basic Books, New York, 1985).
27. J.J. Hopfield, Neurons with graded response have collective computational properties like those of two-state neurons, *Proc. Nat. Acad. Sci. USA* **81** (1984) 3088–3092.
28. P.N. Johnson-Laird, *Mental Models* (Harvard University Press, Cambridge, MA, 1983).
29. J. Keeler, Personal communication (1988).
30. K. Konolige, Bayesian methods for updating probabilities, in: *A Computer-Based Consultant for Mineral Exploration* (SRI International, Menlo Park, CA, 1979) 83–146.
31. H.J. Levesque, Making believers out of computers, *Artificial Intelligence* **30** (1986) 81–108.
32. R. Mac Gregor and R. Bates, The Loom knowledge representation language, Tech. Rept. ISI/RS-87-188, University of Southern California, Information Sciences Institute, Marina del Rey, CA (1987).
33. W. Mark, Representation and inference in the consul system, in: *Proceedings IJCAI-81*, Vancouver, BC (1981) 375–381.
34. J. McCarthy, Programs with common sense, in: M.L. Minsky, ed., *Semantic Information Processing* (MIT Press, Cambridge, MA 1968) 403–418.
35. J.L. McClelland, Retrieving general and specific information from stored knowledge of specifics, in: *Proceedings Third Annual Conference of the Cognitive Science Society*, Berkeley, CA (1981) 170–172.
36. J.L. McClelland and A.H. Kawamoto, Mechanisms of sentence processing: Assigning roles to constituents, in: J.L. McClelland, D.E. Rumelhart and the PDP Research Group, eds., *Parallel Distributed Processing*: *Explorations in the Microstructure of Cognition* **2**: *Applications* (Bradford Books/MIT Press, Cambridge, MA, 1986) 272–326.
37. D. McDermott, Non-monotonic logic II: Non-monotonic modal theories, *J. ACM* **29** (1) (1982) 33–57.
38. M.L. Minsky, A framework for representing knowledge, in: P.H. Winston, ed., *The Psychology of Computer Vision* (McGraw-Hill, New York, 1975) 211–277.
39. A. Newell, The knowledge level, *Artificial Intelligence* **18** (1982) 87–127.
40. P.F. Patel-Schneider, Small can be beautiful in knowledge representation, in: *IEEE Workshop on Principles of Knowledge-Based Systems*, Denver, CO (1984).
41. V. Pigman, Krypton: Description of an implementation, Master's Thesis, Stanford University, Stanford, CA (1984).
42. J.B. Pollack, Personal communication (1988).
43. J.B. Pollack, Recursive auto-associative memory: Devising compositional distributed repre-

sentations, Tech. Rept. MCCS-88-124, Computing Research Laboratory, New Mexico State University, Las Cruces, NM (1988).

44. R. Reiter, On closed world data bases, in: H. Gallaire and J. Minker, eds., *Logic and Data Bases* (Plenum, New York, 1978) 55–76.

45. R. Reiter, A logic for default reasoning, *Artificial Intelligence* **13** (1980) 81–132.

46. R.L. Rivest, Game tree searching by min/max approximation, *Artificial Intelligence* **34** (1988) 77–96.

47. D.E. Rumelhart, Learning ISA hierarchies in a connectionist network, Talk given at the 1986 Connectionist Summer School, Carnegie-Mellon University, Pittsburgh, PA (1986).

48. D.E. Rumelhart, J.L. McClelland and the PDP Research Group, eds., *Parallel Distributed Processing*: *Explorations in the Microstructure of Cognition* **1**: *Foundations* (Bradford Books/ MIT Press, Cambridge, MA, 1986).

49. R.C. Schank, *Dynamic Memory*: *A Theory of Reminding and Learning in Computers and People* (Cambridge University Press, New York, 1982).

50. B. Selman, Analogues, Unpublished manuscript, University of Toronto, Toronto, Ont. (1987).

51. L. Shastri, *Semantic Networks*: *An Evidential Formulation and Its Connectionist Realization* (Morgan Kaufmann, Los Altos, CA/Pitman, London, 1987).

52. E.H. Shortliffe, *Computer-Based Medical Consultations*, *MYCIN* (Elsevier, New York, 1976).

53. D.S. Touretzky, BoltzCONS: Reconciling connectionism with the recursive nature of stacks and trees, in: *Proceedings Eighth Annual Conference of the Cognitive Science Society*, Amherst, MA (1986) 522–530.

54. D.S. Touretzky, *The Mathematics of Inheritance Systems* (Pitman, London, 1986).

55. D.S. Touretzky and S. Geva, A distributed connectionist representation for concept structures, in: *Proceedings Ninth Annual Conference of the Cognitive Science Society*, Seattle, WA (1987) 155–164.

56. D.S. Touretzky and G.E. Hinton, Symbols among the neurons: Details of a connectionist inference architecture, in: *Proceedings IJCAI-85*, Los Angeles, CA (1985) 238–243.

57. A. Tversky and D. Kahneman, Judgements of and by representativeness, in: D. Kahneman, P. Slovic and A. Tversky, eds., *Judgement under Uncertainty*: *Heuristics and Biases* (Cambridge University Press, New York, 1982) 84–98.

58. M. Vilain, Personal communication (1986).

59. W.A. Woods, What's in a link: Foundations for semantic networks, in: D.G. Bobrow and A.M. Collins, eds., *Representation and Understanding*: *Studies in Cognitive Science* (Academic Press, New York, 1975) 35–82.

60. L.A. Zadeh, The role of fuzzy logic in the management of uncertainty in expert systems, *Fuzzy Sets Syst.* **11** (1983) 199–227.

Tensor Product Variable Binding and the Representation of Symbolic Structures in Connectionist Systems

Paul Smolensky

*Department of Computer Science and
Institute of Cognitive Science, University of Colorado,
Boulder, CO 80309-0430, USA*

ABSTRACT

A general method, the tensor product representation, is defined for the connectionist representation of value/variable bindings. The technique is a formalization of the idea that a set of value/variable pairs can be represented by accumulating activity in a collection of units each of which computes the product of a feature of a variable and a feature of its value. The method allows the fully distributed representation of bindings and symbolic structures. Fully and partially localized special cases of the tensor product representation reduce to existing cases of connectionist representations of structured data. The representation rests on a principled analysis of structure; it saturates gracefully as larger structures are represented; it permits recursive construction of complex representations from simpler ones; it respects the independence of the capacities to generate and maintain multiple bindings in parallel; it extends naturally to continuous structures and continuous representational patterns; it permits values to also serve as variables; and it enables analysis of the interference of symbolic structures stored in associative memories. It has also served as the basis for working connectionist models of high-level cognitive tasks.

1. Introduction

Connectionist models rely on parallel numerical computation rather than the serial symbolic computation of traditional AI models, and with the inroads of connectionism has come considerable debate about the roles these two forms of computation should play in AI. While some presume the approaches to be diametrically opposed, and argue that one or the other should be abandoned, others argue that the two approaches are so compatible that in fact connectionist models should just be viewed as implementations of symbolic systems.

In [41] (and also in [36, 38]) I have argued at considerable length for a more complex view of the roles of connectionist and symbolic computation in cognitive science. A one-sentence summary of the implications of this view for AI is this: connectionist models may well offer an opportunity to escape the

Artificial Intelligence **46** (1990) 159–216

brittleness of symbolic AI systems, a chance to develop more human-like intelligent systems—but only if we can find ways of naturally instantiating the sources of power of symbolic computation within fully connectionist systems. If we ignore the connectionist approach, we may miss an excellent opportunity for formally capturing the subtlety, robustness, and flexibility of human cognition, and for elucidating the neural underpinnings of intelligence. If we ignore the symbolic approach, we throw out tremendous insights into the nature of the problems that must be solved in creating intelligent systems, and of techniques for solving these problems; we probably doom the connectionist approach to forever grappling with simple cognitive tasks that fall far short of the true capacity of human intelligence. If we use connectionist systems merely to implement symbolic systems, we might get AI systems that are faster and more tolerant of hardware faults, but they will be just as brittle.

The present paper is part of an effort to extend the connectionist framework to naturally incorporate the ingredients essential to the power of symbolic computation, without losing the virtues of connectionist computation. This extended version of connectionist computation would integrate, in an intimate collaboration, the discrete mathematics of symbolic computation and the continuous mathematics of connectionist computation. This paper offers an example of what such a collaboration might look like.

One domain where connectionist computation has much to gain by incorporating some of the power of symbolic computation is language. The problems here are extremely fundamental. Natural connectionist representation of a structured object like a phrase-structure tree—or even a simple sequence of words or phonemes—poses serious conceptual difficulties, as I will shortly discuss. The problem can be traced back to difficulties with the elementary operation of binding a value to a variable.

I begin in Section 1.1 by discussing why natural connectionist representation of structured objects is a problem. I list several properties of the solution to this problem that is presented in this paper. In Section 1.2, I respond to the possible connectionist criticism that it is misguided to even try to solve this problem. Then, in Section 1.3, I outline the rest of the paper.

Before proceeding it is worth commenting on where the research reported here fits into an overall scheme of connectionist AI. As in the traditional approach, in the connectionist approach several components must be put together in constructing a model. Elements of the task domain must be represented, a network architecture must be designed, and a processing algorithm must be specified. If the knowledge in the model is to be provided by the designer, a set of connections must be designed to perform the task. If the model is to acquire its knowledge through learning, a learning algorithm for adapting the connections must be specified, and a training set must be designed (e.g., a set of input/output pairs). For most of these aspects of connectionist modeling, there exists considerable formal literature analyzing the problem and offering solutions. There is one glaring exception: the representation component. This is a crucial component, for a poor representation will often doom the model to failure, and an excessively generous representation may essentially solve the problem in advance. Representation is particularly critical to understanding the relation between connectionist and symbolic computation, for the representation often embodies most of the relation between a symbolically characterized problem (e.g. a linguistic task) and a connectionist solution.

Not only is the connectionist representation problem a central one, it is also a problem that is amenable to formal analysis. In this paper the problem will be characterized as finding a mapping from a set of structured objects (e.g. trees) to a vector space, the set of states of the part of a connectionist network representing those objects. The mélange of discrete and continuous mathematics that results is reminiscent of a related classical area of mathematics: the problem of representing abstract groups as collections of linear operators on a vector space. The discrete aspects of group theory and the continuous aspects of vector space theory interact in a most constructive way. Group representation theory, with its application to quantum physics, in fact offers a useful analogy for the connectionist representation of symbolic structures. The world of elementary particles involves a discrete set of particle species whose properties exhibit many symmetries, both exact and approximate, that are described by group theory. Yet the underlying elementary particle state spaces are continuous vector spaces, in which the discrete structure is imbedded. In the view that guides the research reported here, in human language processing, the discrete symbolic structures that describe linguistic objects are actually imbedded in a continuous connectionist system that operates on them with flexible, robust processes that can only be approximated by discrete symbol manipulations.

One final note on terminology. In most of this paper the structures being represented will be referred to as *symbolic structures*, because the principal cases of interest will be objects like strings and trees. Except for the consideration of particular symbolic structures, however, the analysis presented here is of structured objects in general; it therefore applies equally well to objects like images and speech trains which are not typically considered "symbolic structures." With this understood, in general discussions I will indiscriminately refer to objects being represented as "structures," "structured objects," or "symbolic structures."

1.1. Distributed representation and variable binding in connectionist systems

I have called the problem considered in this paper that of finding "natural" connectionist representation of structured objects and variable bindings. In fact what I refer to is the problem of finding connectionist representations that are *fully distributed*. The notion of *distributed representation* is central to the power

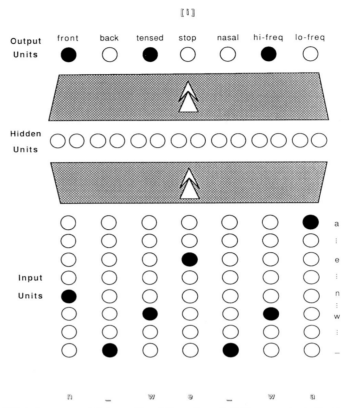

Fig. 1. The NETtalk system of Sejnowski and Rosenberg [35] illustrates both distributed and local connectionist representations.

of the connectionist approach (e.g., [1, 15, 24, 34, 37, 41]; for an opposing view, see [10]). To illustrate the idea of distributed representation, consider the NETtalk system, a connectionist network that learns to pronounce written English [35] (see Fig. 1). Each output of this network is a phonetic segment, e.g. the vowel [i] in the pronunciation of the word *we*. Each phonetic segment is represented in terms of phonetic features; for [i], we have: front = 1, tensed = 1, high-frequency = 1, back = 0, stop = 0, nasal = 0, and so forth. There is one output processor in the network for each of the phonetic features, and its numerical value indicates whether that feature is present (1) or absent (0). Each phonetic segment is therefore represented by a *pattern of activity* over the numerous output processors, and each output processor participates in the representation of many different outputs. This defines a distributed representation of the output phonetic segment.

At the opposite end of a connectionist representational spectrum are *local representations*. These too are illustrated by NETtalk; this time, in the input. Each NETtalk input consists of a letter to be pronounced together with the three preceding and three following letters to provide some context. For each of these seven letters there is a separate pool of input processors in the network, and within each pool there is a separate processor for each letter. In the input representation, in each of the seven pools the single processor corresponding to the letter present is assigned activity 1, and the remaining processors in the pool are all assigned activity 0. This representation is local in two senses. Most obviously, different letters are represented by activity in disjoint localities—in single processing units. Unlike the output activity, there is no overlap of the activity representing alternative values. The other sense of locality is that the activity representing different letter *positions* are all disjoint: each pool localizes the activity representing one letter position.

The input representation in NETtalk illustrates the problems of representing structures and of variable binding in connectionist networks. The input is a string of seven characters (of which the middle one is to be pronounced). There is a pool of processing units dedicated to representing each item in this string. Each pool can be viewed as a slot in the structure: a variable. The value of each variable is a pattern of activity residing in its pool of units. In NETtalk this pattern is localized; we will later consider examples of models in which the corresponding pattern is distributed throughout the pool. Regardless of the patterns used to represent the values, in such systems *the variables are localized regions of the network*. These variables are in fact *registers*, and the great majority of connectionist systems have represented structured data using them. Yet registers are hardly natural or desirable within connectionist models. In order to make available in the processing of structured data the full power of connectionist computation that derives from distributed representation, we need to use *distributed representations of variables* in addition to distributed representations of values.

In this paper a completely distributed representational scheme for variable binding is analyzed: the *tensor product representation*. The tensor product of an n-dimensional vector $\mathbf{v}$ and an m-dimensional vector $\mathbf{w}$ is simply the nm-dimensional vector $\mathbf{v} \otimes \mathbf{w}$ whose elements are all possible products $v_i w_j$ of an element of $\mathbf{v}$ and an element of $\mathbf{w}$. This vector $\mathbf{v} \otimes \mathbf{w}$ is a *tensor of rank two*: its elements are labelled by two indices i and j. A tensor of rank one is simply an ordinary vector labelled by a single index, and a tensor of rank zero is a scalar. Tensors of rank higher than two arise by taking tensor products of more than two ordinary vectors; if $\mathbf{w}$ is an l-dimensional vector, then $\mathbf{u} \otimes \mathbf{v} \otimes \mathbf{w}$ is a tensor of rank three, the nml-dimensional vector consisting of all products $u_i v_j w_k$. The tensor product generalizes the matrix algebra concept of outer product to allow third- and higher-order products; the more general apparatus of tensor algebra is needed here because the recursive use of tensor product representations leads to tensors of rank higher than two.[1]

In the tensor product representation, both the variables and the values can be arbitrarily nonlocal, enabling (but not requiring) representations in which every unit is part of the representation of every constituent in the structure. In this paper, applications of the tensor product scheme to the connectionist representation of complex structured objects are explored. Features of the tensor product representation, most of which distinguish it from existing representations, include the following (corresponding section numbers are indicated in parentheses):

- The representation rests on a principled and general analysis of structure: role decomposition (Section 2.2.1).
- A fully distributed representation of a structured object is built from distributed representations of both the structure's constituents and the structure's roles (Section 2.2.4).
- Nearly all previous connectionist representations of structured data, employing varying degrees of localization, are special cases (Section 2.3).
- If a structure does not saturate the capacity of a connectionist network that represents it, the components of the structure can be extracted with complete accuracy (Section 3.1).
- Structures of unbounded size can be represented in a fixed connectionist network, and the representation will saturate gracefully (Section 3.2).
- The representation applies to continuous structures and to infinite networks as naturally as to the discrete and finite cases (Section 3.3).
- The binding operations can be simply performed in a connectionist network (Section 3.4).
- The representation respects the independence of two aspects of parallelism in variable binding: generating vs. maintaining bindings (Section 4.1).
- The constituents of structure can be simply extracted in a connectionist network (Section 3.4.2).
- A value bound to one variable can itself be used as a variable (Section 3.6).
- The representation can be used recursively, and connectionist representations of operations on symbolic structures, and recursive data types, can be naturally analyzed (Section 3.7).
- Retrieval of representations of structured data stored in connectionist memories can be formally analyzed (Section 3.8).

[1] For treatments of tensor algebra, see [19, 26, 48]; for a short presentation directed to the current work, see [39, Appendix]. While this paper will not make extensive use of tensor calculus, setting the connectionist issues discussed here in the framework of tensor algebra provides a useful link to well-established mathematics. Certain virtues of the tensor calculus, such as the way it systematically manages the multiple indices associated with higher-rank tensors, have already proved important for actual connectionist systems built on tensor product representations [3–7].

- A general sense of optimality for activity patterns representing roles in structures can be defined and analyzed (Section 3.9).
- A connectionist "recirculation" learning algorithm can be derived for finding these optimal representations (Section 3.9).

1.2. Connectionist representation of symbolic structures

The general issue behind the research reported here is the representation in connectionist systems of symbolic structures. This issue figures prominently in the argument of Fodor and Pylyshyn [11] that connectionist models are inadequate on fundamental representational grounds, and the work reported here began as a response to this attack; for responses to Fodor and Pylyshyn based in part on the work reported here, see [40, 42].

A more concrete motivation for pursuing this issue are the challenges facing connectionist modeling of higher cognitive processes such as language. Here our central question takes the form: What are computationally adequate connectionist representations of strings, trees, sentences?

This section is addressed to connectionists who may find this question misguided. The essence of the connectionist approach, they might say, is to expunge symbolic structures from models of the mind. I must agree that the connectionist approach is rather far from a "language of thought" view of cognition in which all mental states are formalized as symbolic structures. However there still remains in connectionism an important role to be played by language and symbolic structures, even if that role is substantially reduced relative to its counterpart in the traditional radically symbolic approach. I have argued this point in some detail in [41], and will only summarize the relevant conclusions here.

Any connectionist model of natural language processing must cope with the questions of how linguistic structures are represented in connectionist models. A reasonable starting point would seem to be to take linguistic analysis of the structure of linguistic objects seriously, and to find a way of representing this structure in a connectionist system. Since the majority of existing representations of linguistic structure employ structures like trees and strings, it is important to find adequate connectionist representations of these symbolic structures. It may well turn out that once such representations are understood, new connectionist representations of linguistic structures will be developed that are not truly representations of symbolic structures but which are more adequate according to the criteria of linguistics, computational linguistics, psycholinguistics, or neurolinguistics. It seems likely, however, that such improvements will rest on prior understanding of connectionist representations of existing symbolic descriptions of linguistic structure.

The importance to the connectionist approach of representing linguistic structures goes well beyond models of natural language processing. Once adequate connectionist representations are found for linguistic structures, then these can serve as the basis for connectionist models of conscious, serial, rule-guided behavior. This behavior can be modeled as explicit (connectionist) retrieval and interpretation of linguistically structured rules. Adequate connectionist models of such behavior are important for connectionist models of higher thought processes.

One line of thought in the connectionist approach implies that analyses of connectionist representations of symbolic structures are unnecessary. The argument goes something like this. Just as a child somehow learns to internally represent sentences with no explicit instruction on how to do so, so a connectionist system with the right learning rule will somehow learn the appropriate internal representations. The problem of linguistic representation is not to be solved by a connectionist theorist but rather a connectionist network.

In response to this argument I have five points.

(1) In the short term, at least, our learning rules and network simulators do not seem powerful enough to make network learning of linguistic representation feasible.

(2) Even if such learning is feasible at some future point, we will still need to *explain* how the representation is done. There are two empirical reasons to believe that such explanation will require the kind of analysis begun in this paper: explanation of the computation of real neural networks has turned out to require much analysis, as mere observation has proved woefully inadequate; the same has turned out to be true even of the self-organized connectionist networks that perform computations vastly simpler than most of natural language processing.

(3) It is important to try to build bridges as soon as possible between connectionist accounts of language processing and existing accounts; the problem is just too difficult to start all over again from scratch.

(4) We would like to be able to experiment *now* with connectionist learning models of rather complex linguistic skills (e.g. parsing, anaphoric resolution, and semantic interpretation, all in complex sentences). For now, at least, such experiments require connectionist representation of linguistic structures to serve as inputs and outputs. We want to study the learning of the operations performed on linguistic structures without waiting many years for the completion of the study of the learning of the linguistic representations themselves.

(5) Language is more than just a domain for building models, it is a foundation on which the entire traditional theory of computation rests. To understand the computational implications of connectionism, it is crucial to know how the basic concepts of symbolic computation and formal language theory relate to connectionist computation.

Of course, exploiting connectionist representations of the sort of symbolic structures used in symbolic AI by no means commits one to a full connectionist implementation of symbolic AI, which, as stated earlier, would miss most of the point of the connectionist approach. The semantic processing of a connectionist representation of a parse tree should not be performed by a connectionist implementation of serially applied symbolic rules that manipulate the tree; rather, the processing should be of the usual connectionist sort: massively parallel satisfaction of multiple soft constraints involving the micro-elements forming the distributed representation of the parse tree. Thus in this paper connectionist representations of *pop* and *cdr* will be mathematical relations between patterns of activity, not processes carried out over time in a connectionist network as part of an extended serial computation (in contrast to [44]). The view behind the present research is not that mental operations are always serial symbol manipulations (although a few are); rather the view is that the information processed often has useful symbolic *descriptions*, and that these descriptions should be taken seriously. (This view is spelled out in detail in [41].)

1.3. Outline of the paper

In Section 2, the notion of connectionist representation is formally defined and the tensor product representation is constructed. Examples are considered, and the various special cases that reduce to previous connectionist representations are discussed. In Section 3, a number of properties of the tensor product representation are proved and several extensions discussed. The connectionist representation of symbolic operations is defined, and examples for strings and trees are considered. Retrieval of symbolic structures represented in connectionist memories by the tensor product representation is analyzed. Finally, work reported elsewhere is briefly summarized concerning a sense of optimality for patterns representing roles in structures, and a connectionist "recirculation" algorithm for learning these optimal representations. Section 4 is a summary and conclusion.

2. Connectionist Representation and Tensor Product Binding: Definition and Examples

In this section I first formally characterize the notion of connectionist representation. Next, the problem of representing structured objects is reduced to three subproblems: decomposing the structures via roles, representing conjunctions, and representing variable/value bindings. First role decompositions are discussed, and then the superpositional representation of conjunction and the tensor product representation for variable/value bindings is defined. Next I show how various special cases of the tensor product representation yield the previous connectionist representations of structured data.

2.1. Connectionist representation

In this paper, the question of how to represent symbolic structures in connectionist systems will be formalized as follows.

Connectionist representations are patterns of activity over connectionist networks; these patterns can extend over many processors in the network, as in distributed representations, or be localized to a single processor, as in a local representation. Such a pattern is a collection of activation values: a vector with one numerical component for every network processor. The space of representational states of a connectionist network thus lies in a vector space, the dimension of which is equal to the number of processors in the network. Each processor corresponds to an independent basis vector; this forms a distinguished basis for the space. In many connectionist networks the processor's values are restricted in some way; such restrictions are important for consideration of the dynamics of the network but are not central to the representational issues considered here, and they will be ignored. (For expositions of the application of vector space theory—linear algebra—to connectionist systems, see, e.g., [16, 37].)

Definition 2.1. The *activity states of a connectionist network* are the elements of a vector space V which has a distinguished basis $\{\hat{\mathbf{v}}_i\}$.

Whenever I speak of a vector space representing the states of a connectionist network, a distinguished basis will be implicitly assumed. Rarely will it be necessary to deal explicitly with this basis. Sometimes it will be useful to use the canonical inner product associated with the distinguished basis: the one in which the basis vectors are orthogonal and of unit norm. (Equivalently, this inner product of two vectors can be computed as the sum of the products of corresponding vector components with respect to the distinguished basis). Whenever I speak of activity patterns being orthogonal, or of their norm, these concepts are taken to be defined with respect to this canonical inner product; the inner product of vectors $\mathbf{u}$ and $\mathbf{v}$ will be denoted $\mathbf{u} \cdot \mathbf{v}$.

Definition 2.2. A *connectionist representation* of the symbolic structures in a set S is a mapping Ψ from S to a vector space V.

The kinds of sets S we will study are sets of strings and sets of binary trees. Of central concern are the images under the mapping Ψ of the relations between symbolic structures and their constituents, and the images of the operations transforming symbolic structures into other structures. Also important are basic questions about the representation mapping such as whether distinguishable symbolic structures have distinguishable representations:

Definition 2.3. A connectionist representation Ψ is *faithful* iff it is one-to-one and there is no structure that it maps to the zero vector $\mathbf{0} \in V$.

2.2. Tensor product representation: Definition

The representation of structured objects explored in this paper requires first that structures be viewed as possesing a number (possibly unbounded) of *roles* which, for particular instances of the structure, are individually bound to particular *fillers*. For example, a string may be viewed as possessing an infinite set of roles $\{r_1, r_2, \ldots\}$ where r_i is the role of the ith element in the string. A particular string of length n involves binding the first n roles to particular fillers. For example, the string *aba* involves the bindings $\{a/r_1, b/r_2, a/r_3\}$, using a notation in which f/r denotes the binding of filler f to role r; in this string, the roles r_i for $i > 3$ are all unbound. Now note that the structure has been characterized as the *conjunction* of an unordered set of variable bindings. The problem of representing the structure has been reduced to the problems of

(1) representing the structure as a conjunction of filler/role bindings;
(2) representing the conjunction operation;
(3) representing the bindings in a connectionist network.

These problems are respectively considered in Sections 2.2.1 through 2.2.3 and brought together in Section 2.2.4.

In Section 3.7.3, we will see that the representations we build using roles and fillers are equivalent to those we would have built by viewing structures as a number of elements engaged in certain structural relations.

2.2.1. *Role decompositions of symbolic structures*

As a formal definition of roles and fillers, I will take the following:

Definition 2.4. Let S be a set of symbolic structures. A *role decomposition F/R* for S is a pair of sets (F, R), the sets of *fillers* and *roles*, respectively, and a mapping

$$\mu_{F/R} : F \times R \rightarrow Pred(S) ; \qquad (f, r) \mapsto f/r .$$

For any pair $f \in F$, $r \in R$, the predicate on S $\mu_{F/R}(f, r) = f/r$ is expressed: f *fills role r.*

The role decomposition has *single-valued roles* iff for any $s \in S$ and $r \in R$, there is at most one $f \in F$ such that $f/r(s)$ holds.

The role decomposition is *recursive* iff $F = S$.

A role decomposition determines a mapping

$$\beta : S \rightarrow 2^{F \times R} ; \qquad s \mapsto \{(f, r) \mid f/r(s)\}$$

that associates to each $s \in S$ the set $\beta(s)$ of *filler/role bindings in s*. The mapping β will be called the *filler/role representation* of S induced by the role decomposition.

The role decomposition is *faithful* iff β is one-to-one.

The role decomposition is *finite* iff for each $s \in S$, the set of bindings in s, $\beta(s)$, is finite.

Throughout this paper all role decompositions will be assumed to be finite, except in sections where the infinite case is explicitly considered.

Recursive role decompositions are heavily used in the standard description of symbolic structures. For example, the description of a LISP S-expression as a structure whose *car* and *cdr* are both S-expressions is a recursive decomposition via the roles *car* and *cdr*. The tensor product representation to be presented shortly will be used to analyze recursive role decompositions (Section 3.7), but in this paper, the representations we consider will not be *defined* using recursive role decompositions; that is possible, but goes beyond the scope of this paper.

Faithful role decompositions are particularly useful because the filler/role representations they induce allow us to identify each symbolic structure with a predicate having a simple conjunctive form which forms the basis of tensor product representation:

Theorem 2.5. *Let F/R be a role decomposition of S. For each $s_0 \in S$, define the predicate π_{s_0} by:*

$$\pi_{s_0}(s) = \bigwedge_{(f,r) \in \beta(s_0)} f/r(s)$$

where $\wedge$ denotes conjunction; $\pi_{s_0}(s)$ is true iff the structure s contains all the filler/role bindings in s_0. Then if the role decomposition is faithful, the structure s_0 can be recovered from the predicate π_{s_0}.

Proof. This result follows immediately from the following lemma:

Lemma 2.6. *The mapping β of the role decomposition maps elements of S into subsets of $F \times R$. These subsets possess a partial order, set inclusion $\subseteq$, which can be pulled back to S via β:*

$$s_1 \leq s_2 \quad \text{iff} \quad \beta(s_1) \subseteq \beta(s_2) .$$

Suppose F/R is faithful. Then with respect to the partial order $\leq$, the set of elements of S for which the predicate π_{s_0} holds has a unique least element, which is s_0. In this way s_0 can be recovered from its corresponding predicate π_{s_0}.

Proof of Lemma 2.6. Since $\beta(s)$ is the set of filler/role bindings in s, $s_1 \leqslant s_2$ iff the bindings in s_1 are a subset of those of s_2:

$$s_1 \leqslant s_2 \quad \text{iff} \quad [\text{for all } f \in F \text{ and } r \in R, f/r(s_1) \Rightarrow f/r(s_2)].$$

Now consider the set of elements s satisfying the predicate π_{s_0}:

$$S(\pi_{s_0}) := \{s \in S \mid \pi_{s_0}(s)\}$$

$$= \{s \in S \mid \text{for all } f \in F \text{ and } r \in R, f/r(s_0) \Rightarrow f/r(s)\}$$

$$= \{s \in S \mid s_0 \leqslant s\}.$$

This set contains s_0, and s_0 is a least element; it remains to show that there is no other least element. Consider any other element s_1 in $S(\pi_{s_0})$. Since μ is faithful and $s_1 \neq s_0$, there is at least one binding f/r not shared by s_0 and s_1. Since $s_1 \in S(\pi_{s_0})$ and s_0 is a least element of $S(\pi_{s_0})$, we must have $f/r(s_1) \wedge \neg f/r(s_0)$. This implies $\neg(s_1 \leqslant s_0)$ so s_1 cannot be a least element in $S(\pi_{s_0})$ □

2.2.2. Connectionist representation of conjunction

The representation of conjunction in connectionist models has traditionally been performed with pattern superposition, i.e. vector addition. If two propositions are each represented in a connectionist system by some pattern of activity, the representation of the conjunction of those propositions is the pattern resulting from superimposing the individual patterns. This paper adopts this method. In terms of the representation mapping Ψ, we can write:

Definition 2.7. A connectionist representation Ψ employs the *superpositional representation of conjunction* iff:

$$\Psi\left(\bigwedge_i p_i\right) = \sum_i \Psi(p_i).$$

The representation of the conjunction of a collection of propositions is the sum of the representations of the individual propositions.

Note that, like conjunction, vector addition is an operation possessing the properties of associativity and commutativity. Were this not so, vector addition could not be used to represent conjunction.

Applying the superpositional representation of conjunction to the case at hand:

Definition 2.8. Suppose S is a set of symbolic structures and F/R is a role decomposition of S with fillers F and roles R. Suppose that Ψ_b is a connectionist representation of the filler/role bindings:

$$\Psi_b : \{ f/r \mid f \in F, r \in R \} \to V$$

where V is a vector space. Then $\Psi_{F/R}$, the connectionist representation of S induced by F/R, the superpositional representation of conjunction, and Ψ_b, is

$$\Psi_{F/R} : S \to V ; \qquad s \mapsto \sum_{(f,r) \in \beta(s)} \Psi_b(f/r) .$$

The use of vector addition to represent conjunction has pervasive implications for the faithfulness of representations. If the representations of $a \wedge b$ and $c \wedge d$ are to be distinguishable, then $\mathbf{a} + \mathbf{b}$ and $\mathbf{c} + \mathbf{d}$ must be different. This constrains the possible patterns $\mathbf{a}$, $\mathbf{b}$, $\mathbf{c}$ and $\mathbf{d}$ that can represent a, b, c and d. It will be guaranteed that $\mathbf{a} + \mathbf{b}$ and $\mathbf{c} + \mathbf{d}$ will be different if the vectors $\mathbf{a}$, $\mathbf{b}$, $\mathbf{c}$ and $\mathbf{d}$ are all *linearly independent*: no one can be expressed as a weighted superposition of the others. In order to guarantee the faithfulness of representations, it will often be necessary to impose the restriction of linearly independent representing patterns for the constituents. This restriction is an expensive one, however, since to have n linearly independent patterns one must have at least n nodes in the network. And, as we will see below in Section 3.8, some sets of structures contain so many shared bindings that they cannot be given linearly independent representations, no matter how the bindings are represented; this is true, for example, of the set of strings $\{ ax, bx, ay, by \}$, decomposed by the roles of *first_position*, *second_position*.

The addition operation used for superposition in this paper is arithmetic addition, in which $1 + 1 = 2$; in other words, the scalars for the vector spaces are real numbers under numerical addition. An important variation of this analysis would be to consider vector spaces over *Boolean* scalars under logical addition (OR): $1 + 1 = 1$. This variation can still be regarded as tensor product representation, but with respect to a different set of scalars; the result would have quite a different character. Boolean tensor product representations are needed to exactly describe a number of existing connectionist models that use Boolean-valued units and correspondingly use Boolean rather than numerical superposition to represent conjunction. Comparing real-valued and Boolean tensor product representations in general is like comparing connectionist models with real-valued units to those with Boolean units: there are a variety of advantages and disadvantages to each. To mention just two, threshold operations can often allow retrievals from lightly-loaded Boolean systems to be exact [50]; but, on the whole, the mathematics of real scalars is simpler. For this reason, this paper begins the analysis of tensor product representations with the real-valued case.

2.2.3. *Connectionist representation of variable binding*

It remains to consider the representation of filler/role bindings; this section introduces the tensor product representation.

The tensor product representation of a value/variable binding is quite simple to define (see Fig. 2). To bind a filler f to a role r we first represent f as a pattern of activity $\mathbf{f}$ over a set of "filler" units $\{\tilde{f}_\phi\}$ and represent r as a pattern of activity $\mathbf{r}$ over a set of "role" units $\{\tilde{r}_\rho\}$. The binding f/r is represented by a pattern of activity $\mathbf{f}/\mathbf{r}$ over a set of "binding" units $\{\tilde{b}_{\phi\rho}\}$, of which there is one for each pair of filler and role units. The activity of the binding unit $\tilde{b}_{\phi\rho}$ is the activity of the filler unit $\tilde{f}_\phi$ in the pattern $\mathbf{f}$ times the activity of the role unit $\tilde{r}_\rho$ in the pattern $\mathbf{r}$.

This procedure is readily characterizable in vector terminology. The representation of the role r is a vector $\mathbf{r}$ in a vector space V_R. V_R is a real vector space with dimension equal to the number of units $\tilde{r}_\rho$. The representation of the filler f is a vector $\mathbf{f}$ in a vector space V_F, a real vector space with dimension equal to the number of units $\tilde{f}_\phi$. The representation of the binding f/r is the *tensor product* vector $\mathbf{f}/\mathbf{r} = \mathbf{f} \otimes \mathbf{r}$ in the tensor product vector space $V_B = V_F \otimes V_R$. V_B is a real vector space with dimension equal to the product of the dimensions of V_F and V_R. The components of the vector $\mathbf{f}/\mathbf{r}$ are related to the components of $\mathbf{f}$ and $\mathbf{r}$ as follows. Each filler unit $\tilde{f}_\phi$ corresponds to a vector $\hat{\mathbf{f}}_\phi$ in V_F (the vector representing the pattern of activity in which that unit has activity 1 and all other units have activity zero). The complete set of vectors

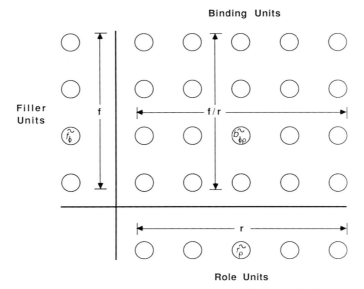

Fig. 2. The tensor product representation for filler/role bindings.

$\{\hat{\mathbf{f}}_\phi\}$ forms the distinguished basis for V_F and any vector $\mathbf{f}$ in V_F can be expressed in terms of this basis as a sequence of real numbers; these are the activities of all the units in the pattern corresponding to $\mathbf{f}$. Exactly the same story holds for the roles. Then the tensor product space $V_B = V_F \otimes V_R$ has as a basis the set of vectors $\{\hat{\mathbf{b}}_{\phi\rho} = \hat{\mathbf{f}}_\phi \otimes \hat{\mathbf{r}}_\rho\}$. The $\phi\rho$ component $(b_{\phi\rho} = (f/r)_{\phi\rho})$ of the vector $\mathbf{b} = \mathbf{f}/\mathbf{r} = \mathbf{f} \otimes \mathbf{r}$ representing the binding is the product of the ϕ component of $\mathbf{f}$ (f_ϕ) and the ρ component of $\mathbf{r}$ (r_ρ):

$$b_{\phi\rho} = f/r_{\phi\rho} = f_\phi r_\rho .$$

Definition 2.9. Let F/R be a role decomposition of S. Let Ψ_F and Ψ_R be connectionist representations of the fillers and roles:

$$\Psi_F : F \to V_F , \qquad \Psi_R : R \to V_R .$$

Then the *tensor product representation of the filler/role bindings* induced by Ψ_F and Ψ_R is the mapping:

$$\Psi_b : \{f/r \mid f \in F, r \in R\} \to V_F \otimes V_R ; \qquad f/r \mapsto \Psi_F(f) \otimes \Psi_R(r) .$$

Fig. 3 shows an example specially chosen for visual transparency. Consider an application to speech processing, and imagine that we are representing the

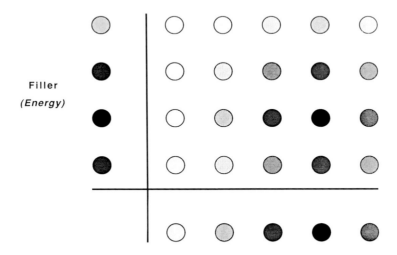

Role *(Time)*

Fig. 3. A visually transparent example of the tensor product representation of a filler/role binding. Darker units are more active.

amount of energy in a particular frequency band over time. For the roles here
we take a series of time points and for the fillers the amount of energy in the
band. In Fig. 3, the roles are represented as patterns of activity over five units.
Each role r_ρ is a time point and is represented as a peaked pattern centered at
unit ρ; the figure shows the case $\rho = 4$. Each filler f_ϕ is an energy level; in Fig. 3
this is represented as a pattern of activity over four units: a single peak
centered at the energy level being represented. The binding pattern is a
two-dimensional peak centered at the point whose x- and y-coordinates are the
time and energy values being bound together.

The example of Fig. 3 is visually transparent because of the simple geometri-
cal structure of the patterns. Of course there is nothing in the binding
mechanism itself that requires this. The distributed representation of roles and
fillers can be arbitrary patterns and in general the tensor product of these
patterns will be even more visually opaque than are the patterns for the roles
and fillers: see Fig. 4. However the mathematical simplicity of tensor product
binding makes the general case as easy to analyze as special cases like that of
Fig. 3.

2.2.4. *Tensor product representation*

Putting together the previous representations, we have:

Definition 2.10. Let F/R be a role decomposition of S, and let Ψ_F and Ψ_R be
connectionist representations of the fillers and roles. Then the corresponding

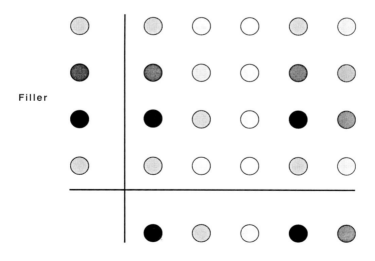

Fig. 4. A generic example of the tensor product representation of a filler/role binding.

tensor product representation of S is

$$\Psi : S \rightarrow V_F \otimes V_R ; \qquad s \mapsto \sum_{(f,\,r)\in\beta(s)} \Psi_F(f) \otimes \Psi_R(r) .$$

If we identify s with the conjunction of the bindings it contains, and if we let $\mathbf{f} = \Psi_F(f)$ and $\mathbf{r} = \Psi_R(r)$, we can write this in the more transparent form

$$\Psi\left(\bigwedge_i f_i/r_i \right) = \sum_i \mathbf{f}_i \otimes \mathbf{r}_i .$$

The interpretation of the activity of binding units in the tensor product representation depends on the interpretation of the filler and role units. If the filler or role representations are local, then each filler or role unit individually represents a particular filler or role, respectively. If the filler or role representation is distributed, the activation of an individual node may indicate the presence of an identifiable feature in the entity being represented. This was true of the example given in Section 1.1: each of the output units represents a phonetic feature in the phonetic segment output by the network. For expository simplicity, we can consider a local representation to be one where a given "feature" is present in exactly one represented object, and a given object possesses exactly one "feature." Then if the binding unit $\tilde{b}_{\phi\rho}$ is active in the tensor product representation of a structure s, the interpretation is that the feature represented by $\tilde{f}_\phi$ is present in a filler of a role possessing the feature $\tilde{r}_\rho$. In this sense, $\tilde{b}_{\phi\rho}$ *represents the conjunction of the features represented by $\tilde{f}_\phi$ and $\tilde{r}_\rho$.*[2] By using the tensor product representation recursively, we can produce conjunctions of more than two features; this will be considered in Section 3.7.3.

2.3. Previous representations and special cases of tensor product representation

Section 3 analyzes the general properties of the tensor product representation. Before proceeding to this general analysis, it is useful to examine a number of special cases of the tensor product representation because these turn out to include nearly all previous cases of connectionist representations of structured objects.

2.3.1. *Role decompositions*

The examples of previous connectionist representations of structured objects that we shall consider employ only a few role decompositions.

---

[2] For a more precise formulation, consider a simple case where the activity of unit $\tilde{f}_\phi$ is 1 or 0, and indicates the truth value of the proposition "there exists x among the represented objects such that the predicate $\tilde{f}_\phi$ holds of x"; and suppose $\tilde{r}_\rho$ can be similarly interpreted. Then $\tilde{b}_{\phi\rho}$ indicates the truth value of the proposition "there exists x among the represented objects such that both predicates $\tilde{f}_\phi$ and $\tilde{r}_\rho$ hold of x." If this is true of n different values of x, in the superposition representing the structure as a whole, the value of $\tilde{b}_{\phi\rho}$ will be n.

Definition 2.11. Suppose S is the set of strings of length no more than n from an alphabet A. Let $F = A$, and let $R = \{r_i\}_{i=1}^{n}$, where r_i is the role "occupies the ith position in the string." Then F/R is the *positional role decomposition* of S.

This is the example given above in Section 2.2, in which the string *aba* is represented by bindings $\{a/r_1, b/r_2, a/r_3\}$. This decomposition is finite, has single-valued roles, and is faithful. This decomposition is the most obvious one, and the one most often used in previous connectionist systems.

The positional decomposition has an obvious extension to the case of finite strings of arbitrary length, where the set of roles becomes infinite; I will treat this as the case of the above definition with $n = \infty$. In the infinite case the decomposition is still faithful, still has single-valued roles, and is still finite, since the strings are all of finite length. The infinite case will be used later to explore saturation of the tensor product representation.

There is a less obvious role decomposition of strings that is used, as we shall shortly see, to advantage by Rumelhart and McClelland [33]; it forms the basis of their "Wickelfeature" representation. (The properties of this role decomposition are crucial to many of the criticisms of this model presented in [17, 27, 28].)

Definition 2.12. Suppose S is the set of strings of length no more than n from an alphabet A. Let $F = A \cup \{<, >\}$, where $<$ and $>$ are two new symbols meaning "left string boundary" and "right string boundary" respectively. Let $R = \{r_{x\_y} \mid x \in F, y \in F\}$, where r_{x_y} is the role "is immediately preceded by x and immediately followed by y." F/R is a role decomposition of S called the *1-neighbor context decomposition*.

Under this decomposition, the string *aba* becomes the set of bindings $\{a/r_{<\_b}, b/r_{a\_a}, a/r_{b\_>}\}$. This decomposition does not have single-valued roles and is not faithful if $n \geq 4$ (the strings a^3 and a^4 can't be distinguished). There is an obvious generalization to the k-neighbor context decomposition: this is faithful if $n < 2k + 2$.[3]

There are also obvious generalizations of the 1-neighbor context decomposition to differing size contexts on the left and right. A special case is the representation of pairs, say strings with $n = 2$, where the roles are $R = \{r_x \mid x \in F\}$: the right-neighbor context. The pair *ab* is represented as the single binding $a/r_{\_b}$. This role decomposition, we shall see, is used in a powerful technique called *conjunctive coding*.

---

[3] This decomposition gives the initial and final substrings of length up to $2k$, and all internal substrings of length $2k + 1$. These substrings uniquely determine strings of length no more than $2k + 1$. The strings a^{2k+1} and a^{2k+2} can't be distinguished, however, so the decomposition is not faithful if $n > 2k + 1$.

While it is true that the positional role decomposition is more faithful than context decompositions for the representation of a *single* structure, it turns out that if multiple structures are to be simultaneously represented, the positional decomposition can be *less* faithful than the context decomposition. Suppose we are to represent the conjunction of *ab* and *cd* by superimposing the representation of the two pairs. What gets represented is the union of the binding sets of the two structures. In the case of positional roles, this union is $\{a/r_1, b/r_2, c/r_1, d/r_2\}$; now it is impossible to distinguish what is being represented from the conjunction of *ad* and *cb*. However, with the right-neighbor context decomposition, the union of the binding sets is $\{a/r_{\_b}, c/r_{\_d}\}$, which is not at all confusable with the conjunction of *ad* and *cb*. With context decompositions confusions can of course also result; these decompositions are not even faithful for representing single structures, when the same fillers appear multiple times in the same context.

An additional virtue of context decompositions is that they give rise to connectionist representations that give the network direct access to the kind of information needed to capture the regularities in many context-sensitive tasks; we shall discuss this below for the specific example of the Rumelhart and McClelland [33] model.

2.3.2. *Connectionist representations*

Having discussed a few of the role decompositions that have been used in connectionist representations of structures, we can now consider a number of examples of such representations. These are grouped according to the degree of locality in the representations of roles and fillers; we therefore start by distinguishing local and distributed connectionist representations in general, and then examine the degree of locality of various existing representations of structured objects.

2.3.2.1. *Local and distributed representations*
Local representations dedicate an individual processor to each item represented. In terms of the vector space of network states, these individual processors correspond to the members of the distinguished basis. Thus:

Definition 2.13. Let Ψ be a connectionist representation of a set X in a vector space V with distinguished basis $\{\hat{\mathbf{v}}_i\}$. Ψ is a *local representation* iff it is a one-to-one mapping of the elements of X onto the set of basis vectors $\{\hat{\mathbf{v}}_i\}$.

A connectionist representation that is not a local representation is a *distributed representation*.

(For a more refined analysis of this distinction, see [43].)

2.3.2.2. *Purely local representations of symbolic structures*
The first special case of the tensor product representation is the most local one.

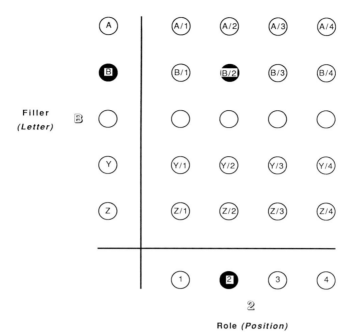

Fig. 5. A purely local tensor product representation of four-letter strings.

Definition 2.14. Let $\Psi_{F/R}$ be the tensor product representation of S induced by a role decomposition F/R of S and two connectionist representations Ψ_F and Ψ_R. Then $\Psi_{F/R}$ is a *purely local tensor product representation* if Ψ_F and Ψ_R are both local representations.

This case is illustrated for the representation of strings in Fig. 5. If the filler and role patterns both involve the activity of only a single processor, then the tensor product pattern representing their binding will also involve only a single unit. In other words, if Ψ_F and Ψ_R are both local representations, then $\Psi_{F/R}$ is a local representation of individual bindings.

Purely local tensor product representations have been used along with the positional role decomposition of strings in many connectionist models; for example:

- As was already mentioned in Section 1.1 and illustrated in Fig. 1, NETtalk [35] uses the purely local representation of Fig. 5 to represent seven-letter input strings.
- The interactive activation model of the perception of letters in words [23, 32] uses the representation shown in Fig. 5 for representing four-letter strings, at its intermediate or "letter" level of representation. This too is a purely local tensor product representation.

- The TRACE model of speech perception [21] uses a purely local representation of strings of phonemes, although some of the positional roles involve overlapping time intervals.
- Fanty's [8] parser uses a purely local tensor product representation involving a positional role decomposition of trees.
- Feldman's [9] connectionist system for visual processing uses a representation that includes the tensor product of a local representation for visual features (including color, size, and shape) and a local representation for position in the visual field.

In many of these models, the local representation of roles is not made explicit in the usual description of the model, but is rather implicit in the structure of the representation. The same is true of the semi-local case we take up next.

2.3.2.3. *Semi-local representations of symbolic structures*
The next most local special case is this.

Definition 2.15. Let $\Psi_{F/R}$ be the tensor product representation of S induced by a role decomposition F/R of S and two connectionist representations Ψ_F and Ψ_R. If Ψ_F is a distributed representation and Ψ_R is a local representation, then $\Psi_{F/R}$ is a *semi-local tensor product representation* or a *role register representation*.

If the filler representation is a distributed pattern and the role representation involves the activity of a single unit, the result is a copy of the filler pattern in a pool of units dedicated to the role: see Fig. 6.
Semi-local tensor product representations have been widely used in conjunction with positional role decompositions:

- The letter perception model [23, 32] uses a semi-local representation of letters at its lowest or "letter feature" level; this is the example shown in Fig. 6. A set of units is dedicated to the representation of the first letter's features; a letter is represented as a pattern of activity over these units, where each unit indicates whether a particular line segment is or is not present in the first letter. There are identical copies of this "first letter register" for the second, third, and fourth letter.
- An early version of NETtalk (Charles Rosenberg, unpublished communication, 1985) used a semi-local representation for the input string: the ith letter was represented by a pattern of activity over a set of units dedicated to the ith position, and each unit indicated whether a particular orthographic feature (e.g., closed loop, ascending line) was present in that letter.
- In Hinton's [13] semantic net model, relationships of the form $R(x, y)$ (e.g., *has_color(clyde, grey)*), are represented by placing three distributed

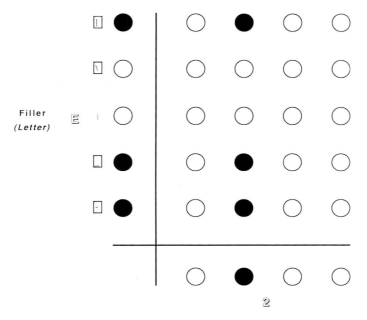

Fig. 6. A semi-local tensor product representation of four-letter strings.

patterns of activity representing the fillers of the roles R, x, and y in pools dedicated to those roles. (There is an additional pool as well.)
- The model of Riley and Smolensky [29] that answers qualitative questions about a fixed simple electric circuit also uses a semi-local representation. Each role is a circuit variable (e.g., the current, or the resistance of one of the resistors) and the fillers are the qualitative values *increases*, *decreases*, *stays_constant*. Each filler is represented as a small pattern in a pool of two units dedicated to the corresponding role.
- Touretzky and Hinton's [46] connectionist production system interpreter uses productions with two symbolic triples on the condition side; each triple is represented by a pattern of activity in a separate pool of units. (The representation of the triples themselves are considered in the next section.)
- The McClelland and Kawamoto [22] model that learns to assign case to the nouns appearing in a standard sentence frame uses a semi-local representation of its input. Each input is an instance of the frame: *The N_1 V the N_2 with the N_3.* The roles here are the three nouns and the verb, and each filler is represented by a pattern of activity in a pool of units dedicated to the corresponding role.

2.3.2.4. *Fully distributed representations of symbolic structures*
Now we come to the most distributed case:

Definition 2.16. Let $\Psi_{F/R}$ be the tensor product representation of S induced by a role decomposition F/R of S and two connectionist representations Ψ_F and Ψ_R. If Ψ_F and Ψ_R are both distributed representations, then $\Psi_{F/R}$ is a *fully distributed tensor product representation*.

Examples of fully distributed representations include the following:

- A visually transparent example of a fully distributed tensor product representation using the positional role decomposition was given in Fig. 3. The patterns representing roles here are examples of *coarse coding* representations described in Hinton, McClelland, and Rumelhart [15]. It is traditional to focus on the numerous positions (roles) that activate a particular role unit (its "receptive field"); the formulation here focuses on the numerous role units activated by a particular positional role. These are merely two perspectives on the many-to-many mapping between positions and units.
- The McClelland and Kawamoto [22] model mentioned earlier can be viewed as using a fully distributed representation of the output. Each output is a set of bindings of noun fillers to the case-frame slots of the verb. This output can be viewed as having roles like *loves-agent, loves-patient, eat-instrument, break-patient*, and so on; these roles can in turn be viewed as structured objects with two sub-roles: *verb* and *case-role*. The patterns representing the overall roles are the tensor product of a distributed pattern representing the verb (built from semantic verb features) and a local representation of the case-role. The representation of the overall roles is thus semi-local. The representation of the output as a whole is the tensor product of this distributed (albeit semi-local) representation of the roles and a distributed representation of the fillers (built of semantic features of nouns). This is an example of the kind of recursive tensor product representation that will be discussed in Section 3.7.3. Because of this recursive structure, the output units in this model represent three-way conjunctions of features for nouns, verbs, and semantic roles. (The "features" of semantic roles used in the model are of the local type mentioned in Section 2.3.2.4: they are in one-to-one correspondence with the semantic roles. A more distributed version of this model would employ real features of semantic roles, where each semantic role is a distributed pattern of features. Then the roles in the output as a whole would have fully distributed representations instead of semi-local ones.)
- An example of a fully distributed representation employing the 1-neighbor context decomposition is the Rumelhart and McClelland [33] model that

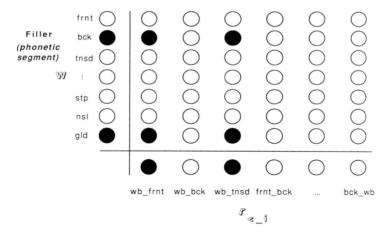

Role *(1-neighbor phonetic context)*

Fig. 7. The principal representation used in Rumelhart and McClelland [33] for phonetic strings. The abbreviations used are $wb = word\_boundary$, $frnt = front$, $bck = back$, $tnsd = tensed$, $stp = stop$; $nsl = nasal$; $gld = glide$.

learns to form the past tense of English verbs; see Fig. 7. In this model, elements of S are strings of phonetic segments. The word "weed" corresponds to the string $[w][i][d]$ which has the bindings $\{w/r_{<\_i}, i/r_{w\_d}, d/r_{i\_>}\}$. The representation of this string is thus

$$\mathbf{w} \otimes \mathbf{r}_{<\_i} + \mathbf{i} \otimes \mathbf{r}_{w\_d} + \mathbf{d} \otimes \mathbf{r}_{i\_>} \, .$$

The filler vectors (e.g. $\mathbf{w}$) are distributed patterns over a set of units representing phonetic features (e.g., *rounded*, *front*, *stop*). The role vectors (e.g. $\mathbf{r}_{<\_i}$) are patterns of activity over a set of units each of which represents the conjunction of a feature of the left neighbor ($<$) and a feature of the right neighbor (i). (In this model, both $<$ and $>$ possess the single feature *word_boundary*.) As in the previous example, since the roles are composite objects, they are in fact themselves further decomposed into sub-roles. The pair of phonetic segments defining the context is decomposed using the right-neighbor context decomposition, and the pattern representing the role r_{a_b} is the tensor product of patterns of phonetic features for $[a]$ and $[b]$. To reduce the number of units in the network, many of the units arising in this further decomposition of the roles were in fact discarded. The overall structure of the representation of the roles can still be productively viewed as a tensor product from which some units have been thrown away.

- Touretzky and Hinton's [46] representation of triples of letters can be viewed as the same sort of third-order tensor product as in the last example, but in which even more binding units are discarded. Their representation involves a set of units $\alpha = 1, \ldots, N$, each of which responds to three groups of letters $(L_\alpha^{(1)}, L_\alpha^{(2)}, L_\alpha^{(3)})$: unit α is active in the representation of $(l^{(1)}, l^{(2)}, l^{(3)})$ iff $l^{(i)} \in L_\alpha^{(i)}$ for $i = 1, 2$ and 3. To relate this to the tensor product representation, imagine three pools of N units, one pool for each letter in the triple. In the ith pool, unit $\tilde{u}_\alpha^{(i)}$ is active iff $l^{(i)} \in L_\alpha^{(i)}$: each letter is represented by a pattern in the corresponding pool. Create a binding unit for each triple of units, one from each pool; it is active iff the corresponding three units are active. This is the tensor product representation of the triples induced by the 1-neighbor context decomposition, with the roles further decomposed by the right-neighbor context decomposition, as in the previous example. Now if we throw out all the binding units corresponding to $(\tilde{u}_\alpha^{(1)}, \tilde{u}_\beta^{(2)}, \tilde{u}_\gamma^{(3)})$, except the N "diagonal" ones corresponding to $(\tilde{u}_\alpha^{(1)}, \tilde{u}_\alpha^{(2)}, \tilde{u}_\alpha^{(3)})$, we get Touretzky and Hinton's representation.
- Hinton [13] suggested an extension to his implemented model using fully distributed representations in which each unit represented a conjunction of features of an object, a relation, and a role.
- Derthick's μKLONE system [2] and Dolan and Dyer's story understanding system [4, 5] both use the fully distributed form of tensor product representation.
- Touretzky and Geva's DUCS system [45] uses fully distributed filler/role bindings that, while currently lacking a mathematical basis like that of tensor product representations, have many of their desirable properties, while requiring potentially far fewer units.

Having mentioned Rumelhart and McClelland's [33] use of context decompositions, it is worth elaborating on remarks of Section 2.3.1 about the advantages of context decompositions over simpler positional decompositions. Many regularities in language depend on the context in which a constituent finds itself, rather than its absolute position. This is particularly true in phonology; the regularities that must be learned in order to form the past tenses of English verbs typically depend on neighbor relations: for example, the rule for "regular" verbs involves replacing $x/r_{y\_>}$ by the bindings $\{x/r_{y\_}$, $^/r_{x\_d}, d/r_{\_>}\}$ if x has feature *dental*, (*weed → weeded*); otherwise, by the bindings $\{\tilde{x}/r_{y\_d}, d/r_{x\_>}\}$ if x has feature *voiced*, (*buzz → buzzed*) or by the bindings $\{x/r_{y\_t}, t/r_{x\_>}\}$ if x does not have feature *voiced*(*bus → bussed*). Thus the featural representation of phonetic segments together with the context decomposition of the string provides the network with just the kind of representation of phonetic strings that it needs in order to learn the regularities characterizing this task (a point elaborated in detail in [17]).

2.4. Relations among purely local, semi-local, and fully distributed representations

Purely local, semi-local and fully distributed representations look quite different on the surface. Are they really as different as they seem? According to the definitions, the only difference is the relation between the representation vectors and the distinguished basis vectors indicating the individual processing units. Does this really matter?

As discussed at length in Smolensky [37], the answer depends on the dynamics driving the connectionist network, and not solely on the representations themselves. If the dynamics is linear, so that the activity of every unit is exactly a weighted sum of the activity of its neighbors in the network, then networks using purely local, semi-local and fully distributed representations will have exactly isomorphic behavior, subject to a few qualifications. Under the linear transformations that map these three cases into each other, locality is not preserved, so that local damage to the networks will have different effects, and what can be learned via the usual local connectionist learning procedures will be different. If the network contains nonlinear units, the isomorphism fails. Also, assuming finite networks, the local case accommodates only a fixed, finite set of fillers and roles; the semi-local case allows an unlimited number of fillers but only a finite set of roles. The fully distributed case, however, can accommodate an infinite set of fillers and roles in a finite network, since the vectors representing both the roles and fillers can be arbitrary activity patterns drawn from vector spaces which, while having finite dimension, contain a continuous infinity of distinct vectors; this will be discussed further in Section 3.2.

3. Tensor Product Representation: Properties

In Section 2, I defined the tensor product representation and showed how a number of representations used in previous connectionist models are various special cases of the tensor product representation. In this section, I will discuss a number of general properties of this representation. The case of interest is fully distributed representation; while some of the results apply also to the more localized special cases, in these cases they become rather trivial.

3.1. Unbinding

Until now I have ignored a crucial and obvious question: if the representations of all the variable bindings necessary for a particular structure are superimposed on top of each other in a single set of binding units, how can we be sure the binding information is all kept straight? In this section we explore this question via the *unbinding* process: taking the tensor product representation for a complex structure and extracting from it the filler for a particular role. Under what conditions can we perform this unbinding operation accurately?

Theorem 3.1. *Let* $\Psi_{F/R}$ *be a tensor product representation induced by a role decomposition with single-valued roles. Suppose the vectors representing the roles bound in a structure s are linearly independent. Then each role can be unbound with complete accuracy: for each bound role* r_i *there is an operation which takes the vector* $\Psi_{F/R}(s)$ *representing s into the vector* $\mathbf{f}_i$ *representing the filler* f_i *bound to* r_i.

Proof. If the role vectors $\{\mathbf{r}_i\}$ being used are linearly independent, then they form a basis for the subspace of V_R that they span. To this basis there corresponds a *dual basis* $\{U_i\}$ [19, p. 82]. Each element in this dual basis is a linear mapping from V_R into the real numbers with the property that

$$U_i(\mathbf{r}_j) = \delta_{ij} = \begin{cases} 1 & \text{if } i = j, \\ 0 & \text{if } i \neq j. \end{cases}$$

That is, U_i maps the single role vector $\mathbf{r}_i$ to 1 and all other role vectors to 0. If we make use of the canonical inner product on the vector space V_R, then the dual vector U_i can be expressed as the operation of taking the inner product with respect to some vector $\mathbf{u}_i$ in V_R:

$$U_i(\mathbf{v}) = \mathbf{v} \cdot \mathbf{u}_i$$

for all $\mathbf{v}$ in V_R. Call $\{\mathbf{u}_i\}$ the *unbinding vectors* for roles $\{r_i\}$. Now let s be the tensor product representation of a structure in which the roles $\{r_i\}$ are bound to the fillers $\{f_i\}$. Then we can extract f_i from s, or unbind r_i, by taking a partial inner product of s with the unbinding vector $\mathbf{u}_i$:

$$\mathbf{s} \cdot \mathbf{u}_i = \left(\sum_j \mathbf{f}_j \otimes \mathbf{r}_j \right) \cdot \mathbf{u}_i$$

$$:= \sum_j \mathbf{f}_j (\mathbf{r}_j \cdot \mathbf{u}_i) = \sum_j \mathbf{f}_j \delta_{ij} = \mathbf{f}_i . \qquad \square$$

Connectionist algorithms for computing the unbinding vectors will be discussed in Section 3.4.2.

Definition 3.2. The procedure defined in the preceding proof is the *exact unbinding procedure*.

Let unbinding of role r_i be performed as in the previous proof, but in place of the unbinding vector $\mathbf{u}_i$ use the role vector $\mathbf{r}_i$ itself. This is the *self-addressing unbinding procedure*.

Unlike the exact unbinding procedure, the self-addressing unbinding procedure is defined for any set of role vectors, even if they are not linearly independent.

Theorem 3.3. *Suppose the self-addressing procedure is used to unbind roles. If the role vectors are all orthogonal, the correct filler pattern will be generated, apart from an overall magnitude factor. Otherwise, the pattern generated will be a weighted superposition of the pattern of the correct filler, $\mathbf{f}_i$, and all the other fillers, $\{\mathbf{f}_j\}_{j \neq i}$. In this superposition, the weight of each erroneous pattern $\mathbf{f}_j$ relative to the correct pattern $\mathbf{f}_i$, the intrusion of role j into role i, is*

$$\frac{\mathbf{r}_i \cdot \mathbf{r}_j}{\|\mathbf{r}_i\|^2} = \cos \theta_{ji} \frac{\|\mathbf{r}_j\|}{\|\mathbf{r}_i\|}$$

where θ_{ji} is the angle between the vectors $\mathbf{r}_j$ and $\mathbf{r}_i$.

Proof.

$$\mathbf{s} \cdot \mathbf{r}_i = \left(\sum_j \mathbf{f}_j \otimes \mathbf{r}_j \right) \cdot \mathbf{r}_i = \sum_j \mathbf{f}_j (\mathbf{r}_j \cdot \mathbf{r}_i)$$

$$= (\mathbf{r}_i \cdot \mathbf{r}_i)\mathbf{f}_i + \sum_{j \neq i} (\mathbf{r}_j \cdot \mathbf{r}_i)\mathbf{f}_j .$$

In this weighted superposition, the ratio of the coefficient of each incorrect filler $\mathbf{f}_j$ to that of the correct filler $\mathbf{f}_i$ is

$$\frac{\mathbf{r}_j \cdot \mathbf{r}_i}{\mathbf{r}_i \cdot \mathbf{r}_i} .$$

The denominator is $\|\mathbf{r}_i\|^2$ and the numerator is $\cos \theta_{ji} \|\mathbf{r}_j\| \|\mathbf{r}_i\|$, giving the claimed result. ☐

Note that if two roles have very similar representations, there can be substantial confusion about what their respective fillers are. The next section provides a quantitative result on the intrusion of one role on another. If the role vectors are linearly independent, the exact unbinding procedure can be used to eliminate intrusions, but the unbinding vectors must be computed.

Since the tensor product binding representation is symmetric between role and filler, the unbinding procedures given above can also be used to retrieve a role pattern from the filler pattern to which it is bound. While there is no asymmetry between role and filler in the representation of a single binding, an asymmetry may however result from the combination of many bindings in the representation of a structured object. For while role decompositions often involve single-valued roles, it is uncommon to encounter single-valued fillers. Thus while there will often be a unique filler indexed by a given role, there will sometimes be several roles associated with a single filler. In the latter case, an unbinding that is performed using the filler pattern as an index will generate the superposition of all the role vectors bound to that filler.[4]

3.2. Graceful saturation

Like a digital memory with n registers, a connectionist system that uses n pools of units to represent a structure with n roles has a discrete saturation point. Structures with no more than n roles filled can be represented precisely, but for larger structures some information must be omitted entirely. The form of saturation characteristic of connectionist systems (e.g., connectionist memories) is less discrete than this; this is one aspect of the "graceful degradation" advertised for connectionist systems.

Aspects of the graceful degradation notion can be formally characterized as follows:

Definition 3.4. Let F/R be a role decomposition of S. A connectionist representation Ψ of S has *unbounded sensitivity* with respect to F/R if for arbitrarily large n,

$$\Psi\left(\bigwedge_{i=1}^{n} f_i/r_i\right)$$

varies as f_i varies, for each $i = 1, 2, \ldots, n$.

If for sufficiently large n the representation of structures containing n filler/role bindings is not faithful, then Ψ *saturates*.

If Ψ saturates and has unbounded sensitivity then Ψ possesses *graceful saturation*.

The tensor product representation, unlike local and role register representations, can exhibit graceful saturation. To show this, I now consider an example that also illustrates how fully distributed tensor product representations can be used to represent an infinite number of roles in a finite-dimensional vector space corresponding to a finite connectionist network.

Theorem 3.5. *Suppose S is the set of finite strings (with no upper bound on length), and let $\{r_i\}_{i=1}^{\infty}$ be the positional roles. Let the vectors $\{\mathbf{r}_i\}_{i=1}^{\infty}$ be unit*

---

[4] Related to unbinding are Mozer's *pullout networks* [25]. These networks take an input that represents a mixture of several coherent objects and "pulls out" the vector representing a single object, suppressing the representation of the others. This is done by setting up connections encoding a set of constraints that define what it means for a vector to represent a coherent object, and using relaxation to settle on a single coherent representation. At least in this normal usage, pullout networks solve a problem that is related to but different from unbinding. The starting point of unbinding is a representation of a single coherent object (structure); the problem is, given a role in the structure, find what fills it (or vice versa).

vectors in N-dimensional space, randomly chosen according to the uniform distribution. Then this tensor product representation possesses graceful saturation. The expected value of the magnitude of the intrusion of role i into role j is proportional to $N^{1/2}$. The number of bindings n that can be stored before the expected total magnitude of intrusions equals the magnitude of the correct pattern increases as $N^{1/2}$.

Proof. Since all role vectors have unit length, from Theorem 3.3, the expected value of the magnitude of the intrusion is

$$EI = \frac{1}{V_{N-1}} \int_0^{\pi} |\cos \theta_{ji}| V(\theta_{ji}) \, d\theta_{ji} .$$

Here V_{N-1} is the $N-1$-dimensional volume of the unit sphere in N-space, and $V(\theta_{ji})$ is the volume of the subset of the unit sphere in N-space consisting of all vectors having angle θ_{ij} with the vector $\mathbf{r}_i$. This subset is in fact a sphere in $N-1$-space with radius $\sin \theta_{ji}$. To see this, choose a Cartesian coordinate system in N-space in which the first coordinate direction lies along $\mathbf{r}_i$. Then the first coordinate x_1 of all points in the subset is $\cos \theta_{ji}$. Since all points lie on the unit sphere, we have

$$1 = \sum_{i=1}^{N} x_i^2 = \cos^2 \theta_{ji} + \sum_{i=2}^{N} x_i^2$$

which implies

$$\sum_{i=2}^{N} x_i^2 = 1 - \cos^2 \theta_{ji} = \sin^2 \theta_{ji} .$$

Thus the subset is a sphere in $N-1$-space with radius $\sin \theta_{ji}$. Therefore

$$V(\theta_{ji}) = V_{N-2} \sin^{N-2} \theta_{ji} .$$

Thus the expected intrusion is

$$EI = \frac{V_{N-2}}{V_{N-1}} 2 \int_0^{\pi/2} \sin^{N-2} \theta \cos \theta \, d\theta$$

$$= \frac{V_{N-2}}{V_{N-1}} 2 \int_0^1 z^{N-2} \, dz = \frac{V_{N-2}}{V_{N-1}} \frac{2}{N-1}$$

(using the substitution $z = \cos \theta$ which implies $dz = -\sin \theta \, d\theta$). The ratio of volumes of spheres of successive dimensions V_{N-2}/V_{N-1} is a complex expression taking different forms depending on whether N is odd or even (see the Appendix of [39]). Since these details are quite irrelevant to the general behavior as N increases, we can look at the mean of two successive such ratios (using the geometric mean since the quantities are ratios) which is given by the simple expression[5]

$$\sqrt{(N-1)/2\pi} \, .$$

The result then is

$$\mathrm{EI} = \sqrt{\frac{2}{\pi(N-1)}} \; .$$

As claimed, the expected interference falls as $N^{-1/2}$.

For a structure involving n bindings, the expected total magnitude of intrusions of all $\{r_j\}_{j \neq i}$ into r_i is $(n-1)\mathrm{EI}$. This equals unity at

$$n = \sqrt{\frac{1}{2}\,\pi}\,(N-1)^{1/2} + 1$$

which increases as the square-root of N. $\square$

The estimate of interference given in the preceding theorem is a very conservative one, since it computes the expected sum of the *absolute values* of all intrusions. In fact, for any given component of the desired filler, the errors caused by intrusions will be of both signs, producing a net error much smaller than the worst case analyzed above.

3.3. Continuous structures and infinite-dimensional representations

Certain structures are characterized by a continuum of roles. Strings, for example, have a natural extension to a continuum of positions. Examples of such continuous one-dimensional "strings" include speech input and motor output; a two-dimensional example is an image.

The tensor product representation extends naturally to the case of a continuum of roles. The representation of the conjunction of bindings extends naturally from the sum over a discrete set of bindings to an integral over a continuum of bindings.

---

[5] There is a rough calculation that suggests that, as the dimension N grows, the expected inner product of unit-length role vectors should decrease with the square root of N. Suppose for the first N role vectors we chose an orthonormal basis. For the next vector, suppose we choose one that is equidistant from all the others; an example is the vector whose components in the orthonormal basis are $C^{-1}(1, 1, \ldots, 1)$. In order for this vector to have unit length, the normalization constant C must be $\sqrt{N}$. Now the inner product of this vector with any of the others is $C^{-1} = N^{-1/2}$.

Definition 3.6. Let F/R be a role decomposition of S, not necessarily finite, and let $d\mu(r)$ be a measure on R. Let $\text{supp}_R(s)$ be the subset of R containing roles which are bound in s, and suppose F/R has single-valued roles. Suppose given the connectionist representations

$$\Psi_F : F \to V_F ; \qquad f \mapsto \mathbf{f} ,$$

$$\Psi_R : R \to V_R ; \qquad r \mapsto \mathbf{r}$$

and assume these functions are measurable with respect to $d\mu(r)$. Then the corresponding tensor product representation of S is

$$\Psi_{F/R}(s) = \int_{\text{supp}_R(s)} \mathbf{f}(r) \otimes \mathbf{r} \, d\mu(r) .$$

$\Psi_{F/R}(s)$ is defined only for those s for which the integral is well-defined: $\text{supp}_R(s)$ must be a measurable set and the integral must converge.

If the role decomposition is finite, and $d\mu$ is counting measure, then this reduces to the previous definition of the tensor product representation.

In the case of a continuous string, we can take the roles to be $r(t)$ for a continuous time index t. For the measure we can use ordinary Lebesque measure on t. Then if each role is represented by a pattern $\mathbf{r}(t)$ and the fillers by the patterns $\mathbf{f}(t)$, the entire continuous string is represented by $\int \mathbf{f}(t) \otimes \mathbf{r}(t) \, dt$. This representation of the continuous structure goes over exactly to the discrete case if it happens that the fillers are discrete step-functions of time. Suppose the filler $\mathbf{f}(t)$ is constant over the interval $[t_i, t_{i+1}]$ with value $\mathbf{f}_i$. Then the representation of the string is

$$\int_t \mathbf{f}(t) \otimes \mathbf{r}(t) \, dt = \sum_i \int_{t_i}^{t_{i+1}} \mathbf{f}(t) \otimes \mathbf{r}(t) \, dt$$

$$= \sum_i \int_{t_i}^{t_{i+1}} \mathbf{f}_i \otimes \mathbf{r}(t) \, dt$$

$$= \sum_i \mathbf{f}_i \otimes \int_{t_i}^{t_{i+1}} \mathbf{r}(t) \, dt = \sum_i \mathbf{f}_i \otimes \mathbf{r}_i$$

where the vector representing the discrete role for the time slot $[t_i, t_{i+1}]$ is the integral of the vectors representing the time points in the slot:

$$\mathbf{r}_i := \int_{t_i}^{t_{i+1}} \mathbf{r}(t)\, dt .$$

The representation of a continuous string can be visualized with the help of the example illustrated in Fig. 3, which shows a tensor product binding between a time and the energy level of a speech formant. The patterns representing the energy level and time are peaks centered at the values being represented; this can apply to continuous represented values as well as discrete ones. The pattern $\mathbf{r}_4$ representing time $i = 4$ (shown in Fig. 3) is a peak centered on the fourth role unit; a pattern $\mathbf{r}(4.2)$ representing time $t = 4.2$ would be derived by taking a peak on the continuous line centered at 4.2 and evaluating it at the integer values $i = 1, 2, \ldots, 5$. One can similarly generate patterns representing continuous energy levels $\mathbf{f}(t)$. As in the discrete case, the tensor product representation of the binding $f(t)/r(t)$ then becomes a two-dimensional peak centered at $(t, f(t))$, evaluated at points with integer coordinates. Superimposing the representation of the bindings for all t, we get the representation of the continuous string of energy levels: it resembles a smeared-out version of the graph of energy versus time, the activity of each unit in the grid of Fig. 3 being greater the closer it lies to the actual graph.

In the representation illustrated in Fig. 3, the role and filler vector spaces have finite dimensions (5 and 4, respectively). In such a case it is of course impossible for all the role vectors to be linearly independent; that would require an infinite-dimensional role vector space. The tensor product representation applies as well to infinite-dimensional vector spaces as to finite-dimensional ones. In that case the patterns representing roles (and possibly also fillers) would not be patterns defined by a finite number of values as shown in Fig. 3 but could rather be curves defined over a continuous segment. The peaked patterns representing energy levels and times could be smooth Gaussians over a fixed interval, with mean equal to the quantity being represented and with variance, say, some fixed value. Then the representation of each binding would be a two-dimensional smooth Gaussian with mean at the point with x- and y-coordinates equal to the time and energy values, respectively.

If the role space is infinite-dimensional, then so too will be the binding space. To view this space as the states of a connectionist network would require postulating an infinite number of units, one for each dimension of the space. The infinite-dimensional case is of interest not for computer simulation but for analysis; patterns which are functions of a continuous variable pose no particular difficulty for analysis relative to patterns which are finite-dimensional vectors.

It is significant that the tensor product representation extends so naturally to continuous collections of roles, continuous sets of fillers, and vectors for representing roles and fillers that are continuous patterns. As I have argued elsewhere [41], an important characteristic of a number of connectionist networks is the existence of an underlying continuous model. Thus one indication that a connectionist representational scheme is well-motivated is that it has a natural continuous extension, even if particular simulation models take advantage only of the discrete case.

3.4. Connectionist mechanisms for binding and unbinding

The tensor product representation has so far been characterized mathematically, without any discussion of how such a representation might be set up and used in a connectionist system. In this section I consider first the creation of bindings and then I take up unbinding.

3.4.1. *Parallel binding in connectionist systems*

The most immediate application of the tensor product representation is to models learning to map some structured input to structured output; for example, the surface form of a sentence to its parsed form. Here it is not the job of the network to set up the tensor product representations: in presenting the input/output pairs to the network during training, the modeler must convert the symbolic inputs and outputs to their vector representations, and this can be done directly by using the mathematical definition of the tensor product representation.

In more complex applications, a network might be so constructed as to internally perform variable binding via the tensor product. A convenient way to achieve this is to use so-called *sigma-pi* processing units [30]. Such a unit has a number of input sites at each of which connections from a number of other processors converge. For each site σ, the sigma-pi unit takes the *product* of all the inputs $\{I_{\sigma i}\}$ there; it then adopts as its value ν a weighted *sum* over all sites, with one weight w_σ per site:

$$\nu = \sum_\sigma w_\sigma \prod_i I_{\sigma i}$$

Using sigma-pi units, tensor product binding can be easily achieved in a connectionist network: see Fig. 8. The network consists of a set of filler units $\tilde{f}_\phi$, a set of role units $\tilde{r}_\rho$, and set of binding units $\tilde{b}_{\phi\rho}$, one for each pair of filler and role units. Each binding unit is a sigma-pi unit with a single site with unit weight. Converging on the site of the binding unit $\tilde{b}_{\phi\rho}$ are two connections, one from $\tilde{f}_\phi$ and one from $\tilde{r}_\rho$. Then if the filler and role patterns $\mathbf{f}$ and $\mathbf{r}$ are set up on the filler and role units, the binding units will set up the representation of the binding $\mathbf{f}/\mathbf{r}$.

Fig. 9 shows a network equivalent to the one shown in Fig. 8. Here the

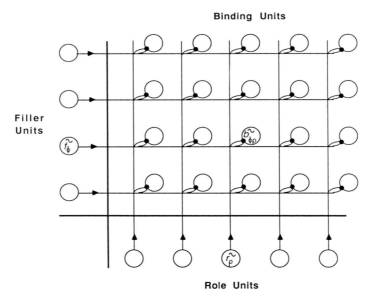

Fig. 8. A network using sigma-pi binding units to perform tensor product binding.

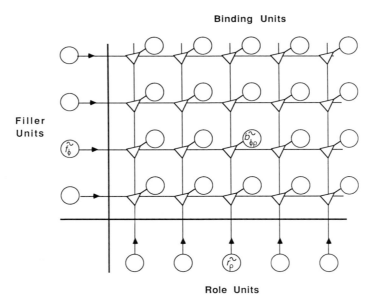

Fig. 9. A network using multiplicative junctions to perform tensor product binding.

product occurs not at the unit but at the junction of two connections; the two activities entering the triangular junction [12] from the filler and role units are multiplied together and the result is sent along the third line to the binding unit.

The representation of complex structures requires superimposing multiple filler/role bindings. There are two obvious ways of doing this: sequentially and in parallel. In the sequential case, one binding is performed at a time, and the binding units accumulate their activity over time. This can be achieved with the network shown in Fig. 8 if we use accumulating sigma-pi binding units obeying

$$\frac{dv}{dt} = \sum_{\sigma} w_{\sigma} \prod_{i} I_{\sigma i} .$$

Equivalently, serial binding can be performed by the network of Fig. 9 if the binding units accumulate activity over time.

In order to superimpose all N bindings in parallel, we need to extend the network shown in Fig. 8, creating nodes $\{f_{\phi}^{(\sigma)}\}_{\sigma=1}^{N}$ and $\{r_{\rho}^{(\sigma)}\}_{\sigma=1}^{N}$: see Fig. 10, which illustrates the simplest case, $N = 2$. Now each sigma-pi binding unit has N sites instead of one; each site has unit weight. Each site σ on binding unit $\tilde{b}_{\phi\rho}$ receives a pair of connections from the nodes $\tilde{f}_{\phi}^{(\sigma)}$ and $\tilde{r}_{\rho}^{(\sigma)}$. Now we can bind N pairs of roles and fillers in parallel. In the σth filler pool we set up the pattern

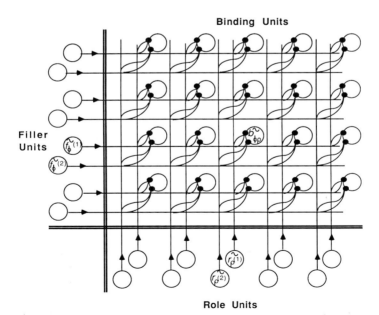

Binding Units

Filler Units

Role Units

Fig. 10. An extension of the network of Fig. 8 that can perform two variable bindings in parallel.

$\mathbf{f}_\sigma$ representing f_σ and on the σth role pool we set up the pattern $\mathbf{r}_\sigma$ representing r_σ. The value of binding unit $\tilde{b}_{\phi\rho}$ is then

$$\tilde{b}_{\phi\rho} = \sum_\sigma 1 \prod \{\tilde{f}_\phi^{(\sigma)}, \tilde{r}_\rho^{(\sigma)}\} = \sum_\sigma (\mathbf{f}_\sigma)_\phi (\mathbf{r}_\sigma)_\rho .$$

The pattern of activity on the binding units is thus the correct tensor product representation of the structure. Fig. 11 is the equivalent of Fig. 10 using multiplicative junctions instead of sigma-pi units.

There is no need to perform *all* the binding serially or in parallel; the mechanisms of sequential and parallel combination of bindings are independent, and can be combined. If there are N pools of filler and role units, N bindings can be established in parallel, and if the binding units accumulate activity over time, further bindings can be added sequentially, up to N at a time.

There are two senses in which bindings are occurring in parallel here. Bindings are *generated* in parallel, N at a time; the *generation capacity* is sharply defined by N. At the same time, multiple bindings are being *maintained* in parallel; the binding units can simultaneously support multiple bindings superimposed on each other. The *maintenance capacity* of the representation is

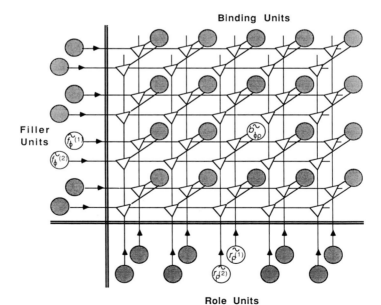

Fig. 11. An extension of the network of Fig. 9 that can perform two variable bindings in parallel. (Unlabelled units have been shaded to enhance readability.)

not sharply defined, due to the graceful saturation of the representation. The scale of the maintenance capacity is, however, set by n, the number of role units in each of the N sets.

For the network shown in Fig. 10, the generation and maintenance capacities are independent; this contrasts with most existing connectionist systems. For example, the McClelland and Rumelhart letter perception model processes exclusively four letter words. Strings of length $n = 4$ can be represented; the maintenance capacity is precisely defined at four letters. The binding of all four letters to their positions are all performed in parallel; the generation capacity is also $N = 4$. If different roles correspond to different regions of a parallel network, as in local and semi-local representations, it is natural that these roles should all be sent activation in parallel. If the different roles share a common set of units, as in fully distributed representations, there comes the space/time trade-off we have seen above: duplicate machinery to permit parallel binding, or wait while multiple bindings are performed serially.

It seems intuitive that the two binding capacities ought to be independent characteristics of the degree of parallelism in a processing system. In many human cognitive processes, for example, the generation capacity of binding appears to be much smaller than the maintenance capacity: $N \ll n$. In visual perception we are able to maintain rich percepts involving a huge number of bindings of properties to locations, but it turns out that at any one time (requiring approximately 50 msec) our visual systems can only establish the bindings for a small region of the visual field [47]. The large number of bindings that we maintain in parallel are generated a small fraction at a time through an extended sequential process. In discourse processing, syntactic and semantic processes seem to indicate that many constituents in complex structures are being maintained and processed in parallel, yet only a small fraction of these constituent/role bindings are generated at once. If one looks at the processing of small linguistic and/or visual items whose size fits within the binding generation capacity (e.g. four-letter words), the distinction between the generation and maintenance capacities does not assert itself. However, connectionist models of more complex, extended tasks such as reading whole passages must respect the distinction between these two aspects of parallelism; the tensor product representation offers a natural way to do so, because the machinery needed to create one binding can also create the others: there is no need to build separate hardware to create each binding, as is typically done with local or semi-local representations.

3.4.2. Connectionist unbinding mechanisms

The mathematics of the unbinding procedure was described in Section 3.1. It is easy to implement this procedure in a connectionist network; in fact, the network of Fig. 9 can be used for unbinding as well as for binding. We presume that the binding units are supporting a pattern of activity which is the tensor product representation of a structure. To unbind role r_i, a pattern of activity is first set up on the role units: for the exact unbinding procedure, this pattern should be that of the unbinding vector $\mathbf{u}_i$; for the self-addressing unbinding procedure, the pattern should be $\mathbf{r}_i$. As a result of the activity in the role and binding units, a pattern of activity arises on the filler units. At each triangular junction, the activity of the connected role and binder units are multiplied together and sent to the connected filler unit, which adds up all the inputs it so receives (I assume, following [12], that the triangle junctions operate symmetrically, multiplying the activities arriving on any two lines and sending the product out along the third line.) Thus the activity of filler unit $\tilde{f}_\phi$ is

$$\tilde{f}_\phi = \sum_\rho \tilde{r}_\rho \tilde{b}_{\phi\rho} \; .$$

This is the correct activity to implement the unbinding procedures of Section 3.1. With the extended network shown in Fig. 11, N roles can be unbound simultaneously.

This procedure has been defined for retrieving a filler from a role. By interchanging roles and fillers, it can also be used to retrieve a role from a filler, subject to the caveat of Section 3.1 about non-single-valuedness.

The unbinding vectors needed for the exact unbinding procedure can be stored in a network in a number of ways. Using an additional group of units, a local representation of roles for unbinding could be used, so that when it was desired to unbind a given role, the corresponding unit could be activated, and the weights on connections emanating from that unit could be used to set up the corresponding unbinding vector on the role units. Alternatively, the additional group of units could be used with a distributed representation; the actual vector representing r_i could be set up on these units, and feedforward connections could then set up the corresponding unbinding vector $\mathbf{u}_i$ on the role units. It is always possible to perform this mapping linearly when the role vectors are linearly independent, which is also the condition required for the unbinding vectors to be defined in the first place. In fact, the Widrow–Hoff learning rule can be used to learn the weights necessary to map the $\{\mathbf{r}_i\}$ into the $\{\mathbf{u}_i\}$, provided a teacher can present the target vectors $\{\mathbf{u}_i\}$. Since the matrix of $\{\mathbf{u}_i\}$ is just the inverse of the matrix of $\{\mathbf{r}_i\}$, iterative matrix inversion algorithms implemented in a connectionist network can be used to compute the $\{\mathbf{u}_i\}$ from the $\{\mathbf{r}_i\}$. One simple way to do this is as follows (see also [18]). Using Widrow–Hoff learning, train a simple linear associator to map each $\mathbf{r}_i$ to the ith unit vector, i.e., to a local representation of roles with a unique unit active per role. When the $\mathbf{r}_i$ are linearly independent, this is always possible. Now, we make the connections in this linear associator bi-directional and symmetric. If a role vector $\mathbf{r}_i$ is placed on the input units of the associator, it will create a local pattern on the output units. If we send this activity backwards along the same connections, then the new pattern set up on the input units will be exactly $\mathbf{u}_i$.[6]

3.5. Binding unit activities as connection weights

In Section 3.4.1 we discussed one way of generating the tensor product representation of a structure: sequentially representing individual filler/role pairs on the role and filler units, while each binding unit takes the product of the activities of its corresponding pair of role and filler units. These products then accumulate on the binding units as the individual pairs are presented. This procedure is formally identical to the *Hebbian learning procedure* for storing the associations between roles and corresponding fillers: each binding unit plays the role of the *connection* between a role and filler unit, and its activity plays the role of the weight or strength of that connection. Furthermore, the self-addressing unbinding mechanism described in Section 3.4.2 is formally identical to the use of the Hebbian weight matrix to associate a pattern over the role units with the corresponding pattern on the filler units.

This relationship between binding units and connections suggests avenues for further exploration, two of which will now be briefly described.

3.5.1. *From Hebbian to Widrow–Hoff weights*

In Section 3.1 it was pointed out that the pattern needed for exact unbinding of role r_i, the unbinding vector $\mathbf{u}_i$, is not in general equal to the role vector $\mathbf{r}_i$; the retrieval and role patterns are equal only if the role vectors are orthonormal. This corresponds to a well-known property of the Hebbian weight matrix: associations will be correctly formed by the Hebbian learning procedure if and only if the input patterns are orthogonal. There is a more complex learning procedure than the Hebbian one which produces a matrix with better retrieval capability than the Hebbian matrix: the Widrow–Hoff [49] or delta rule [30]. This suggests replacing the Hebbian matrix corresponding to the tensor product representation with the Widrow–Hoff matrix. With this new representation, the self-addressing unbinding procedure would produce correct results as long as the role vectors are *linearly independent*: orthogonality is not required. Unfortunately, this Widrow–Hoff representation is considerably more difficult to write down, analyze, and actually construct in a connectionist network. For example, the Widrow–Hoff learning procedure, unlike the Hebbian one, requires repeated presentations of the set of items to be stored.

---

[6] The weights $\{W_{kj}\}$ needed to map the $\{\mathbf{r}_i\}$ to the output basis vectors satisfy $\Sigma_j W_{kj}(\mathbf{r}_i)_j = \delta_{ki}$. In other words, $\mathbf{W}$ is the inverse of the matrix of role vectors. The kth row of $\mathbf{W}$ is thus just the unbinding vector $\mathbf{u}_k$; i.e., if we define $(\mathbf{u}_k)_j = W_{kj}$, then $\mathbf{u}_k \cdot \mathbf{r}_i = \delta_{ki}$ which is the defining property of the unbinding vectors. When $\mathbf{r}_i$ is sent through $\mathbf{W}$, it sets up the ith unit vector, and when this is sent back through the same connections, the jth activity is $\Sigma_k W_{kj}(\delta_{ki}) = W_{ij} = (\mathbf{u}_i)_j$. That is, the vector $\mathbf{r}_i$ has been replaced by the vector $\mathbf{u}_i$.

A relaxation process could be used to do Widrow–Hoff binding [D. Rumelhart, personal communication], but it would require that all filler/role pairs be simultaneously presented to the relaxation network. This would break the independence, discussed in Section 3.4.1, of the generation and maintenance capacities for binding.

3.5.2. *Relation to Connection Information Distribution*

The relation between tensor product binding units and Hebbian weights suggests another development of the present analysis. In McClelland's [20] Connection Information Distribution (CID) scheme, the activity of certain units determine the weights between others. Unbinding could be naturally carried out in a CID as follows. The represented structure would be active in a set of binder units which would set the weights between role and filler units. This would create a machine that transforms role patterns to filler patterns (to the approximation to which unbinding vectors equal role vectors). Figure 11 can be viewed as a CID in which the binder units are setting weights in a collection of N role/filler associators.

Despite the intimate relation between tensor product binding units and connection weights, it should be emphasized that the primary purpose of the tensor product representation is not to serve as an apparatus for filler/role associations: it is rather to provide a pattern of activity representing a structured object which can then be used for processing the object as a whole. This is the reason why the elements of the tensor product representation have been viewed as the activities of units rather than the strength of connections. The CID allows us to use unit activities as connection strengths, giving us simultaneous access to both aspects of the representation.

3.6. Values as variables

It is often important for the value bound to a variable to in fact itself be a variable to which a value is to be bound. The tensor product binding representation allows for this in the following way. Out of the representation for the variable/value binding can be extracted the pattern of activity that represents the value. This pattern can in turn be used as the pattern representing a variable, and used in another binding on other binding units where it is bound to a value. The situation is depicted in Fig. 12.

3.7. Representation of symbolic operations; recursive decompositions

So far we have not considered the representation of symbolic *operations*: mappings from S to itself. Examples that will now be considered are the stack operations *push* and *pop* and the LISP operators *car*, *cdr*, and *cons*. Understanding such operations are important for treating recursive role decomposi-

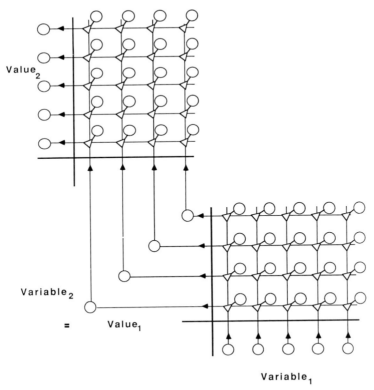

Fig. 12. A network capable of representing two value/variable bindings in which the same entity—the pattern of activity over the diagonally-aligned units—serves as the value in the first binding (*Value₁*) and the variable in the second binding (*Variable₂*).

tions, since in such a decomposition each role is in fact an operator mapping S into S.

The definition we need to get started is

Definition 3.7. Let $O : S \to S$ be an operator on S and $\Psi : S \to V$ be a connectionist representation of S. Then a corresponding *representation of O* is an operator

$$\mathbf{O} : V \to V ; \quad \mathbf{v} \mapsto \mathbf{Ov}$$

with the property

$$\Psi(O(s)) = \mathbf{O}\Psi(s) .$$

3.7.1. *Stack operations: push and pop*

In this section we consider the basic stack operations, *push* and *pop*. To keep complications to a minimum, two simplifications will be made. In place of a stack containing complex elements, simple strings from a fixed alphabet will be used to model the essential stack structure of linear ordered elements with a first element. The second simplification will be to consider an infinite stack, i.e., no limit to the length of the strings modeling the stack.

Let S be the set of finite-length strings from an alphabet A. Let F/R be the positional role decomposition of Definition 2.11. Let Ψ_F be a faithful representation of F, and let Ψ_R be a representation of R in which the role vectors $\{\mathbf{r}_i\}_{i=0}^{\infty}$ representing the positional roles $\{r_i\}_{i=0}^{\infty}$ are all linearly independent. This means that V_R is an infinite-dimensional space. (The analysis can easily be modified to strings of length no more than n, in which case V_R can be n-dimensional; the finite case just introduces uninteresting complications.) For simplicity, assume that the role vectors span the space V_R and therefore form a basis.

The positional role decomposition has the property that if r_i is unbound, so is r_j if $j > i$. Thus the representations of strings are all in a restricted subspace of V:

Definition 3.8. The *string subset* of V is

$$V_S = \left\{ \sum_i \mathbf{f}_i \otimes \mathbf{r}_i \mid \text{for all } i, \text{ if } \mathbf{f}_i = \mathbf{0}, \text{ then for all } j > i, \mathbf{f}_j = \mathbf{0} \right\}.$$

Theorem 3.9. *The pop operation on S is represented by a linear transformation* **pop** *on V:*

$$\mathbf{pop} : V \to V ; \qquad \sum_i \mathbf{f}_i \otimes \mathbf{r}_i \mapsto \sum_i \mathbf{f}_i \otimes \mathbf{r}_{i-1} .$$

The operation push$_a$ on S is represented by an affine transformation **push$_a$** *on V:*

$$\mathbf{push_a} : V \to V ; \qquad \sum_i \mathbf{f}_i \otimes \mathbf{r}_i \mapsto \mathbf{a} \otimes \mathbf{r}_0 + \sum_i \mathbf{f}_i \otimes \mathbf{r}_{i+1} .$$

Both **pop** *and* **push$_a$** *map V_S into V_S, for all $\mathbf{a} \neq \mathbf{0}$.*

Proof. First note that the definitions of **pop** and **push** given in the theorem are adequate because every vector in $V = V_F \otimes V_R$ can be uniquely expressed in the form $\sum_i \mathbf{f}_i \otimes \mathbf{r}_i$ since $\{\mathbf{r}_i\}$ is a basis of V_R. That **pop** is linear and **push** is affine is easily checked.

Suppose s is the string $a_0 a_1 \ldots a_n$ and that the characters have representations $\Psi_F(a_i) = \mathbf{a}_i$. Then

$$\Psi(pop(s)) = \Psi(a_1 a_2 \ldots a_n)$$

$$= \sum_{i=1}^{n} \mathbf{a}_i \otimes \mathbf{r}_{i-1} = \mathbf{pop} \sum_{i=0}^{n} \mathbf{a}_i \otimes \mathbf{r}_i = \mathbf{pop}\,\Psi(s) \,.$$

Thus **pop** is a representation of *pop*. Similarly, **push**$_a$ is a representation of *push*$_a$.

$$\Psi(push_a(s)) = \Psi(aa_0 a_1 \ldots a_n)$$

$$= \mathbf{a} \otimes \mathbf{r}_0 + \sum_{i=0}^{n} \mathbf{a}_i \otimes \mathbf{r}_{i+1}$$

$$= \mathbf{push_a} \sum_{i=0}^{n} \mathbf{a}_i \otimes \mathbf{r}_i = \mathbf{push_a}\,\Psi(s) \,. \qquad \Box$$

3.7.2. *LISP binary tree operations: car, cdr, and cons*

Let S be the set of LISP S-expressions built from a set of atoms A. We define a role decomposition as follows. For the fillers, take $F = A$. A typical role, r_{011011}, is defined as follows. The predicate a/r_{011011} is "the *caddaddr* is the atom a." The roles are indexed by finite bit strings, and correspond to compositions of *car* and *cdr* operations, with 0 indicating *car* and 1 indicating *cdr*. Note that these roles are to be filled only by *atoms*. Thus, for example, the S-expression $s = (a.(b.c))$ contains the bindings $\{a/r_0, b/r_{01}, c/r_{11}\}$; the role r_1 is unbound—not because s has no *cdr*, but because the *cdr* is not an atom. The role indexed by the empty string ε is special: the predicate a/r_ε is "is the atom a."

This decomposition is faithful and has single-valued roles. If objects like circular lists are considered valid S-expressions, then the decomposition is not finite.

This role decomposition has the property that if r_x is bound, then r_{yx} is unbound, where yx is the concatenation of the bit strings y and x. In particular, if r_ε is bound, no other role can be; this is exactly the case for atoms. Lists are S-expressions for which the *cdr* is never a non-nil atom, at all levels of imbedding; in other words, for all bit strings x, r_{1x} is unbound or bound to *nil*.

Let Ψ_R map each r_x into a corresponding vector $\mathbf{r}_x$ in a basis of an infinite-dimensional vector space V_R. Let Ψ_F be a faithful representation of $F = A$ in V_F, and let $\mathbf{nil} := \Psi_F(nil)$. Now we investigate the properties of the induced tensor product representation Ψ.

Definition 3.10. The *atomic subspace* of V is

$$V_a = \{\mathbf{f} \otimes \mathbf{r}_\varepsilon \mid \mathbf{f} \in V_F\} = V_F \otimes \mathrm{span}(\{\mathbf{r}_\varepsilon\}) \,.$$

The *non-atomic subspace* of V is

$$V_{na} = \left\{ \sum_{x \neq \varepsilon} \mathbf{f}_x \otimes \mathbf{r}_x \,|\, \mathbf{f}_x \in V_F \right\} = V_F \otimes \mathrm{span}(\{\mathbf{r}_x \,|\, x \neq \varepsilon\}) \,.$$

The *S-subset* of V is

$$V_S = \left\{ \sum_x \mathbf{f}_x \otimes \mathbf{r}_x \,|\, \text{for all } x, \text{ if } \mathbf{f}_x = \mathbf{0}, \text{ then for all } y, \, \mathbf{f}_{yx} = \mathbf{0} \right\} \,.$$

The *list subset* of V is

$$V_l = \left\{ \sum_x \mathbf{f}_x \otimes \mathbf{r}_x \in V_S \,|\, \text{for all } x, \mathbf{f}_{1x} \neq \mathbf{0} \Rightarrow \mathbf{f}_{1x} = \mathbf{nil} \right\} \,.$$

Note that V_S is not closed under vector addition. For example, $\Psi((a)) + \Psi(((b)))$ corresponds to a mixture of two list structures; it possesses the bindings $\{a/r_0, b/r_{00}\}$, violating the condition defining V_S. Thus V_S is not a vector space. The same example also shows that V_l is not a vector space.

Now we are ready for representations of the operators *car*, *cdr*, and *cons*.

Definition 3.11. Define two linear transformations $\mathbf{T}_0$ and $\mathbf{T}_1$ on V_R by the following actions on the basis $\{\mathbf{r}_x\}$:

$$\mathbf{T}_0 : V_R \rightarrow V_R ; \qquad \mathbf{r}_{x0} \mapsto \mathbf{r}_x ; \quad \mathbf{r}_{x1} \mapsto \mathbf{0} ; \quad \mathbf{r}_\varepsilon \mapsto \mathbf{0}$$

$$\mathbf{T}_1 : V_R \rightarrow V_R ; \qquad \mathbf{r}_{x1} \mapsto \mathbf{r}_x ; \quad \mathbf{r}_{x0} \mapsto \mathbf{0} ; \quad \mathbf{r}_\varepsilon \mapsto \mathbf{0}$$

Theorem 3.12. *The following linear transformations on V are representations of the operators car and cdr:*

$$\mathbf{car} : \sum_x \mathbf{f}_x \otimes \mathbf{r}_x \mapsto \sum_x \mathbf{f}_x \otimes \mathbf{T}_0 \mathbf{r}_x \,, \qquad \mathbf{cdr} : \sum_x \mathbf{f}_x \otimes \mathbf{r}_x \mapsto \sum_x \mathbf{f}_x \otimes \mathbf{T}_1 \mathbf{r}_x \,.$$

Proof. The representation of an *S*-expression s can be written

$$\Psi(s) = \sum_y \mathbf{f}_y \otimes \mathbf{r}_y = \mathbf{f}_\varepsilon \otimes \mathbf{r}_\varepsilon + \sum_x \mathbf{f}_{x0} \otimes \mathbf{r}_{x0} + \sum_x \mathbf{f}_{x1} \otimes \mathbf{r}_{x1} \,.$$

Now $f_{x0} = cxr(car(s))$, where cxr denotes the composition of *cars* and *cdrs* corresponding to the bit string x. So if $t = car(s)$, then $f_{x0} = cxr(t)$. Thus the filler of r_{x0} in s is the filler of r_x in $t = car(s)$. Conversely, any filler of r_x in t is a filler of r_{x0} in s. Thus the representation of $car(s)$ is

$$\Psi(car(s)) = \sum_x \mathbf{f}_{x0} \otimes \mathbf{r}_x$$

$$= \mathbf{car}\left[\mathbf{f}_\varepsilon \otimes \mathbf{r}_\varepsilon + \sum_x \mathbf{f}_{x0} \otimes \mathbf{r}_{x0} + \sum_x \mathbf{f}_{x1} \otimes \mathbf{r}_{x1} \right] = \mathbf{car}\Psi(s) \,.$$

This shows that **car** represents *car*. By replaying this argument with *car* replaced by *cdr* and with 0 and 1 interchanged, we see that **cdr** represents *cdr*. The linearity of **car** and **cdr** are immediate consequences of the linearity of $\mathbf{T}_0$ and $\mathbf{T}_1$. $\square$

Remark. The operators **car** and **cdr** treat **nil** like all other atoms: they map it to **0**. This corresponds to the *car* and *cdr* of all atoms, including *nil*, being *undefined*. If *car* and *cdr* are defined to be *undefined* on all non-nil atoms, but to take *nil* to *nil*, then the above definitions of **car** and **cdr** have to be changed if they are to represent *car* and *cdr*: the definitions must include the *ad hoc* stipulation that $\mathbf{nil} \otimes \mathbf{r}_\varepsilon$ is mapped to itself, while $\mathbf{a} \otimes \mathbf{r}_\varepsilon$ is mapped to **0** for all vectors **a** representing non-nil atoms. This does not destroy the linearity of **car** and **cdr** as long as the vector **nil** is linearly independent of the representations of all non-nil atoms. It does however destroy the property that $\mathbf{f} \otimes \mathbf{r} \mapsto \mathbf{f} \otimes \mathbf{Tr}$, where the transformation of the role is independent of its filler.

Theorem 3.13. *Let $\mathbf{u}_0$ and $\mathbf{u}_1$ be two vectors in V. Then there is a unique vector* **v** *in V_{na} such that*

$$\mathbf{car}\ \mathbf{v} = \mathbf{u}_0\ ,$$

$$\mathbf{cdr}\ \mathbf{v} = \mathbf{u}_1\ .$$

Define

$$\mathbf{cons} : V \times V \to V_{na}\ ; \qquad (\mathbf{u}_0, \mathbf{u}_1) \mapsto \mathbf{v}\ .$$

Then this function is:

$$\mathbf{cons} : \left(\sum_x \mathbf{f}_x \otimes \mathbf{r}_x, \sum_y \mathbf{f}'_y \otimes \mathbf{r}_y \right) \mapsto \sum_x \mathbf{f}_x \otimes \mathbf{r}_{x0} + \sum_y \mathbf{f}'_y \otimes \mathbf{r}_{y1}\ .$$

cons *is a representation of the cons function on S.*

Proof. Let

$$\mathbf{u}_0 = \sum_x \mathbf{f}_x \otimes \mathbf{r}_x\ ,$$

$$\mathbf{u}_1 = \sum_y \mathbf{f}'_y \otimes \mathbf{r}_y\ ,$$

$$\mathbf{v} = \sum_x \mathbf{f}_x \otimes \mathbf{r}_{x0} + \sum_y \mathbf{f}'_y \otimes \mathbf{r}_{y1}\ .$$

Then

$$\mathbf{car}\ \mathbf{v} = \mathbf{car}\left[\sum_x \mathbf{f}_x \otimes \mathbf{r}_{x0} + \sum_y \mathbf{f}'_y \otimes \mathbf{r}_{y1}\right] = \sum_x \mathbf{f}_x \otimes \mathbf{r}_x = \mathbf{u}_0$$

and

$$\mathbf{cdr}\ \mathbf{v} = \mathbf{cdr}\left[\sum_x \mathbf{f}_x \otimes \mathbf{r}_{x0} + \sum_y \mathbf{f}'_y \otimes \mathbf{r}_{y1}\right] = \sum_y \mathbf{f}'_y \otimes \mathbf{r}_y = \mathbf{u}_1\ .$$

Furthermore, $\mathbf{v} \in V_{na}$ so $\mathbf{v}$ satisfies the required conditions. These conditions completely determine $\mathbf{v}$: the **car** condition determines the fillers of all $\{r_{x0}\}$, the **cdr** condition determines the fillers of all $\{r_{x1}\}$, and the condition that $\mathbf{v}$ be in V_{na} implies that the only remaining role, r_ε, must be unfilled.

Since **car** and **cdr** represent *car* and *cdr*, it follows that **cons** represents *cons*. To see this, let

$$s = cons(s_0, s_1)\ ,$$

$$\mathbf{u}_0 = \Psi(s_0)\ ,$$

$$\mathbf{u}_1 = \Psi(s_1)\ .$$

Then, since **car** represents *car*, and $car(s) = s_0$,

$$\mathbf{car}\ \Psi(s) = \Psi(car(s)) = \Psi(s_0) = \mathbf{u}_0$$

and similarly

$$\mathbf{cdr}\ \Psi(s) = \mathbf{u}_1\ .$$

By the previous part of the proof, this implies that

$$\Psi(s) = \mathbf{cons}(\mathbf{u}_0, \mathbf{u}_1)\ .$$

In other words,

$$\Psi(cons(s_0, s_1)) = \mathbf{cons}(\Psi(s_0), \Psi(s_1))\ .$$

Thus **cons** represents *cons*. □

Just as complex structures in S can be constructed from atoms by successive applications of *cons*, so the tensor product representation of these items can similarly be constructed by successive applications of **cons** on the vectors representing atoms:

$$\Psi(a) = \Psi_F(a) \otimes \mathbf{r}_\varepsilon .$$

Using **cons** to build up complex representations from simpler ones allows us to exploit the recursive role decomposition of S provided by car and cdr.

The analysis of strings in Section 3.7.1 can be viewed as a subset of this analysis of S-expressions. The alphabet is identified with the set of atoms, and the ith positional role r_i of the string is identified with r_{0i_u}, where i_u is the unary representation of i: $i_u = 11\ldots1$ (i times). The operator pop becomes cdr and $push_a(s)$ becomes $cons(a, s)$.

As emphasized in the introduction, the primary goal of this research is representations of structured data that can support effective massively parallel processing. As an example, with the representation of binary trees discussed here, it is possible to determine in one operation whether the atom a appears anywhere in the tree; as pointed out in Section 3.1, the unbinding operations can be performed with respect to fillers as well as roles, and with a simple linear unbinding operation we can compute what role is filled by a. (As mentioned in Section 3.1, if there are multiple roles filled by a, the pattern computed will be the superposition of the vectors representing those roles).[7]

3.7.3. *Recursive construction of tensor product representations*

Related to recursive decomposition is the recursive construction of tensor product representations. This occurs when the fillers or roles are themselves structures that are decomposed by a new role decomposition. In other words, having decomposed S in terms of F and R, we now take F or R as a new S' and decompose it in terms of new fillers F' and roles R'. Consider the case of decomposition of R. If the role decomposition of R is F'/R', then the binding f/r is itself a set of bindings $f/(f'/r')$. The tensor product representation of such a finer-grained binding is then

$$\mathbf{f} \otimes (\mathbf{f}' \otimes \mathbf{r}') .$$

In this case we are led to third-order (or, by further recursion, higher-order) tensor products, that is, to tensors of rank three or higher. The binding units can be interpreted as representing third- (or higher-) order conjunctions of features.

This recursive structure is just what we see in the Rumelhart and McClelland [33] past-tense learning model. Here the original role decomposition of phonetic strings is the 1-neighbor context decomposition. Each role r_{x_y} is itself

---

[7] Determining whether a tree contains a certain subtree (rather than a certain atom) can also be done in a single operation, if the role vectors are chosen in an appropriately recursive fashion; however this requires further development of the analysis that goes beyond the scope of this paper.

a structured object, whose structure is determined by the pair (x, y). These pairs can be decomposed by the right-neighbor role decomposition, in which x fills the role *has right neighbor y*, $r'_{\_y}$. Thus the binding i/r_{w_d} (the vowel in *weed*) becomes $i/(w/r'_{\_d})$ and the final representation is the third-order tensor product

$$\mathbf{i} \otimes \mathbf{w} \otimes \mathbf{r}'_{\_d} \,.$$

In fact, in this model, this is just $\mathbf{i} \otimes \mathbf{w} \otimes \mathbf{d}$, since the role vector $\mathbf{r}'_{\_d}$ is just $\mathbf{d}$. Equivalently, we can take the more naturally ordered product $\mathbf{w} \otimes \bar{\mathbf{i}} \otimes \mathbf{d}$ as the representation of the subsequence *wid*. (This same result could have been arrived at through other routes, e.g., a left-neighbor decomposition of the 1-neighbor contextual roles.)

At this point we can now consider whether it would not have been better to view a structure not as a set of roles and fillers, but rather as a set of constituents engaged in certain mutual *relations*. The letter sequence *abc*, e.g., could be viewed as the constituents *a*, *b*, and *c* engaged in the relations *left-of(a, b)* and *left-of(b, c)*. This could be used to construct a tensor product representation in which *left-of(a, b)* was represented by the tensor product of three vectors representing *left-of*, *a* and *b*.

This variation of the role/filler construction adopted above has certain advantages, but in the end produces a representation which is just a special case of the role/filler construction. As we have just seen, using contextual roles, we can view *abc* as having roles *left_of_b*, *left_of_c* filled, respectively, by *a* and *b*. Then, considering the roles in turn as structures, we view *left_of_b* as having a subrole *left_of* filled by *b*. Then the recursive role/filler construction leads to a representation of *a/left_of_b* which is the tensor product of the three vectors representing *left_of*, *b* and *a*; this representation is equivalent to that of *left_of(a, b)*.

Essentially, applying the role/filler construction recursively using contextual roles amounts to a standard trick from mathematical logic for reducing functions and relations taking multiple arguments—e.g., the two-place relation *left_of*—to nested functions and relations taking only one argument—e.g., the one-place relation *left_of_b* constructed from the one-place function *left_of*: *left_of(a, b) = left_of_b(a)*; *left_of_b = left_of(b)*. In this sense, structural decomposition via multiple-argument functions and relations can be seen as syntactic sugar for certain kinds of recursive filler/role decompositions.

3.8. Storage of structured data in connectionist memories

One of the primary uses of connectionist representations is as objects of associations in associative memories: associative memories are connectionist-implemented mappings from a vector representing a cue to a vector representing the retrieved item. Because of its mathematical simplicity it is possible to analyze the use of tensor product representations in such memories. Here I analyze the case of pair association since it is simpler than the content-addressed auto-association case which is perhaps a purer example of connectionist "memory" [30].

We start with the simplest possible case.

Theorem 3.14. *Suppose $\Psi_{F/R}$ is a tensor product representation of S induced by a decomposition with single-valued roles, with representations of fillers and roles in which all filler vectors are mutually orthogonal as are all role vectors. Let $\{s^{(k)}\}$ be a subset of S, and let the vectors representing these structures, $\{\mathbf{s}^{(k)}\}$, be associated in a connectionist network using the Hebb rule with the patterns $\{\mathbf{t}^{(k)}\}$. Then if the structures $\{s^{(k)}\}$ share no common fillers (i.e., for each role, all structures have different fillers), the associator will function perfectly; otherwise there will be cross-talk that is monotonic in the degree of shared fillers. In particular, the output associated with $s^{(l)}$ is proportional to*

$$\mathbf{t}^{(l)} + \sum_{k \neq l} \mu_{lk} \mathbf{t}^{(k)}$$

where

$$\mu_{lk} = \frac{\displaystyle\sum_{i : f_i^{(l)} = f_i^{(k)}} \|\mathbf{f}_i^{(l)}\|^2 \|\mathbf{r}_i\|^2}{\displaystyle\sum_i \|\mathbf{f}_i^{(l)}\|^2 \|\mathbf{r}_i\|^2} .$$

Proof. The Hebbian weights are

$$\mathbf{W} = \sum_k \mathbf{t}^{(k)} \mathbf{s}^{(k)\mathrm{T}} .$$

Thus the output generated from the input representing $s^{(l)}$ is:

$$\mathbf{W}\mathbf{s}^{(l)} = \sum_k \mathbf{t}^{(k)} \mathbf{s}^{(k)\mathrm{T}} \mathbf{s}^{(l)}$$

$$= \sum_k \mathbf{t}^{(k)} \left[\sum_i \mathbf{f}_i^{(k)} \otimes \mathbf{r}_i \right] \cdot \left[\sum_j \mathbf{f}_j^{(l)} \otimes \mathbf{r}_j \right]$$

$$= \sum_k \mathbf{t}^{(k)} \sum_i \sum_j (\mathbf{f}_i^{(k)} \cdot \mathbf{f}_j^{(l)})(\mathbf{r}_i \cdot \mathbf{r}_j)$$

$$= \sum_k \mathbf{t}^{(k)} \sum_i \sum_j (\delta_{\mathbf{f}_i^{(k)}, \mathbf{f}_j^{(l)}} \|\mathbf{f}_i^{(k)}\|^2)(\delta_{ij} \|\mathbf{r}_i\|^2)$$

$$= \sum_k \mathbf{t}^{(k)} \sum_i \delta_{\mathbf{f}_i^{(k)}, \mathbf{f}_i^{(l)}} \|\mathbf{f}_i^{(k)}\|^2 \|\mathbf{r}_i\|^2$$

$$= \left[\sum_i \|\mathbf{f}_i^{(l)}\|^2 \|\mathbf{r}_i\|^2 \right] \mathbf{t}^{(l)} + \sum_{k \neq l} \left[\sum_i \|\mathbf{f}_i^{(l)}\|^2 \|\mathbf{r}_i\|^2 \, \delta_{\mathbf{f}_i^{(k)}, \mathbf{f}_i^{(l)}} \right] \mathbf{t}^{(k)} .$$

The first term here is the correct associate $\mathbf{t}^{(l)}$ weighted by a positive coefficient. The second term is a sum of all other (incorrect) associates $\{\mathbf{t}^{(k)}\}_{k \neq l}$, each weighted by a nonnegative coefficient. These coefficients will all vanish if there are no common fillers. Taking the ratio of the coefficient of $\mathbf{t}^{(k)}$ to that of $\mathbf{t}^{(l)}$ gives the desired result. ☐

The Hebb rule is capable of accurately learning associations to patterns that are orthogonal. If the patterns are not necessarily orthogonal but are still linearly independent, the associations can be accurately stored in a connectionist memory using the more complex Widrow–Hoff [49] or delta learning procedure [30]. So the question is, what collections of symbolic structures have linearly independent representations under the tensor product representation? To answer this question, it turns out to be important to define the following concept:

Definition 3.15. Let F/R be a role decomposition of S and let $k \mapsto s^{(k)}$ be a sequence of elements in S. An *annihilator* of $k \mapsto s^{(k)}$ with respect to R/F is a sequence of real numbers $k \mapsto \alpha^{(k)}$, not all zero, such that, for all fillers $f \in F$, and all roles $r \in R$,

$$\sum_{k \,:\, f/r \in \beta(s^{(k)})} \alpha^{(k)} = 0 .$$

For example, consider the sequence of strings (ax, bx, ay, by). With respect to the positional role decomposition, this has annihilator $(+1, -1, -1, +1)$, since for each filler/role binding in $\{a/r_1, b/r_1, x/r_2, y/r_2\}$, the corresponding annihiulator elements are $\{+1, -1\}$, which sum to zero.

Theorem 3.16. *Suppose Ψ is a tensor product representation of the structures S, and that $k \mapsto s^{(k)}$ is a sequence of distinct elements in S. Suppose that the filler vectors $\mathbf{f}$ representing the fillers bound in the elements $\{s^{(k)}\}$ are all linearly independent, and that the same is true of the role vectors $\mathbf{r}$ representing the roles bound in the elements $s^{(k)}$. If $k \mapsto s^{(k)}$ has no annihilator with respect to F/R, then associations to the tensor product representations $\{\Psi(s_i)\}$ can all be simultaneously and accurately stored in a connectionist memory by using the Widrow–Hoff learning rule.*

Proof. Let

$$\Psi(s^{(k)}) = \sum_i \mathbf{f}_i^{(k)} \otimes \mathbf{r}_i .$$

Here we use the same set of roles $\{\mathbf{r}_i\}$ for all structures $\{s^{(k)}\}$; this can always be done provided we allow the filler vector $\mathbf{f}_i^{(k)}$ to equal the zero vector whenever the role $\mathbf{r}_i$ is unbound in structure $s^{(k)}$.

By the remarks immediately preceding Definition 3.15, it is sufficient to show that the patterns $\{\Psi(s^{(k)})\}$ are all linearly independent. Suppose on the contrary that there are coefficients $\{\alpha^{(k)}\}$, not all zero, such that

$$\mathbf{0} = \sum_k \alpha^{(k)} \Psi(s^{(k)})$$

$$= \sum_k \alpha^{(k)} \left[\sum_i \mathbf{f}_i^{(k)} \otimes \mathbf{r}_i \right] = \sum_i \left[\sum_k \alpha^{(k)} \mathbf{f}_i^{(k)} \right] \otimes \mathbf{r}_i .$$

Then, because the role vectors $\{\mathbf{r}_i\}$ are linearly independent, this implies that for all i,

$$\sum_k \alpha^{(k)} \mathbf{f}_i^{(k)} = \mathbf{0} .$$

Now we rewrite this as a sum over all distinct filler vectors:

$$\sum_\gamma \mathbf{f}_\gamma \sum_{k \, : \, \mathbf{f}_i^{(k)} = \mathbf{f}_\gamma} \alpha^{(k)} = \mathbf{0} .$$

But since the filler vectors $\{\mathbf{f}_\gamma\}$ are linearly independent, this implies, for all i and for all γ,

$$\sum_{k \, : \, \mathbf{f}_i^{(k)} = \mathbf{f}_\gamma} \alpha^{(k)} = 0 .$$

This means exactly that $\{\alpha^{(k)}\}$ is an annihilator of the sequence of structures $k \mapsto s^{(k)}$. Since by hypothesis such an annihilator does not exist, it must be that the representations $\{\Psi(s^{(k)})\}$ are linearly independent. $\square$

It was remarked above that the strings $\{ax, bx, ay, by\}$ possess an annihilator with respect to the positional role decomposition. This means that the tensor product representations of these strings are not linearly independent, even under the preceding theorem's assumptions of linearly independent filler and role vectors. They cannot therefore be accurately associated with arbitrary patterns even using the Widrow–Hoff learning rule. On the other hand, it is easy to see that the strings $\{ax, bx, ay\}$ do *not* possess an annihilator; the preceding theorem shows that their tensor product representations can therefore be accurately associated with arbitrary patterns.

3.9. Learning optimal role representations

The tensor product representation is constructed from connectionist representations of fillers and roles. As indicated in Section 2.3.2.3, distributed representation of fillers have been used in many connectionist models for some time; usually, these representations are built from an analysis of the fillers in terms of features relevant for the task being performed. But what about distributed representations of roles? This, a problem raised in [13], becomes a major question in tensor product representation. For many applications, it is easy to imagine task-appropriate features for roles that could serve well as the basis for distributed role representations. For example, Fig. 3 shows a distributed representation of positional roles with the useful property that nearby positions are represented by similar patterns. Algorithms such as back-propagation [31] can also be used to learn role representations for a given task, using a network such as that shown in Fig. 11 and backpropagating through the multiplicative junctions.

It is also possible to analyze the question of distributed representations for roles from a domain-independent perspective. One rather general sense in which a set of role vectors might be considered "optimal" can be characterized as those representations for which fillers can be unbound in a way that minimizes the total error introduced by non-linearly independent role vectors. In [39], I introduce this error measure, give algebraic and geometric characterizations of optimal sets of role vectors, and show how a simple recurrent linear network can perform gradient descent in the error measure to find the optimal vectors. This learning algorithm is an example of a "recirculation algorithm" [14] in which activity cycles in a loop, and the change in a weight w_{ji} from i to j is proportional to the activity at i times the *rate of change* of activity at j. Space does not allow presentation of this analysis here, and the reader is referred to [39] for full detail.

4. Conclusion

The limitations of the results reported here are many. The theoretical analyses of role decompositions, graceful saturation, connectionist representations of symbolic operators and recursive structures, retrieval of tensor product representations in connectionist memories, and optimal role vectors are just beginnings. An analysis is needed of the consequences of throwing away binding units and other means of controlling the potentially prohibitive growth in their number. A further analysis is needed of the possibility of having a value for one variable serve as another variable, without an unbinding of the first variable. The relations between tensor product binding units and connection weights, briefly considered in Section 3.5, need to be pursued. Furthermore, for reasons such as those discussed in [13], it will often happen that for storing representations of structures in content-addressed memories, the tensor product representation alone will be insufficient, and hidden units will need to be added to capture higher-order conjunctions that distinguish different structures from each other; the current framework needs to be extended to adequately treat such cases. Also, the analysis of recursive structures needs to be further developed to ensure that imbedded structures can be effectively processed.

The viability of the tensor product representation has been confirmed in an implemented connectionist model, the tensor product production system (TPPS) [6, 7]. TPPS performs a number of fundamental aspects of symbolic processing, such as condition matching against symbolic structures, variable binding on the condition side and substitution into the action side of productions, conflict resolution, and insertion and deletion of structures. TPPS can be viewed as a reimplementation of Touretzky and Hinton's distributed connectionist production system (DCPS) [46], intended to show that a tensor-product-based system would be simpler from both mathematical and implementation perspectives, and would also perform well.[8]

In summary, the tensor product representation enables truly distributed representations of complex symbolic structures in connectionist systems, in a natural way that generalizes existing representations and is simple enough to permit analyses of a number of properties. Tensor product representations are determined by a number of parameters which can be productively analyzed separately: the role decomposition of the structures being represented, the method for connectionist representation of conjunction, and the connectionist representations of fillers and roles being used. Such conceptual tools for analyzing alternative connectionist representations are necessary if we are to deepen our understanding of the representational component of connectionist modeling. Most importantly, the tensor product framework allows a crucial aspect of symbolic computation, the representation and processing of structured data based on the binding of values to variables, to be incorporated into the connectionist approach in a natural way that adds to the power of connectionist computation without sacrificing its advantages.

ACKNOWLEDGEMENT

This paper attempts to formalize and analyze ideas on distributed representation that have been articulated and exploited in various ways by a number of connectionist researchers. I have benefitted in particular from many ideas of Geoff Hinton, both published and personally communicated. The responsibility for the formulation pursued here is of course entirely my own.

This work has been supported by NSF grants IRI-8609599 and ECE-8617947 to the author, by a

---

[8] In this paper, "variable binding" refers to the creation of an object that links a variable to its value; this can be applied to *implicit* bindings such as that between a letter and the position it occupies in a string, or to *explicit* bindings such as that between a symbol denoting a variable in the condition or action side of a production and a symbol denoting the value of that variable. In implicit bindings, the "variable" (or "role") involved is not usually explicitly represented in a symbolic system by a symbol, but rather is implicit in the datastructures used in the implementation. This needn't be the case, of course; instead of writing a list as (a b c), we *could* use a frame-like structure such as *list*: el_1 = a, el_2 = b, el_3 = c; then the implicit binding of the filler a to its role would become explicit. Explicit variable binding was the primary issue in DCPS and later TPPS.

grant to the author from the Sloan Foundation's computational neuroscience program, and by the Optical Connectionist Machine Program of the NSF Engineering Research Center for Optoelectronic Computing Systems at the University of Colorado at Boulder, supported in large part by NSF grant CDR 8622236.

Many thanks to Géraldine Legendre for crucial support.

REFERENCES

1. J.A. Anderson and G.E. Hinton, Models of information processing in the brain, in: G.E. Hinton and J.A. Anderson, eds., *Parallel Models of Associative Memory* (Erlbaum, Hillsdale, NJ, 1981).
2. M. Derthick, A connectionist architecture for representing and reasoning about structured knowledge, in: *Proceedings Ninth Annual Conference of the Cognitive Science Society*, Seattle, WA (1987).
3. C.P. Dolan, Tensor manipulation networks: Connectionist and symbolic approaches to comprehension, learning, and planning, AI Lab Tech. Rept., University of California, Los Angeles, CA (1989).
4. C.P. Dolan and M.G. Dyer, Symbolic schemata, role binding, and the evolution of structure in connectionist memories, in: *Proceedings First International Conference on Neural Networks*, San Diego, CA (1987).
5. C.P. Dolan and M.G. Dyer, Parallel retrieval of conceptual knowledge, in: D. Touretzky, G.E. Hinton and T.J. Sejnowski, eds., *Proceedings Connectionist Models Summer School* (Morgan Kaufmann, Los Altos, CA, 1988).
6. C.P. Dolan and P. Smolensky, Implementing a connectionist production system using tensor products, in: D.Touretzky, G.E. Hinton and T.J. Sejnowski, eds., *Proceedings Connectionist Models Summer School* (Morgan Kaufmann, Los Altos, CA, 1988).
7. C.P. Dolan and P. Smolensky, Tensor product production system: A modular architecture and representation, *Connection Sci.* **1** (1989) 53–68.
8. M. Fanty, Context-free parsing in connectionist networks, Tech. Rept. 174, Department of Computer Science, University of Rochester, Rochester, NY (1985).
9. J.A. Feldman, Four frames suffice: A provisional model of vision and space, *Behav. Brain Sci.* **8** (1985) 265–289.
10. J.A. Feldman, Neural representation of conceptual knowledge, Tech. Rept. 189, Department of Computer Science, University of Rochester, Rochester, NY (1986).
11. J.A. Fodor and Z.W. Pylyshyn, Connectionism and cognitive architecture: A critical analysis, *Cognition* **28** (1988) 3–71.
12. G.E. Hinton, A parallel computation that assigns canonical object-based frames of reference, in: *Proceedings IJCAI-81*, Vancouver, BC (1981).
13. G.E. Hinton, Implementing semantic networks in parallel hardware, in: G.E. Hinton and J.A. Anderson, eds., *Parallel Models of Associative Memory* (Erlbaum, Hillsdale, NJ, 1981).
14. G.E. Hinton and J.L. McClelland, Learning representations by recirculation, in: D.Z. Anderson, ed., *Neural Information Processing Systems* (American Institute of Physics, New York, 1988).
15. G.E. Hinton, J.L. McClelland and D.E. Rumelhart, Distributed representations, in: J.L. McClelland, D.E. Rumelhart and the PDP Research Group, eds., *Parallel Distributed Processing: Explorations in the Microstructure of Cognition* **2**: *Psychological and Biological Models* (MIT Press/Bradford Books, Cambridge, MA, 1986).
16. M.I. Jordan, An introduction to linear algebra in parallel distributed processing, in: D.E. Rumelhart, J.L. McClelland and the PDP Research Group, eds., *Parallel Distributed Processing: Explorations in the Microstructure of Cognition* **1**: *Foundations* (MIT Press/Bradford Books, Cambridge, MA, 1986).

17. J. Lachter and T.G. Bever, The relation between linguistic structure and associative theories of language learning: A constructive critique of some connectionist learning models, *Cognition* **28** (1988) 195–247.
18. Y. Le Cun, C.C. Galland and G.E. Hinton, GEMINI: Gradient estimation through matrix inversion after noise injection, in: D.S. Touretzky, ed., *Advances in Neural Information Processing Systems* **1** (Morgan Kaufmann, San Mateo, CA, 1989).
19. L.H. Loomis and S. Sternberg, *Advanced Calculus* (Addison-Wesley, Reading, MA, 1968) 305–320.
20. J.L. McClelland, The programmable blackboard model of reading, in: J.L. McClelland, D.E. Rumelhart and the PDP Research Group, eds., *Parallel Distributed Processing: Explorations in the Microstructure of Cognition* **2**: *Psychological and Biological Models* (MIT Press/ Bradford Books, Cambridge, MA, 1986).
21. J.L. McClelland and J.L. Elman, Interactive processes in speech perception: The TRACE model, in: J.L. McClelland, D.E. Rumelhart and the PDP Research Group, eds., *Parallel Distributed Processing: Explorations in the Microstructure of Cognition* **2**: *Psychological and Biological Models* (MIT Press/Bradford Books, Cambridge, MA, 1986).
22. J.L. McClelland and A.H. Kawamoto, Mechanisms of sentence processing: Assigning roles to constituents, in: J.L. McClelland, D.E. Rumelhart and the PDP Research Group, eds., *Parallel Distributed Processing: Explorations in the Microstructure of Cognition* **2**: *Psychological and Biological Models* (MIT Press/Bradford Books, Cambridge, MA, 1986).
23. J.L. McClelland and D.E. Rumelhart, An interactive activation model of context effects in letter perception, Part 1: An account of the basic findings, *Psychol. Rev.* **88** (1981) 375–407.
24. J.L. McClelland, D.E. Rumelhart and the PDP Research Group, eds., *Parallel Distributed Processing: Explorations in the Microstructure of Cognition* **2**: *Psychological and Biological Models* (MIT Press/Bradford Books, Cambridge, MA, 1986).
25. M.C. Mozer, *The Perception of Multiple Objects: A Parallel, Distributed Processing Approach* (MIT Press/Bradford Books, Cambridge, MA, 1990).
26. E. Nelson, *Tensor Analysis* (Princeton University Press, Princeton, NJ, 1967).
27. S. Pinker and A. Prince, On language and connectionism: Analysis of a parallel distributed processing model of language acquisition, *Cognition* **28** (1988) 73–193.
28. A. Prince and S. Pinker, Wickelphone ambiguity, *Cognition* **30** (1988) 189–190.
29. M.S. Riley and P. Smolensky, A parallel model of (sequential) problem solving, in: *Proceedings Sixth Annual Conference of the Cognitive Science Society*, Boulder CO (1984).
30. D.E. Rumelhart, G.E. Hinton and J.L. McClelland, A general framework for parallel distributed processing, in: D.E. Rumelhart, J.L. McClelland and the PDP Research Group, eds., *Parallel Distributed Processing: Explorations in the Microstructure of Cognition* **1**: *Foundations* (MIT Press/Bradford Books, Cambridge, MA, 1986).
31. D.E. Rumelhart, G.E. Hinton and R.J. Williams, Learning internal representations by error propagation, in: D.E. Rumelhart, J.L. McClelland and the PDP Research Group, eds., *Parallel Distributed Processing: Explorations in the Microstructure of Cognition* **1**: *Foundations* (MIT Press/Bradford Books, Cambridge, MA, 1986).
32. D.E. Rumelhart and J.L. McClelland, An interactive activation model of context effects in letter perception, Part 2: The contextual enhancement effect and some tests and extensions of the model, *Psychol. Rev.* **89** (1982) 60–94.
33. D.E. Rumelhart and J.L. McClelland, On learning the past tenses of English verbs, in: J.L. McClelland, D.E. Rumelhart and the PDP Research Group, eds., *Parallel Distributed Processing: Explorations in the Microstructure of Cognition* **2**: *Psychological and Biological Models* (MIT Press/Bradford Books, Cambridge, MA, 1986).
34. D.E. Rumelhart, J.L. McClelland and the PDP Research Group, eds., *Parallel Distributed Processing: Explorations in the Microstructure of Cognition* **1**: *Foundations* (MIT Press/ Bradford Books, Cambridge, MA, 1986).

35. T.J. Sejnowski and C.R. Rosenberg, Parallel networks that learn to pronounce English text, *Complex Syst.* **1** (1987) 145–168.

36. P. Smolensky, Information processing in dynamical systems: Foundations of harmony theory, in: D.E. Rumelhart, J.L. McClelland, and the PDP Research Group, eds., *Parallel Distributed Processing: Explorations in the Microstructure of Cognition* **1**: *Foundations* (MIT Press/ Bradford Books, Cambridge, MA, 1986).

37. P. Smolensky, Neural and conceptual interpretations of parallel distributed processing models, in: J.L. McClelland, D.E. Rumelhart and the PDP Research Group, eds., *Parallel Distributed Processing: Explorations in the Microstructure of Cognition* **2**: *Psychological and Biological Models* (MIT Press/Bradford Books, Cambridge, MA, 1986).

38. P. Smolensky, Connectionist AI, symbolic AI, and the brain, *AI Rev.* **1** (1987) 95–109. Special Issue on the Foundations of AI.

39. P. Smolensky, On variable binding and the representation of symbolic structures in connectionist systems, Tech. Rept. CU-CS-355-87, Department of Computer Science, University of Colorado at Boulder, CO (1987).

40. P. Smolensky, The constituent structure of connectionist mental states: A reply to Fodor and Pylyshyn, *Southern J. Philos.* **26**, Supplement (1987) 137–163.

41. P. Smolensky, On the proper treatment of connectionism, *Behav. Brain Sci.* **11** (1988) 1–23.

42. P. Smolensky, Connectionism, constituency, and the language of thought, in: B. Loewer and G. Rey, eds., *Fodor and His Critics* (Blackwell, Oxford, 1991).

43. P. Smolensky and M.C. Mozer, *Lectures on Connectionist Cognitive Modeling* (Erlbaum, Hillsdale, NJ, to appear).

44. D.S. Touretzky BoltzCONS: Reconciling connectionism with the recursive nature of stacks and trees, in: *Proceedings Eighth Annual Conference of the Cognitive Science Society*, Amherst, MA (1986).

45. D.S. Touretzky and S. Geva, A distributed connectionist representation for concept structures, in: *Proceedings Ninth Annual Conference of the Cognitive Science Society*, Seattle, WA (1987).

46. D.S. Touretzky and G.E. Hinton, Symbols among the neurons: Details of a connectionist inference architecture, in: *Proceedings IJCAI-85*, Los Angeles, CA (1985).

47. A.M. Treisman and H. Schmidt, Illusory conjunctions in the perception of objects, *Cognitive Psychol.* **14** (1982) 107–141.

48. F.W. Warner, *Foundations of Differentiable Manifolds and Lie Groups* (Scott, Foresman, Glenview, IL, 1971) 54–62.

49. G. Widrow and M.E. Hoff, Adaptive switching circuits, in: *Institute of Radio Engineers, Western Electronic Show and Convention, Convention Record, Part 4* (1960) 96–104.

50. D. Willshaw, Holography, associative memory, and inductive generalization, in: G.E. Hinton and J.A. Anderson, eds., *Parallel Models of Associative Memory* (Erlbaum, Hillsdale, NJ, 1981).

Learning and Applying Contextual Constraints in Sentence Comprehension*

Mark F. St. John** and James L. McClelland

Department of Psychology, Carnegie-Mellon University, Pittsburgh, PA 15213, USA

ABSTRACT

A parallel distributed processing model is described that learns to comprehend single clause sentences. Specifically, it assigns thematic roles to sentence constituents, disambiguates ambiguous words, instantiates vague words, and elaborates implied roles. The sentences are pre-segmented into constituent phrases. Each constituent is processed in turn to update an evolving representation of the event described by the sentence. The model uses the information derived from each constituent to revise its ongoing interpretation of the sentence and to anticipate additional constituents. The network learns to perform these tasks through practice on processing example sentence/event pairs. The learning procedure allows the model to take a statistical approach to solving the bootstrapping problem of learning the syntax and semantics of a language from the same data. The model performs very well on the corpus of sentences on which it was trained, and generalizes to sentences on which it was not trained, but learns slowly.

1. Introduction

The goal of our research has been to develop a model that can learn to convert a simple sentence into a conceptual representation of the event that the sentence describes. Specifically, we have been concerned with the later stages of this process: the conversion of a sequence of sentence constituents, such as noun phrases, into a representation of the event. A number of problems make this process difficult. First, the words of a sentence may be ambiguous or vague. In the sentence, "The pitcher threw the ball," each content word is ambiguous. "Pitcher" could either refer to a ball-player or a container;

*The authors would like to thank Geoffrey Hinton, Brian MacWhinney, Andrew Hudson, and the members of the PDP Research Group at Carnegie-Mellon. This research was supported by NSF Grant BNS 86-09729, ONR Contracts N00014-86-G-0146, N00014-86-K-00167, and N00014-86-K-0349, and NIMH Career Development Award MH00385 to the second author.

**Present address: Department of Cognitive Science, University of California at San Diego, La Jolla, CA 92093, USA.

Artificial Intelligence 46 (1990) 217–257
0004-3702/90/$03.50 © 1990 — Elsevier Science Publishers B.V. (North-Holland)

"threw" could either refer to toss or host; and "ball" could refer to a sphere or a dance. How are the appropriate meanings selected so that a single, coherent interpretation of the sentence is produced? Vague words also present difficulties. In the sentences, "The container held the apples" and "The container held the cola," the word "container" refers to two different objects [1]. How does the context affect the interpretation of vague words?

A third problem is the complexity of assigning the correct thematic roles [9] to the objects referred to in a sentence. Consider:

(1) The teacher ate the spaghetti with the busdriver.
(2) The teacher ate the spaghetti with the red sauce.
(3) The busdriver hit the fireman.
(4) The busdriver was hit by the fireman.

In the first two examples, semantics play an important role. In the first sentence, it is the reader's knowledge that busdrivers are people that precludes the reader from deciding the busdriver is to be served as a condiment. Instead, it must be that both he and the teacher are eating the spaghetti. Semantic constraints work conversely in the second sentence. In the third sentence, semantics do not help determine who is the agent and who is the patient. Instead, word order determines the thematic role assignments. The busdriver is the agent because "the busdriver" is the pre-verbal constituent. Finally, in the fourth sentence, the influence of other morphological features can be seen. The passive verb tense and the "by" preposition, in conjunction with the word order, determine that the busdriver is the patient. Thematic role assignment, then, requires the joint consideration of a variety of aspects of the sentence.

A fourth problem for processing sentences is that a sentence may leave some thematic constituents implicit that are nevertheless present in the event. For example in sentences (1) and (2) above, the spaghetti was undoubtedly eaten with forks. Psychological evidence indicates that missing constituents, when strongly related to the action, are inferred and added to the description of the event. McKoon and Ratcliff [23] found, for example, that "hammer" was inferred after subjects read "Bobby pounded the boards together with nails."

Our model of the comprehension process centers on viewing the process as a form of constraint satisfaction. The surface features of a sentence, its particular words and their order and morphology, provide a rich set of constraints on the sentence's meaning. Each feature constrains the meaning in a number of respects. Conjunctions of features, such as word order and passive-voice morphology, provide additional constraints. Together, the constraints lead to a coherent interpretation of the sentence [17]. These constraints are not typically all-or-none. Instead, constraints tend to vary in strength: some are strong and others are relatively weak. An example adapted from Marcus [18] provides an illustration of the competition between constraints.

(1) Which dragon did the knight give the boy?

(2) Which boy did the knight give the dragon?
(3) Which boy did the knight give the sword?
(4) Which boy did the knight give to the sword?

Apparently, in the first two sentences, a weak syntactic constraint makes us prefer the first noun as the patient and the noun after the verb as the recipient. The subtle semantics in the second sentence, that knights don't give boys to dragons, does not override the syntactic constraint for most readers, though it may make the sentence seem ungrammatical to some. In sentence (3), a stronger semantic constraint overrides this syntactic constraint: swords, which are inanimate objects, cannot receive boys. Finally, in the fourth sentence, a stronger syntactic constraint overrides the semantics. It is clear from this example that constraints vary in strength and compete to produce an interpretation of a sentence. A good method for capturing this competition is to assign real-valued strengths to the constraints, and to allow them to compete or cooperate according to their strength.

Parallel distributed processing, or connectionist, models are particularly good for modeling this style of processing. They allow large amounts of information to be processed simultaneously and competitively, and they allow evidence to be weighted on a continuum [20, 22]. A number of researchers have pursued this idea and have built models to apply connectionism to sentence processing [5, 6, 35]. The development of this approach, however, has been retarded because it is difficult to determine exactly what constraints are imposed by each feature or set of features in a sentence. It is even more difficult to determine the appropriate strengths each of these constraints should have. Connectionist learning procedures, however, allow a model to learn the appropriate constraints and assign appropriate strengths to them.

To take advantage of this feature, learning was added to our list of goals. The model is given a sentence as input. From the sentence, the model must produce a representation of the event to which the sentence refers. The actual event that corresponds to the sentence is then used as feedback to train the model. But learning is not without its own problems. Several features of the learning task make learning difficult. One problem is that the environment is probabilistic. On different occasions, a sentence may refer to different events, that is, it may be referentially ambiguous. For example, a sentence like, "The pitcher threw the ball," may refer to either the tossing of a projectile or the hosting of a party. The robust, graded, and incremental character of connectionist learning algorithms leads us to hope that they will be able to cope with the variability in the environment in which they learn.

A second learning problem concerns the difficulty of learning the mapping between the parts of the sentence and the parts of the event [10, 26]. Learning the mapping is sometimes referred to as a boot-strapping problem since the meaning of the content words and significance of the syntax must be acquired from the same set of data. To learn the syntax, it seems necessary to already know the word meanings. Conversely, to learn the word meanings it seems necessary to know how the syntax maps the words onto the event description. The connectionist learning procedure takes a statistical approach to this problem. Through exposure to large numbers of sentences and the events they describe, the mapping between features of the sentences and characteristics of the events will emerge as statistical regularities. For instance, in the long run, the learning procedure should discover the regularity that sentences beginning with "the boy" and containing a transitive verb in the active voice refer to events in which a young, male human participates as an agent. The discovery of the entire ensemble of such regularities provides a joint solution to the problems of learning the syntax and the meanings of words.

Some aspects of these goals have been addressed by our own earlier work [21, 30]. However, these previous models used a cumbersome *a priori* representation of sentences that proved unworkable (see [30] for discussion). Given the recent successes in using connectionist learning procedures to learn internal representations [12, 28], we decided to explore the feasibility of having a network learn its own representation of sentences.

A final characteristic of language comprehension we wanted to capture is sometimes called the principle of immediate update [3, 19, 34]. As each constituent of the sentence is encountered, the interpretation of the entire event is adjusted to reflect the constraints arising from the new constituent in conjunction with the constraints from constituents already encountered. Based on all of the available constraints, the model should try to anticipate upcoming constituents. It should also adjust its interpretation of preceding constituents to reflect each new bit of information. In this way, particular sentence interpretations may gain and lose support throughout the course of processing as each new bit of information is processed. This immediate update should be accomplished while avoiding the difficulty of performing backtracking.

In sum, the model addresses six goals:

- to disambiguate ambiguous words;
- to instantiate vague words;
- to assign thematic roles;
- to elaborate implied roles;
- to learn to perform these tasks;
- to immediately adjust its interpretation as each constituent is processed.

2. Description of the SG Model

2.1. Task

The model's task is to process a single clause sentence without embeddings into a representation of the event it describes. The sentence is presented to the model as a temporal sequence of constituents. A constituent is either a simple noun phrase, a prepositional phrase, or a verb (including the auxiliary verb, if any). The information each of these sentence constituents yields is immediately used as evidence to update the model's internal representation of the entire event. This representation is called the sentence gestalt because all of the information from the sentence is represented together within a single, distribut-ed representation; the model is called the Sentence Gestalt, or SG, model because it contains this representation. This general concept of sentence representation comes from Hinton's pioneering work [11]. From the sentence gestalt, the model can produce, as output, a representation of the event. This event representation consists of a set of pairs. Each pair consists of a thematic role and the concept that fills that role. Together, the pairs describe the event.

2.2. Architecture and processing

The model consists of two parts. One part, the sequential encoder, sequentially processes each constituent to produce the sentence gestalt. The second part is used to produce the output representation from the sentence gestalt.

2.2.1. Producing the sentence gestalt

To process the constituent phrases of a sentence, we adapted an architecture from Jordan [15] that uses the output of previous processing as input on the next iteration (see Fig. 1). Each constituent is processed in turn to update the sentence gestalt. To process a constituent, it is first represented as a pattern of activation over the *current constituent* units. Activation from these units projects to the first hidden unit layer and combines with the activation from the *sentence gestalt* created as the result of processing the previous constituent. The actual implementation of this arrangement is to copy the activation from the *sentence gestalt* to the *previous sentence gestalt* units, and allow activation to feed forward from there. Activation in the hidden layer then creates a new

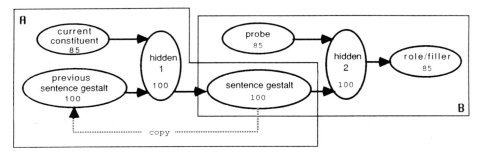

Fig. 1. The architecture of the network. The boxes highlight the functional parts: Area *A* processes the constituents into the sentence gestalt, and Area *B* processes the sentence gestalt into the output representation. The numbers indicate the number of units in each layer.

pattern of activation over the *sentence gestalt* units. The sentence gestalt, therefore, is not a superimposition of each constituent. Rather, each new pattern in the sentence gestalt is computed through two layers of weights and represents the model's new best guess interpretation of the meaning of the sentence.

2.2.2. *Producing the output*

As noted previously, several other models have used a type of sentence gestalt to represent a sentence. McClelland and Kawamoto [21] used units that represented the conjunction of semantic features of the verb with the semantic features of a concept. To encode a sentence, the patterns of activity produced for each verb/concept conjunction were activated in a single pool of units that contained every possible conjunction. St. John and McClelland [30] used a similar conjunctive representation to encode a number of sentences at once. These representations suffer from inefficiency and scale badly because so many units are required to represent all of the conjunctions. The current model's representation is far more efficient.

The model's efficiency comes from making the sentence gestalt a trainable, hidden unit layer. Making the sentence gestalt trainable allows the network to create the primitives it needs to represent the sentence efficiently. Instead of having to represent every possible conjunction, only those conjunctions that are useful will be learned and added to the representation. Further, these primitives do not have to be conjunctions between the verb and a concept. A hidden layer could learn to represent conjunctions between the concepts themselves or other combinations of information if they were useful for solving its task.

Since a layer of hidden units cannot be trained by explicitly specifying its activation values, we invented a way of "decoding" the sentence gestalt into an output layer. Backpropagation can then be used to train the hidden layer. The output layer represents the event as a set of thematic role and filler pairs. For example, the event described by "The pitcher threw the ball" would be represented as the set {agent/pitcher(ball-player), action/threw(toss), patient/ball(sphere)}. The words in parentheses indicate which concepts the ambiguous words correspond to.

The output layer can represent one role/filler pair at a time. To decode a particular role/filler pair, the sentence gestalt is probed with half of the pair, either the role or the filler. Activation from the probe and the *sentence gestalt* combine in the second hidden layer which in turn activates the entire role/filler pair in the output layer. The entire event can be decoded in this way by successively probing with each half of each pair.

When more than one concept can plausibly fill a role, we assume that the correct response is to activate each possible filler to a degree. The degree of activation of the units representing each filler corresponds to the filler's conditional probability of occurring in the given context. The network should learn weights to produce these activations through training. To achieve this goal, we employed an error measure in the learning procedure, cross-entropy [13], that converges on this goal:

$$C = -\sum_j [T_j \log_2(A_j) + (1 - T_j)\log_2(1 - A_j)]$$

where T_j is the target activation and A_j is the output activation of unit j. As with many connectionist learning procedures, the goal is to minimize the error measure or cost-function [13]. The minimum of C occurs at the point in weight space where the activation value of each output unit equals the conditional probability that the unit should be on in the current context. In the model, when the network is probed with a particular role, several of the output units represent the occurrence of a particular filler of that role. When C is at its minimum, the units' activation values represent the conditional probability of the occurrence of that filler, in that role, given the current situation.[1] Note, however, that on any particular training trial, the target of training is one particular event. The minimum of C, then, is defined across the ensemble of training examples the model is shown.

Probing with the filler works similarly. The activation value of each role unit in the output layer represents the conditional probability of the probed filler playing that role in the current situation. In performing gradient descent in C, the network is searching for weights that allow it to match activations to these conditional probabilities.

2.3. Environment and training regime

Training consists of trials in which the network is presented with a sentence and the event it describes. The rationale is that the language learner experiences some event and then hears a sentence about it. The learner processes the sentence and compares the conceptual representation its comprehension mechanism produces to the conceptual representation it obtained from experiencing the event. Discrepancies are used as feedback for the comprehension mechanism. These sentence/event pairs were generated on-line for each training trial. Some pairs are more likely to be generated than others. Over training, these differences in the likelihood of generation translate into differences in training frequency.

The network is trained to generate the event from the sentence as input. To

---

[1] The situation, as defined in the learning procedure, is the combination of the previous sentence gestalt, the current constituent, and the current probe. It would be desirable to define the situation solely in terms of the sequence of sentence constituents. While our results suggest that the sentence gestalt learns to save all the relevant information from earlier constituents, we have no proof that it does.

promote immediate processing, a special training regime is used. After each constituent has been processed, the network is trained to predict the set of role/filler pairs of the entire event. From the first constituent of the sentence, then, the model is forced to try to predict the entire event. This training regime, therefore, assumes that the complete event is available to the learning procedure as soon as sentence processing begins, but it does not assume any special knowledge about which aspects of the event correspond to which sentence constituents. Of course, after processing only the first constituent, the model generally cannot correctly guess the entire event. By forcing it to try, this training procedure requires the model to discover the mapping between constituents and aspects of the event, as it forces the model to extract as much information as possible from each constituent. Consequently, as each new constituent is processed, the model's predictions of the event are refined to reflect the additional evidence it supplies.

2.4. An illustration of processing

An example of how a trained network processes a sentence will help illustrate how the model works. To process the sentence, "The teacher ate the soup," the constituents of the sentence are processed in turn. As each constituent is processed, the network performs a type of pattern completion. The model tries to predict the entire event by augmenting the information supplied by the constituents processed so far with additional information that correlates with the information supplied by the constituents.

With each additional constituent, the model's predictions improve. Early in the sentence, many possible events are consistent with what little is known about the sentence so far. The completion process activates each of these alternatives slightly, according to their support. As more constituents are processed, the additional evidence more strongly supports fewer possible events.

The pattern of activation over the sentence gestalt can be observed directly, and responses to probes can be examined, to see what it is representing after processing each constituent of the sentence (see Fig. 2). After processing the first constituent, "The teacher," of our example sentence, the network assumes the sentence is in the active voice and therefore assigns *teacher* to the agent role. The network also fills in the semantic features of teachers (person, adult, and female) according to its previous experience with teachers. When probed with the action role, the network weakly activates a number of possible actions which the teacher performs. The network similarly makes guesses about the other roles for which it is probed.

When the second constituent, "ate," is processed, the sentence gestalt is refined to represent the new information. In addition to representing both that *teacher* is the agent and that *ate* is the action, the network is able to make better guesses about the other roles. For example, it infers that the patient is

The teacher ate the soup.

Sentence unit	Gestalt Activations #1	#2	#3		Role/Filler Activations #1	#2	#3
1				**agent**			
2				person			
3				adult			
4				male			
5				female			
6				bus driver			
7				teacher			
8				**action**			
9				consumed			
10				ate			
11				gave			
12				threw(host)			
13				drove(motiv.)			
14				**patient**			
15				person			
16				adult			
17				child			
18				female			
19				schoolgirl			
20				thing			
21				food			
22				ball(party)			
23				steak			
24				soup			
25				crackers			

Fig. 2. The evolution of the sentence gestalt during processing. On the left, the activation of part of the sentence gestalt is shown after each sentence constituent has been processed. On the right, the activation of selected output units is shown when the evolving gestalt is probed with each role. The #s correspond to the number of constituents that have been presented to the network at that point. #1 means the network has seen "The teacher;" #2 means it has seen "The teacher ate;" etc. The activations (ranging between 0 and 1) are depicted as the darkened area of each box.

food. Since, in the network's experience, teachers typically eat soup, the network produces activation corresponding to the inference that the food is *soup*. After the third constituent is processed, the network has settled on an interpretation of the sentence. The thematic roles are represented with their appropriate fillers.

2.5. Specifics of the model

2.5.1. *Input representation*

Each sentence constituent can be thought of as a surface role/filler pair. It consists of one unit indicating the surface role of the constituent and one unit representing each word in the constituent. One unit stands for each of 13 verbs, 31 nouns, 4 prepositions, 3 adverbs, and 7 ambiguous words. Two of the ambiguous words have two verb meanings, three have two noun meanings, and two have a verb and a noun meaning. Six of the words are vague terms (e.g. someone, something, and food). For prepositional phrases, the preposition and the noun are each represented by a unit in the input. For the verb constituent, the presence of the auxiliary verb "was" is likewise encoded by a separate unit. Articles are not represented, and nouns are assumed to be singular and definite throughout.

The surface role, or location, of each constituent is coded by four units that represent location respective to the verb: pre-verbal, verbal, first-post-verbal, and n-post-verbal. The first-post-verbal unit is active for the constituent immediately following the verb, and the n-post-verbal unit is active for any constituent occurring after the first-post-verbal constituent. A number of constituents, therefore, may share the n-post-verbal position. The sentence, "The ball was hit by someone with the bat in the park," would be encoded as the following ordered set in which the words in parentheses represent units in the input that are on for each constituent {(pre-verbal, ball), (verbal, was, hit), (first-post-verbal, by, someone), (n-post-verbal, with, bat), (n-post-verbal, in, park)}. Without the surface roles, the network must learn to use the temporal order of the constituents to produce syntactic constraints. Additional simulation has shown that the network can learn the corpus without the surface roles. Interestingly, removing the surface roles did not slow down learning.

2.5.2. *Output representation*

The output has one unit for each of 9 possible thematic roles (e.g., agent, action, patient, instrument) and one unit for each of 45 concepts, including 28 noun concepts, 14 actions, and 3 adverbs. Additionally, there is a unit for the passive voice. Finally, there are 13 "feature" units, such as male, female, and adult. These units are included in the output to allow the demonstration of more subtle effects of constraints on interpretation (see Appendix A for the complete set of roles and concepts). This representation is not meant to be comprehensive. Instead, it is meant to provide a convenient way to train and demonstrate the processing abilities of the network. Any one role/filler pattern, then, consists of two parts. For the role, one of the 9 role units should be active, and for the filler, a unit representing the concept, action, or adverb should be active. If relevant, some of the feature units or the passive voice unit should be active.[2]

2.5.3. *Training environment*

While the sentences often include ambiguous or vague words, the events are always specific and complete: each event consists of a specific action and each

---

[2] A second output layer was included in the simulations. This layer reproduced the sentence constituent that fits with the role/filler pair being probed. Consequently, the model was required to retain the specific words in the sentence as well as their meaning. Since this aspect of the processing does not fit into the context of the current discussion, these units are not discussed further. Additional simulation has shown that this extra demand on the network does not qualitatively affect its performance.

thematic role related to this action is filled by some specific concept. Accordingly, each event occurs in a particular location, and actions requiring an instrument always have a specific instrument.

Sentence/event pairs are created on-line during training from scaffoldings called sentence-frames. The sentence-frames specify which thematic roles and fillers can be used with that action. Each of the 14 actions has a separate sentence-frame. Four additional frames were made to cover passive versions of sentences involving the actions *kissed*, *shot*, *hit*, and *gave*.

To create a sentence/event pair, a sentence-frame is picked at random and then each thematic role is processed in turn. (Appendix B contains a sample sentence-frame.) For example, let's assume that the *Ate* sentence-frame is chosen. Agent is the first role processed. First, a concept to fill the role is selected from the set of concepts that can play the agent role in the *Ate* sentence-frame. This role/filler pair is added to the event description. Since some roles, such as instrument and location, may not be mentioned in the sentence, it is randomly determined, according to a preset probability, whether a role will be included in the sentence. If the role is to be included, a word is chosen to represent the filler in the sentence. Otherwise, the role is left out of the sentence, but it is still included in the event description. Since the agent role must be included in sentences about eating, it is placed in the sentence, and a word is chosen. Assuming *busdriver* is chosen as the filler concept, a word to describe *busdriver* is selected. For example, the word "someone" might be chosen.

Next, the action role is processed. Since the *Ate* sentence-frame is being used, the action must be *ate*. A word to describe *ate* is then chosen: "consumed," for example. Then the patient is chosen. The probabilities of choosing particular patients depend upon what has been selected for the agent and action. Given the selection of *busdriver* as the agent, *steak* is a much more likely patient than *soup*. Let's assume that *steak* is selected, and that the word "steak" is chosen to represent it. In general, by changing the probabilities of selecting specific fillers according to which other fillers have been selected so far, statistical regularities among the fillers will develop across the corpus.

In the same way, the remaining role/filler pairs for the sentence-frame are generated. Assuming only the first three roles are chosen to be included in this sentence, the input sentence will be, "Someone consumed the steak." The event will be the entire set of role/filler pairs {agent/busdriver, action/ate, patient/steak, instrument/knife, location/living-room, etc.}.

In this way, 120 different events can be generated from the set of frames with some being more likely to appear than others. The most frequent event occurs, on average, 5.5 times per 100 trials, but the least frequent event occurs only 9 times per 10,000. The number of words that can be chosen to describe an event and the option to include or eliminate optional constituents from the sentence brings the number of sentence/event pairs to 22,645.

In training the model on this corpus, sentence-frames were picked at random, and sentence/event pairs were generated according to the random procedure described above. No specific sentences or events were set aside to not be trained.

The sentences are limited in complexity because of the limitations of the event representation. Only one filler can be assigned to a role in a particular sentence. Also, all the roles are assumed to belong to the sentence as a whole. Therefore, no embedded clauses or phrases attached to single constituents are possible.

2.5.4. *Training procedure details*

Each training trial consists of first generating a sentence/event pair, and then presenting the sentence to the model for training. The constituents are presented to the model sequentially, one at a time. After the model processes a constituent, the model is probed with each half of each role/filler pair for the entire event. The error produced on each probe is collected and propagated backward through the network (cf. [28]). The weight changes from each sentence trial are added together and used to update the weights after every 60 trials. The learning rate, ε, was set to 0.0005, and momentum was set to 0.9. No attempt was made to optimize these values, so it is likely that learning time could be improved by tuning these parameters.

3. Results

3.1. Overall performance

First, we will assess the model's ability to comprehend sentences generally. Then we will examine the model's ability to fulfill our specific processing goals, and we will examine the development of the model's performance across training trials. Finally, we will discuss the model's ability to generalize.

Once the model was able to process correctly both active and passive sentences, the simulation was stopped and evaluated. Correct processing was defined as activating the correct units more strongly than the incorrect units. After 330,000 random sentence trials, the model began correctly processing the passive sentences in the corpus.

A set of 100 test sentence/event pairs were generated randomly from the corpus. These sentence/event pairs were generated in the same way the training sentences were generated except that they were generated without regard to their frequency during training, so seldom practiced pairs were as likely to appear in the test set as frequently practiced pairs. Of these pairs, 45 were set aside for separate analysis because they were ambiguous: at least two different interpretations could be derived from each (e.g. Someone ate something). Of the remaining sentence/event pairs, every sentence contained at least one vague or ambiguous word, yet each had only one interpretation. These unambiguous sentence/event pairs were tested by first allowing the model to process all of the constituents of the sentence. Then the model was probed with each half of each constituent that was mentioned in the sentence. The output produced in response to each probe was compared to the target output. Figure 3 presents a histogram of the results.

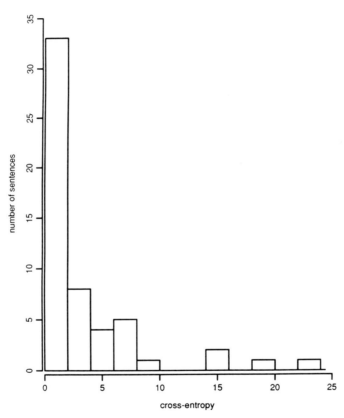

Fig. 3. Histogram of the cross-entropy error for random sentences after 330,000 sentence trials. The sentences were drawn randomly from the corpus without regard to their frequency. A cross-entropy measure of between 0 and 10 results from sentences that are processed almost perfectly. Only small errors occur when an output unit should be completely activate (with a value of 1), but only obtains an activation of 0.7 or 0.8, or when a unit should have an activation of 0, but has an activation of 0.1 or 0.2. Cross-entropy errors of between 15 and 20 occur when one of the role/filler pairs is incorrect. For example, if *teacher* were supposed to be the agent, but the network activates *busdriver*, an error of about 15 would result.

For these unambiguous sentences, the cross-entropy, summed over constituents, averaged 3.9 per sentence. Another measure of performance is the number of times an output unit that should be on is less active than an output unit that should be off. The idea behind this measure is that as long as the correct unit within any set, such as people or gender, is the most active, it can win a competition with the other units in that set. Checking that all of the correct units are more active than any of the incorrect units is a quick, and conservative, way of calculating this measure. An incorrect unit was more active in 14 out of the 1710 possible cases, or on 0.8% of the opportunities.

The 14 errors were distributed over 8 of the 55 sentences. In 5 of the 8 sentences, the error involved the incorrect instantiation of the specific concept, or a feature of that concept, referred to by a vague word. Two other errors involved the incorrect activation of the concept representing a nonvague word. In each case, the incorrect concept was similar to the correct concept. Therefore, errors were not random; they involved the misactivation of a similar concept or the misactivation of a feature of a similar concept. The errors in the remaining sentence involved the incorrect assignment of thematic roles in a passive, reversible sentence: "Someone hit the pitcher" (see the section on learning for a discussion of this problem).

Additional practice, of course, improved the model's performance. Improvement is slow, however, because the sentences processed incorrectly are relatively rare. After a total of 630,000 trials, the number of sentences having a cross-entropy higher than 15 dropped from 3 to 1. The number of errors dropped from 14 to 11.

3.2. Performance on specific tasks

Our specific interest was to develop a processor that could correctly perform several important language comprehension tasks. Five typical sentences were drawn from the corpus to test each processing task. The categories and one example sentence for each are presented in Table 1. The parentheses denote the implicit, to be inferred, role.

Table 1
Task categories

Category	Example
Role assignment	
Active semantic	The schoolgirl stirred the kool-aid with a spoon.
Active syntactic	The busdriver gave the rose to the teacher.
Passive semantic	The ball was hit by the pitcher.
Passive syntactic	The busdriver was given the rose by the teacher.
Word ambiguity	The pitcher hit the bat with the bat.
Concept instantiation	The teacher kissed someone.
Role elaboration	The teacher ate the soup (with a spoon).

The first category involves role assignment. The category was divided into four sub-categories based on the type of information available to help assign the correct thematic roles to constituents. Sentences in the active semantic group contain semantic information that can help assign roles. In the example from Table 1, of the concepts referred to in the sentence, only the schoolgirl can play the role of an agent of stirring. The network can therefore use that semantic information to assign schoolgirl to the agent role. Similarly, kool-aid is something that can be stirred, but cannot stir or be used to stir something else. After each sentence was processed, the sentence gestalt was probed with the filler half of each role/filler pair. The network then had to complete the pair by filling in the correct thematic role. For each pair, in each sentence, the unit representing the correct role was the most active. Sentences in the passive semantic category are processed equally well. Of course the semantic knowledge necessary to perform this task is never provided in the input or programmed into the network. Instead, it must be developed internally in the sentence gestalt as the network learns to process sentences.

Syntactic information does not have to be used in these cases; the semantic constraints suffice. In fact, if the surface location of the constituents is removed from the input, the roles are still assigned correctly. Further, if the constituents are presented in different orders, the activation values in the output are affected only slightly. Sentence processing that can rely on semantic information, therefore, essentially does, though confusing the syntax appears to have a slight corrupting effect.

The relative strengths of syntactic and semantic constraints are determined by their reliability in the training corpus. The more reliable a constraint, the more potent its influence in processing. This effect of the corpus on later processing is also found in natural languages. Word order in English is very reliable and is a very strong constraint on the meaning of a sentence. In Italian, however, word order is less reliable and is a much weaker constraint which can be over-ridden by semantic constraints. Consequently, the sentence "The pencil kicked the cow" in English is taken to mean that the pencil did the kicking because of the word order, while in Italian it is taken to mean that the cow did the kicking because of the semantics of the situation [17].

To process sentences in the active and passive syntactic categories, however, the network cannot rely entirely on semantic constraints to assign thematic roles. Sentences in these categories were created by including in the corpus pairs of reversible events, such as the busdriver giving a rose to the teacher, and the teacher giving a rose to the busdriver. Both of these events were trained with equal frequency. Without a difference in frequency, there is no semantic regularity to help predict which of the two events a sentence refers to. The model must rely on syntactic information, such as word order, to assign the thematic roles. Passive sentences further complicate processing by making word order, by itself, unpredictive. The past participle and the "by" preposition provide cues designating the passive, but in themselves do not cue which person plays which role either. The word order information must be used in conjunction with the passive cues to determine the correct role assignments.

When sentences in the syntactic categories were tested, for each role/filler pair in each test sentence, the correct role was the most active. Figure 4 provides an example of role assignment in the semantic and syntactic categories.

The remaining three categories involve the use of context to help specify the concepts referred to in a sentence. Sentences in the word ambiguity category contain one or more ambiguous words. After processing a sentence, the network was probed with the role half of each role/filler pair. The output patterns for the fillers were then examined. Figure 5 provides an example sentence with ambiguous words. For all pairs in each test sentence, the correct filler was the most active.

Disambiguation requires the competition and cooperation of constraints from both the word and its context. While the word itself cues two different interpretations, the context fits only one. In "The pitcher hit the bat with the bat," "pitcher" cues both *container* and *ball-player*. The context cues both *ball-player* and *busdriver* because the model has seen sentences involving both people hitting bats. All the constraints supporting *ball-player* combine, and

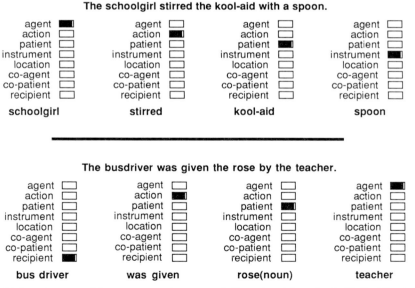

Fig. 4. Role assignment. After a sentence is processed, the network is probed with the filler half of each role/filler pair. The activation over a subset of the thematic role units is displayed. The first sentence contains semantic information useful for role assignment, while the second sentence contains only syntactic information useful for role assignment.

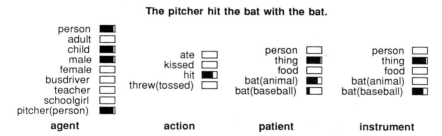

Fig. 5. Word disambiguation. The sentence "The pitcher hit the bat with the bat" is processed by the network. The network is then probed with each thematic role in the event. The activation over a subset of the fillers is displayed. The network correctly disambiguates each word.

together they win the competition for the interpretation of the sentence. As can be seen from the present example, even when several words of a sentence are ambiguous, the event which they support in common dominates the disparate events that they support individually. The processing of both instances of "bat" work similarly: the word and the context mutually support the correct interpretation. Consequently, the final interpretation of each word fits together into a globally consistent event.

Concept instantiation works similarly. Though the word cues a number of more specific concepts, only one fits the context. Again, the constraints from the word and from the context combine to produce a unique, specific interpretation of the term. As with the disambiguation task, each test sentence was processed, and then the network was probed with the role half of each role/filler pair. The output filler patterns were examined to see if the correct concept and semantic features were instantiated (see Fig. 6). In each case, the correct concept and features were the most active.

Depending upon the sentence, however, the context may only partially constrain the interpretation. Such is the case in "The teacher kissed someone." "Someone" could refer to any of the four people found in the corpus. Since, in the network's experience, females only kiss males, the context constrains the interpretation of "someone" to be either the busdriver or the pitcher, but no further. Consequently, the model can activate the *male* and *person* features of the patient while leaving the units representing *busdriver* and *pitcher* only partially active. The features *adult* and *child* are also partially and equally active because the busdriver is an adult while the pitcher is a child (see Fig. 6). While *pitcher* is slightly more active in this example, neither is activated above 0.5 (see the section on ambiguous sentences for an explanation of the difference in activations). In general, the model is capable of inferring as much information as the evidence permits: the more evidence, the more specific the inference.

Word disambiguation can be seen as one type of this general inference

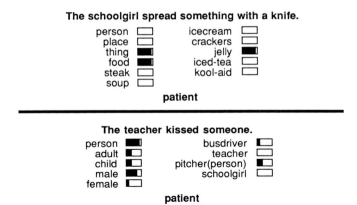

Fig. 6. Concept instantiation. The network has learned that *jelly* is always the patient of *spread*. When the network processes "The schoolgirl spread something with a knife," it instantiates "something" as *jelly*. For the sentence "The teacher kissed someone," the network partially instantiates "someone" as a *male* and *person*, and activates both *pitcher* and *busdriver* partially.

process. The only difference is that for ambiguous words, both the general concept and the specific features differ between the alternatives, while for vague words, the general concept is the same and only some of the specific features differ.

Finally, sentences in the role elaboration category test the model's ability to infer thematic roles not mentioned in the input sentence. For example, in "The teacher ate the soup," no instrument is mentioned, yet a spoon can be inferred. For each test sentence, after the sentence was processed, the network was probed with the role half of the to-be-inferred role/filler pair. The correct filler was the most active in each case. Figure 7 provides an example. For role

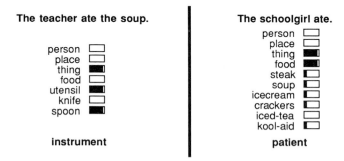

Fig. 7. Role elaboration. After processing the sentence "The teacher ate the soup," the network is probed with the instrument role. The filler activations are displayed. The network correctly infers *spoon*. For "The schoolgirl ate," the model must infer a patient. Because the schoolgirl is likely to eat a variety of foods, no particular food is well activated.

elaboration, the context alone provides the constraints for making the inference. Extra roles that are very likely will be inferred strongly. When the roles are less likely, or could be filled by more than one concept, they are only weakly inferred.

As it stands, there is nothing to keep the network from generalizing to infer extra roles for every sentence, even for events in which these roles make no sense. For instance, in "The busdriver drank the iced-tea," no instrument should be inferred, yet the network infers knife because of its association with the busdriver. It appears that since the busdriver uses a knife in many events about eating, the network generalizes to infer the knife as an instrument for his drinking. However, in events further removed from eating, instruments are not inferred. For example, in "The busdriver rose," no instrument is activated. It appears, then, that generalization of roles is affected by the degree of similarity between events. When events are similar, elaborative roles may be generalized. When events are distinct, roles do not generalize, and the model has no reason to activate any particular filler for a role.

3.3. Immediate update

As each constituent is processed, the information it conveys modifies the sentence gestalt and strengthens the inferences it supports. But the beginning of a sentence may not always accurately predict its eventual full meaning. For example, in "The adult ate the steak with daintiness," the identity of the adult is initially unknown. After "The adult ate" has been processed, *busdriver* and *teacher* are equally active. After processing "The adult ate the steak," the model guesses that the agent is the *busdriver* since steak is typically eaten by busdrivers. At this point, the model has sufficient information to instantiate "the adult" to be the *busdriver*. Along with this inference, *gusto* is inferred as the manner of eating, since busdrivers eat with gusto. Here the model demonstrates its ability to infer additional thematic roles.

The model has, at this point, been led down the garden path toward an ultimately incorrect interpretation of the sentence. The next constituent processed, "with daintiness," only fits with the teacher and the schoolgirl. Since the sentence specifies an adult, the agent must be the *teacher*. The model must revise its representation of the event to fit with the new information by de-activating *busdriver* and activating *teacher* (see Fig. 8).

In general, as each constituent is processed, the information it explicitly conveys is added to the representation of the sentence along with implicit information implied by the constituent in the current situation. When the evidence is ambiguous and supports many conflicting inferences (such as after "The adult ate" has been processed) all the inferences are weakly activated in the sentence gestalt. When new evidence suggests a different interpretation, the sentence gestalt is revised.

The adult ate the steak with daintiness.

Sentence Gestalt Activations					Role/Filler Activations				
unit	#1	#2	#3	#4		#1	#2	#3	#4
1					**agent**				
2					person				
3					adult				
4					child				
5					male				
6					female				
7					bus driver				
8					teacher				
9					**action**				
10					ate				
11					shot				
12					drove(trans)				
13					drove(motiv)				
14					**patient**				
15					person				
16					adult				
17					child				
18					bus driver				
19					schoolgirl				
20					thing				
21					food				
22					steak				
23					soup				
24					crackers				
25					**adverb**				
26					gusto				
27					pleasure				
28					daintiness				

Fig. 8. The sequential processing of a garden-path sentence. After "the steak" has been processed, the network instantiates "the adult" with the concept *busdriver*. When "with daintiness" is processed, the network must reinterpret "the adult" to mean *teacher*.

3.4. Ambiguous sentences

The ambiguous sentences in the test set were tested separately. As noted above, an ambiguous sentence has more than one consistent interpretation. For example, the adult in the sentence, "The adult drank the iced-tea in the living-room," can be instantiated with either *busdriver* or *teacher* as the agent, but the sentence offers no clues that *teacher* is the correct agent in this particular sentence/event pair in the test set. In these ambiguous cases, the model should compromise and activate *busdriver* and *teacher* partially and equally, causing two small errors. What the network typically did, however, was to activate one concept slightly more than the other.

One reason for these differences in activations is the recent training history of the network. The sentence/event pairs trained more recently have a greater impact on the weights and, therefore, on subsequent processing. Because selection of training examples occurs randomly, several sentences involving a particular agent may occur before a sentence/event involving a different agent is trained. Such training biases can lead to a bias in the activation of alternatives in ambiguous sentences. We tested this explanation by training the network on sentence/event pairs that consisted of an ambiguous sentence and the subordinate, weakly activated, event. From one to three training trials were required to balance the activation of the subordinate event with that of the previously dominant event.

The sensitivity of the network to recent training on ambiguous sentences is due to the dynamics of the activation function. Because the activation function is sigmoidal, it is sensitive to changes in the value of its input when the value is in the middle of its range. Since each meaning of an ambiguous sentence should be activated partially, its inputs to the activation function must lie in this middle range. Consequently, minor changes to the weights that determine the input value will have a major impact on the activation value.

Conversely, in the extremes of the range of the activation function, changes in the input value will have little discernible effect on the activation value. Since the one meaning of an unambiguous sentence should be activated fully, its inputs to the activation function lie in the extremes of the function's range. Minor changes in the weights, therefore, will have only minor changes on the activation value, making the processing of unambiguous sentences robust to recent training.

3.5. Learning

As the network learns to comprehend sentences correctly, a number of developmental phenomena can be observed. In fact, the only real failures in performance stem from a developmental effect. Problems in processing only arise in processing infrequent and irregular sentences. For example, sentences about the busdriver eating soup are rare. The network is seven times more likely to see a sentence about the busdriver eating steak than eating soup. This frequency difference creates a strong regularity between "The busdriver ate" and the concept *steak*. In a sentence about the busdriver eating soup, the word "soup" constrains the patient to be *soup*, while "The busdriver ate" partially constrains the patient to be *steak*. The constraints compete for an interpretation of the sentence. When the regularities are particularly strong, the contextual constraints can win the competition and cause the bottom-up activation from the word itself to be overridden.

Though this effect seems like a serious flaw, it is a flaw that the model shares with people. In an illuminating experiment, Erickson and Mattson [8] asked subjects questions like, "How many animals of each kind did Moses take on the Ark?" Subjects typically answered, "Two," despite their knowledge, when later asked, that Moses had nothing to do with the Ark. Constraints from the context overwhelmed the constraint from the word "Moses."

Erickson and Mattson also describe a second order effect in that subjects will balk when asked, "How many animals of each kind did Nixon take on the Ark?" Apparently, the degree of semantic overlap between the correct concept and the foil affects how easily subjects will be misled. The model demonstrates the second order effect as well. Given "The busdriver ate the ball," the model fails to activate any patient. The model cannot explicitly balk, but its failure to represent the sentence accurately or misinterpret it is similar to balking. This example suggests that the SG model holds promise for demonstrating interesting human-like errors in comprehension.

In the model, this frequency or regularity effect diminishes with training: the reliability of a constraint, its probability of correctly predicting the output, rather than its overall frequency, becomes increasingly important. The word "soup" perfectly predicts the concept *soup*: whenever "soup" appears in a sentence, the event contains the concept *soup*. On the other hand, the busdriver eats a variety of foods: "the busdriver ate" is only 70% reliable as a predictor of *steak*. With increased training, even low frequency constraints are practiced. If they are reliable, they gain strength and eventually outweigh more frequent but less reliable constraints. Similar developmental trends occur as children learn language [17]. Progress is slow, but after a total of 630,000 trials even these very infrequent and irregular sentences are processed correctly.

The early effect of frequency works for syntactic constraints as well as semantic constraints. As shown in Fig. 9, the model masters sentences in the active voice sooner than it masters sentences in the passive voice. This difference is due to the greater frequency of sentences in the active voice in the corpus. While 14 sentence frames use the active voice, only 4 frames use the passive voice. After 330,000 trials, though, both voices are handled correctly.

The syntactic constraints develop more slowly than the regular semantic constraints. Yet while every sentence contains word order constraints, only an occasional sentence will contain a particular semantic constraint. Based on the

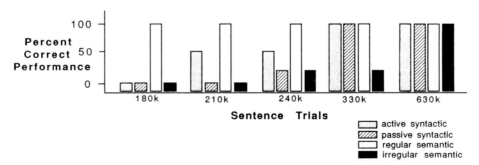

Fig. 9. Development of performance. active syntactic—The busdriver kissed the teacher; passive syntactic—The teacher was kissed by the busdriver; regular semantic—The busdriver ate the steak; irregular semantic—The busdriver ate the soup. Correct performance means the correct concepts are more active than incorrect concepts.

frequency of practice with particular constraints, then, the word order constraints should be learned much earlier than the semantic constraints. Two caveats to the frequency rule help explain this result. First, the syntactic constraints involve the conjunction of word order with the presence or absence of the passive markers, and such conjunctions are difficult to learn. Second, learning tends to generalize across semantically similar words, so training on one word can facilitate the learning of similar words.

The large number of training trials required to achieve good performance led us to look for ways to improve the speed of learning. One experiment consisted of removing the first hidden layer from the architecture. The input and the previous sentence gestalt then fed directly into the sentence gestalt layer. It was hoped that by making the network one layer more shallow, and by reducing the number of weights, error correction would proceed more quickly. Training of the modified network was stopped when it became apparent that the model did not learn the semantic constraints more quickly, and it had not learned the syntactic constraints at all. It is possible that the network could still learn the syntactic constraints given more training. The point of the modification, however, was to speed learning, and this goal was not fulfilled.

The reason for the utility of the first hidden layer in computing the syntactic constraints lies in the conjunctive nature of the constraints. The hidden layer is useful in computing the conjunction of word order and active/passive voice markers. Without the hidden layer, the sentence gestalt would have to compute the conjunction as well as represent the meaning of the sentence. Such a representation is apparently difficult for the network to find.

3.6. Representations

While the input to the network is a local encoding where each word is represented by a different unit, the network can create internal representations that are distributed and that explicitly encode helpful semantic information. The weights running from the input layer to the first hidden layer can be seen as "constraint vectors" which determine how each word influences the evolution of the sentence gestalt. These constraint vectors are the model's bottom-up representation of each word. Words that impose similar constraints should develop similar constraint vectors. A cluster analysis of the weight vectors reveals their similarity. Separate cluster analyses were performed for unambiguous verbs and nouns (see Fig. 10).

The verbs cluster into a number of hierarchical groups. One cluster contains the consumption verbs. Another contains stirred and spread. These two clusters then combine into a cluster of verbs involving people and food. Kissed, hit, and shot formed another cluster. For each of these verbs there were passive-voice sentences in the corpus, and each could take an animate object. Gave, the only dative verb, stands apart from the other verbs. This clustering reflects the similarity of the case frames of the members of the different clusters.

The constraint vectors of nouns further reflect similarities in the constraints they impose on the evolving sentence gestalt. This similarity is reflected in two ways. As with the verbs, semantically similar words cluster: all of the people cluster, and dog and spot are very similar. Words that occur together in the same context also have similar constraint vectors. For example, ice cream clusters with park, and jelly clusters with knife. In the corpus, ice cream is always eaten in the park, and jelly is always spread with a knife. Their similar constraint vectors follow from the similar constraints they impose on the events described by the sentences in which they appear.

3.7. Generalization

An important remaining question is whether the model is actually learning useful constraints that it can apply to novel sentences or whether it is simply memorizing sentence/event pairs. Since sentences in the first simulation were

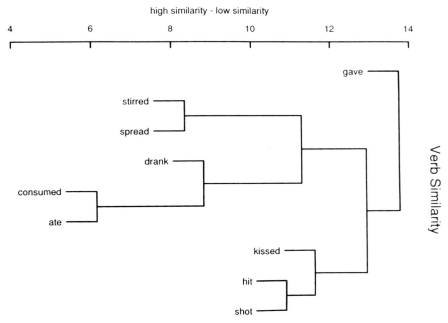

Fig. 10. Cluster analyses. The analysis computes the similarity between the weight vectors leading from each input unit to the first hidden layer. The more similar two vectors or clusters of vectors (in euclidean distance), the sooner they are combined into a new cluster. Physical distance in the figure is irrelevant; only the clustering is important. For instance, "stirred" is not notably more similar to "drank" than it is to "ate."

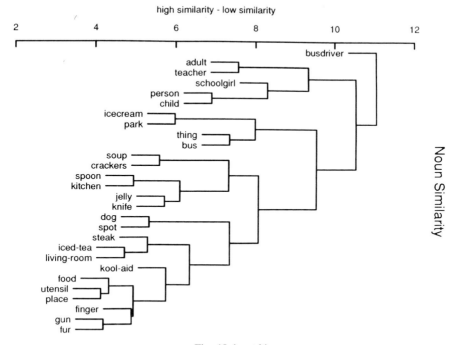

high similarity - low similarity

Fig. 10 (contd.)

generated randomly and none were set aside to not be trained, the first simulation cannot be used to evaluate generalization. Two new corpora were developed to test the model's generalization abilities. One of the new corpora was designed to test the model's ability to generalize syntactic regularities and the other was designed to test its ability to generalize semantic regularities. The model was trained and evaluated on each corpus separately.

3.7.1. Syntax

For syntax, we tested the model's ability to learn and use the syntax of active and passive sentences. Could the model learn to use the active/passive voice markers and the temporal order of the constituents, word order, productively on novel sentences? This is a test of compositionality. The model must learn to compose the familiar constituents of sentences in new combinations. To perform this generalization task, the model must learn several types of information. First, it must learn the concept referred to by each word in a sentence: "John" refers to *John* and "saw" refers to *saw*. Second, the model must learn that the order of the constituents, which constituent comes before the verb and which after, is important to assigning the agent and patient. Third, the model must learn the relevance of the passive markers: the past participle of the verb and the prepositional phrase beginning with "by." Fourth, the model must learn to integrate the order information and the passive marker information to correctly assign the thematic roles.

The model was trained on a corpus of sentences composed of ten people and ten reversible actions, such as "John saw Mary." These sentences could appear in the active or passive voice. The basic corpus consisted of all 2000 sentences (10 people by 10 actions by 10 people by 2 voices). Before training began, though, 250 of these sentences (12.5%) were set aside for later testing: they were not trained. The model was then trained on the remaining sentences. Once the training corpus was mastered (after 100,000 trials), the 250 test sentences were presented to the model. The model processed 97% of these sentences correctly. In only 11 sentences did the model incorrectly assign a thematic role. In these sentences, when probed with one of the fillers, the model activated an incorrect role more strongly than the correct role.

3.7.2. Semantics

Semantic regularities may also provide the basis for generalization. We tested the model's ability to learn some semantic regularities and apply them in novel contexts. There are two basic generalization effects we would like to see in the model's behavior. First, as with syntax, the trained model should exhibit compositionality: the model should be able to represent successfully sentences it has never seen before. Secondly, the model should make predictions: it should be able to use information presented early in a sentence to help it process subsequent information.

To test these generalization effects, we again created a simple corpus for the model to learn. This corpus consisted of 8 adults and 8 children, 5 actions, and 8 objects for each action. The corpus was arranged to make age a semantic regularity. For each action, 3 objects were presented with adults, 3 were presented with children, and 2 were presented with both adults and children. This arrangement created a corpus of 400 sentences (8 adults by 5 actions by 5 objects plus 8 children by 5 actions by 5 objects). For example,

George watched the news.	Bobby watched He-Man.
George watched Johnny Carson.	Bobby watched Smurfs.
George watched David Letterman.	Bobby watched Mighty Mouse.
George watched Star Trek.	Bobby watched Star Trek.
George watched the Road Runner.	Bobby watched the Road Runner.

The regularity is that the age of the agent, in conjunction with the verb, predicts a set of objects. Age, though, is not explicitly encoded in the input or the output representations. Instead, it is a "hidden" feature (Unlike people in the first simulation, people in this corpus are represented by a single unit, i.e. locally.). The model must learn which agents are the adults and which are the children based on its experience seeing the objects with which each is paired. The children all watch one set of shows, and the adults all watch another set. Age, therefore, organizes the sentences into sets. Since age does not appear in the input, however, it must be induced by the model and accessed as each sentence is processed.

Before the model was trained on the corpus of sentences, 50 of the 400 sentences (12.5%) were randomly picked to be set aside as the generalization set. The model was then trained on the remaining sentences. When these sentences were processed correctly (after 90,000 trials), the model was tested for compositional and predictive generalization.

Again, to be compositional, the model should be able to process correctly the sentences on which it had not been trained. The model processed 86% of these sentences correctly. On the remaining 14%, or 7 sentences, the model activated the wrong object more strongly than it activated the correct object. At the point in training when the model was stopped, then, it could compose novel sentences reasonably well.

Semantic generalization should allow the model to predict subsequent information. There are two types of regularities that the model should discover to help make predictions. One is the general regularity that children do children's activities and that adults do adult activities. To test the learning of this regularity we observed which objects the model predicted after the model had processed the agent and action. Given an agent and an action, the model should predict the objects appropriate for that action and an agent of that age. For example, given the partial sentence, "Bobby watched...," the model should predict the object to be either He-Man, Smurfs, Mighty Mouse, the Road Runner, or Star Trek. Specifically, this regularity suggests that the model should activate each of these subjects 1/5 or 0.2.

What makes this a generalization task is that some of the sentences in the corpus were set aside and not trained: some agents were never paired with certain objects. For example, the network was never trained on the sentence, "Bobby watched He-Man." To activate each object in the age appropriate set to 0.2, the model must generalize. It must generalize both to discover the complete set of five children's shows, and to associate that set to each of the eight children. This generalization can be tested by observing whether He-Man is activated as a predicted object for "Bobby watched. . . ."

The other type of regularity is specific to each agent. The fact that the training corpus does not contain, "Bobby watched He-Man," is also a regularity that the model can learn. It learns that it should not predict He-Man as an object for "Bobby watched. . . ." Since, for Bobby, there are only four shows that he actually watches, each should be given an activation level of 1/4 or 0.25. The model's tendency to generalize by using the general regularity about children's viewing habits, therefore, is counteracted by the specific regularity about Bobby's personal viewing habits. The activation of the appropriate/untrained (e.g. He-Man for Bobby) objects should be a compromise between the two competing forces. The appropriate/untrained objects, then, should have an activation somewhat less than 0.2. For the appropriate/trained (e.g. Mighty Mouse for Bobby) objects, the activation level should lie between 0.2 and 0.25, and the activation level for the inappropriate/untrained objects (e.g. the news for Bobby) should be close to 0.

The model's predictions on each of the five actions for four of the people in the corpus were tabulated. The activation values for the model's object predictions were categorized into three groups: the appropriate/trained, the appropriate/untrained, and the inappropriate/untrained. The average activation in each group is shown in Table 2. The means are significantly different from one another.

Three conclusions can be drawn from these data. One, the appropriate/trained objects are activated to the appropriate degree. The model correctly predicts the correct set of objects for the action and the age of the agent. Two, the model generalizes in that it also activates age-correct objects it has not actually seen in that context before. The substantially weaker activation of these appropriate/untrained objects demonstrates the competition between the general and specific regularities. The general regularity activates the objects, but the agent-specific regularities reduce that activation. Three, the set of inappropriate/untrained objects for each action is turned off.

The difference in activation between the appropriate/untrained and inappropriate/untrained objects understates their difference in the network. As the activation of a unit approaches 1 or 0, the non-linearity of the activation function requires that exponentially more activation be added to move closer to 1 or 0. A large change in the net input, therefore, would be required to reduce the activation level of an appropriate/untrained object to that of an inappropriate/untrained object. Consequently, the two types of objects are substantially different, and the general regularity is having a significant impact on prediction.

Interestingly, there is a trade-off during training between compositional generalization and predictive generalization. During training the model improves its ability to compose novel sentences, but loses the ability to make general predictions. The general predictions are lost as the model learns the

Table 2
Semantic prediction

Appropriateness	Training	
	Trained	Untrained
Appropriate	0.210	0.036
Inappropriate	—	0.006

specific regularities of the training corpus. Compositionality is gained as the input constituents become lexeme-like. As the network trains, it slowly learns which parts of the input are responsible for which parts of the output. The network slowly hones the meanings of the input constituents until they are essentially represented as lexemes.

The model's training procedure encourages predictive generalization for both types of regularities by explicitly requiring the model to predict the object after processing the agent and action. Recall that the model must answer questions about the entire sentence after processing each constituent. The model learns that all of the untrained objects, both appropriate and inappropriate, should not be predicted because they never occur.

It may seem that the model diverges from human behavior as it reduces the influence of the general regularity in favor of the person-specific regularities. It must be remembered, though, that the model is trained on a set of only 16 people. If there were many more people, the person-specific regularities would receive less practice and the general regularity would receive more practice. This change would make the age generalization much stronger.

The model can clearly learn and productively apply regularities from its training corpus to novel sentences. However, the degree to which the model composes novel sentences, 97% in the syntactic corpus, but only 86% in the semantic corpus, is far from the degree we expect from people. Again, this performance may be due to the size and content of the corpus. The effects of these factors on generalization are not well understood. Our simulation should be taken only as an indication that some degree of compositionality can be acquired.

As demonstrated by learning the rule for the passive voice construction, it can learn syntactic regularities, and as demonstrated by learning the meaning of each word and the hidden-feature age, it can learn semantic regularities. Generalization based on these regularities takes two forms. When the regularity consists of input/output pairings, generalization leads to compositionality. Input/output pairings are like lexemes in that the specific input constrains a specific part of the output. There are few, if any, constraints on other parts of the output. Lexemes will compose in novel combinations easily because each one makes a separate and independent contribution to the interpretation.

When the regularity consists of input/input pairings, generalization can lead to prediction. For input/input pairings, one part of the input affects multiple parts of the output. Some of the parts may be future constituents, so the input, in effect, predicts future inputs. These input/input pairings may not compose easily. The parts may make mutually contradictory predictions. For example in, "Bobby watched the news," "Bobby" predicts that *the news* will not be watched, and "the news" predicts that *Bobby*, a child, will not be watching. These contradictory predictions will create conflict in the sentence gestalt and make the interpretation hard to represent.

Additionally, a novel pairing may not compose easily because the constraints specific to a pair may not have been learned. In other words, there may be constraints, in the environment, that pertain to a pair of input constituents. If the model has never experienced this pair, it cannot know these constraints, and they will not affect the interpretation.

3.8. Variable syntactic frames

The model is able to learn and use syntactic information. It can correctly apply syntactic information to assign thematic roles in sentences with reversible verbs. But how complex syntax can the model learn? Since the model can only represent simple sentences in the output layer, it cannot learn or use the complex syntax involved in sentences with embedded clauses. The syntax of sentences involving "gave," however, is relatively complex because of the variability in the location of roles in the sentence. Because it need only involve simple sentences, it is representable in the output layer, and because it is representable, it can be used as the target for error correction. The question is, will the model be able to learn?

We created a corpus consisting of the different legal constructions of "gave."

> The busdriver gave the rose to the teacher.
> The busdriver gave the teacher the rose.
> The teacher was given the rose by the busdriver.
> The rose was given to the teacher by the busdriver.
> The rose was given by the busdriver to the teacher.

The corpus consisted of 56 events of this type. Each event was equally frequent so that there were no semantic regularities for the model to detect and use to help it assign the agent and recipient thematic roles. The model was able to master this corpus. It learned to correctly assign each of the thematic roles in the event described by the sentence.

There are still many more phenomena on which the model has not been trained or tested. The general point, though, is that the model appears to have the capability to learn and use syntactic constraints productively. Where its limits are is presently unknown.

4. Discussion

The SG model has been quite successful in meeting the goals that we set out for it, but it is of course far from being the final word on sentence comprehension. Here we briefly review the model's accomplishments. Following this review, we consider some of its limitations and how they might be addressed by further work.

4.1. Accomplishments of the model

One of the principle successes of the SG model is that it correctly assigns constituents to thematic roles based on syntactic and semantic constraints. The syntactic constraints are more difficult for the model to master than the semantic constraints even though we have provided explicit cues to the syntax, in the form of the surface location of the constituents, in the input. The model does, however, come to master these constraints as they are exemplified in the corpus of training sentences. Though syntactic constraints can be significantly more subtle than those our model has faced thus far, those it has faced are fairly difficult. To correctly handle active and passive sentences, the model must map surface constituents onto different roles depending on the presence of various surface cues elsewhere in the sentence.

The model also exhibits considerable capacity to use context to disambiguate meanings and to instantiate vague terms in contextually appropriate ways. Indeed, it is probably most appropriate to view the model as treating each constituent in a sentence as a clue or set of clues that constrain the overall event description, rather than as treating each constituent as a lexical item with a particular meaning. Although each clue may provide stronger constraints on some aspects of the event description than on others, it is simply not the case that the meaning associated with the part of the event designated by each constituent is conveyed by only that constituent itself.

The model likewise infers unspecified arguments roughly to the extent that they can be reliably predicted from the context. Here we see very clearly that constituents of an event description can be cued without being specifically designated by any constituent of the sentence. These inferences are graded to reflect the degree to which they are appropriate given the set of clues provided. The drawing of these inferences is also completely intrinsic to the basic comprehension process: no special separate inference processes must be spawned to make inferences, they simply occur implicitly as the constituents of the sentence are processed.

The model demonstrates the capacity to update its representation as each new constituent is encountered. Our demonstration of this aspect of the model's performance is somewhat informal; nevertheless, its capabilities seem impressive. As each constituent is encountered, the interpretation of all aspects of the event description is subject to change. If we revert to thinking in terms of meanings of particular constituents, both prior and subsequent context can influence the interpretation of each constituent. Unlike most conventional sentence processing models, the ability to exploit subsequent context is again an intrinsic part of the process of interpreting each new constituent. There is no backtracking; rather, the representation of the sentence is simply updated to reflect the constraints imposed by each constituent as it is encountered.

While avoiding backtracking, the model also avoids the computational explosion of computing each possible interpretation of a sentence as it encounters ambiguous words and thematic role assignments. A simpler model helps explain how the SG model avoids these dual pitfalls. Kawamoto [16] describes an auto-associative model of lexical access. In his model, patterns of activation represent a word and its meaning. For each ambiguous word, there are two patterns, each representing the association of the word with one of its meanings. Positive weights interconnect the units representing a pattern, and negative weights interconnect units between patterns.

When an ambiguous word is processed, it initially activates semantic units representing both meanings. The resulting pattern of activation is a combination of the semantic features of both meanings, so the bindings among the features of a meaning are lost in the activation pattern. These bindings, however are preserved in the weights, and the model will settle into one interpretation of the word or the other. One can think of the alternative interpretations as minima in an energy landscape. The initial pattern of activation falls on the high energy ridge between the minima. The settling process moves the pattern of activation down one side of the ridge to one of the minima.

The SG model does not settle, but the idea is similar. When there is not sufficient information to resolve an ambiguity, the sentence interpretations may become conflated in the pattern of activation over the sentence gestalt and in the output responses to probes. The bindings within an interpretation, however, are preserved in the weights. When sufficient new information for disambiguation is provided, the sentence gestalt computes a single interpretation with correct thematic role and semantic feature bindings. For example, given "The adult ate," and with *agent* as the probe, the model partially activates *busdriver*, *teacher*, *male*, and *female*. Which is male and which is female is lost in the activation pattern over the output layer. (It is not clear to what extent the bindings are lost in the activation pattern over the sentence gestalt. In general, the representation over the sentence gestalt is an area for further inquiry.). After the model is further given ". . . the steak with gusto," it is clear that the agent is the busdriver. When probed for the agent, the model unambiguously activates *busdriver* in the output layer.

For the unambiguous sentences in the corpus, the model predominately achieves the correct bindings and interpretations. For the ambiguous sentences, the model conflates, in the output layer, the patterns for each possible role filler for the role being probed. Theoretically, the model should set the activations to match the conditional probabilities for the aspects of the event that remain underspecified. Instead, these activations tend to vacillate based on recent, related training trials. This vacillation toward alternate interpretations is reminiscent of the frequent finding that humans generally do not notice the ambiguity of sentences. Instead, they generally settle for one interpretation or the other, unless their attention is explicitly drawn to the ambiguity. In sum, the long-term, average probabilities of picking particular interpretations may reflect the statistical properties of the environment, while the moment to moment fluctuations of interpretations reflect recent experience.

The gradual, incremental learning capabilities of the network underlie its ability to solve the bootstrapping problem, that is, to learn simultaneously about both the syntax and semantics of constituents. The problem of learning syntax and semantics is central for developmental psycholinguistics. Naigles, Gleitman and Gleitman [25] state that learning syntax and semantics using only statistical information seems impossible because, "at a minimum, it would require such extensive storage and manipulation of contingently categorized event/conversation pairs as to be unrealistic." Yet it is exactly by using such information that our model solves the problem. The model learns the syntax and semantics of the training corpus simultaneously. Across training trials, the model gradually learns which aspects of the event description each constituent of the input constrains and in what ways it constrains these aspects.

The problem of discovering which event in the world a sentence describes when multiple events are present would be handled in a similar way, though we have not modeled it. Again, the aspects of the world that the sentence actually describes would be discovered gradually over repeated trials, while those aspects that spuriously co-occur with these described aspects would wash out. For both the bootstrapping and the ambiguous reference problem, then, our model takes a gradual, statistical approach. We do not want to overstate the case here, since the child learning a language confronts a considerably more complex version of these problems than our model does. Our sentences are pre-segmented into constituents, are very simple in structure, and are much fewer in number than the sentences a child would hear. However, the results demonstrate that the bootstrapping and ambiguous reference problems might ultimately be overcome by an extension of the present approach.

Many of the accomplishments of the SG model are shared by predecessors. Cottrell, [5] Cottrell and Small [6], Waltz and Pollack [35], and McClelland and Kawamoto [21] have all demonstrated the use of syntactic and semantic constraints in role assignment and meaning disambiguation. Of these, the first two embodied the immediate update principle, but did not learn, while the third learned in a limited way, and had a fixed set of input slots.

The greater learning capability of our model allows it to find connection strengths that solve the constraints embodied in the corpus without requiring the modeler to induce these constraints and without the modeler trying to build them in by hand. It also allows the model to construct its own representations in the sentence gestalt, and this ability allows these representations to be considerably more compact than in other cases.

Some previous models have used conjunctive representations in which role/filler pairs are explicitly represented by units pre-assigned to represent either specific role/filler pairs [5, 6, 35] or particular combinations of role features and filler features [21]. Particularly, when such representations are extended so that triples, rather than simply pairs, can be represented [30, 33], these networks can become intractably large even with small vocabularies. The present model avoids intractable size by learning to use its representational capacity sparingly to represent just those role/filler pairings that are consistent with its experience. This ability prevents the model from being able to represent totally arbitrary events: its representational capacities are strongly constrained by the range of its experience. In this regard the model seems similar to humans: it is widely known that human comprehension is strongly influenced by experience [2, 4].

The major simulation reported here contained explicit surface role markings in the input. These markings were designed to make the learning of the syntactic information easier. Additional simulations, though, showed that the network could learn the syntactic information from only the temporal sequences of constituents. In a different task, where the network must attempt to anticipate the next input, there have been several demonstrations that networks can learn to keep track of parse position, at least for small finite-state grammars [7, 29]. Extracting information from the temporal order of input sequences, then, is a function generally within the computational limits of recurrent networks.

Finally, the model is able to generalize the processing knowledge it has learned and apply it to novel sentences. Generalization can come in two varieties: compositional and predictive generalization. Compositional generalization occurs when the model has learned the constraints on sentence interpretation contributed by each element of the sentence, including both syntax and semantics, and has learned how to combine that information in novel sequences. The cluster analysis of the input weights confims that the network is learning the semantic constraints imposed by constituents. It seems likely that a considerable part of the specification of these constraints might be derivable by the network from experience on a subset of the possible contexts where a word can occur. The interpretation acquired in these experiences would then cause the new word to behave like other similar words in contexts in which it was not trained. Illustrations that backpropagation networks can generalize in this way are provided by Hinton [12], Taraban, McDonald and MacWhinney [31], and Rumelhart [27]. In both the syntactic and the semantic generalization corpora, the model demonstrates its ability to learn this information and compose it.

The second variety of generalization is predictive generalization. It occurs when the model can use a regularity to predict upcoming sentence constituents. In the semantic generalization experiment, the model learned regularities about the age of agents in the corpus. The model then used these regularities to predict appropriate objects.

4.2. Deficiencies and limitations of the model

The model has several limitations and a few obvious deficiencies. The model only addresses a limited number of language phenomena. It does not address quantification, reference and co-reference, coordinate constructions, or many other phenomena. Perhaps the most important limitation is the limitation on the complexity of the sentences, and of the events that they describe. In general, it is necessary to characterize the roles and fillers of sentences with respect to their superordinate constituents. Similarly in complex events, there may be more than one actor, each performing an action in a different sub-event of the overall event or action. Representing these structures requires head/role/filler triples instead of simple role/filler pairs.

One solution is to train the model using triples rather than pairs as the sentence and event constituents. The difficulty lies in specifying the non-sentence members of the triples. These non-sentence members would stand for entire structures. Thus they would be very much like the patterns that we are currently using as sentence gestalts. It would be desirable to have the learning procedure induce these representations, but this is a bootstrapping problem that we have not yet attempted to solve.

Another limitation of the model is the use of local representations both for concepts and for roles. The present model used predominantly local representations of concept meanings only for convenience; in reality we would suppose that the conceptual representations underlying events would be represented by distributed patterns [14]. This kind of representation would have several advantages. Context has the capability not only of selecting among highly distinct meanings such as between flying bats and baseball bats, but also, we believe, of shading meanings, emphasizing certain features and altering properties slightly as a function of context [21]. Both of these phenomena are easily captured if we view the representation of a concept as a distributed pattern.

Similarly, there are several problems with the concept of role which are solved if distributed representations are used. It is often difficult to determine whether two roles are the same, and it is very difficult to decide exactly how many different roles there are. If roles were represented as distributed patterns, these issues would simply fall by the wayside. In earlier work [21], it was necessary to invent distributed representations for concepts, but recently a number of researchers have shown that such representations can be learned [12, 24, 28]. The procedure should also apply to distributed representations of roles.

A final limitation is the small size of the corpus used in training the model. Given the length of time required for training, one might be somewhat pessimistic about the possibility that a network of this kind could master a substantial corpus. However, it should be noted that the extent to which learning time grows with corpus size is extremely hard to predict for connectionist models, and is highly problem dependent. For some problems (e.g. parity), learning time per pattern increases more than linearly with the number of training patterns [32], while for other problems (e.g. negation), learning time per pattern actually can decrease as the number of patterns increases [27].

Where the current problem falls on this continuum is not yet known. A comparison of the learning times between the general corpus and the syntactic corpus used in the generalization experiments, however, is suggestive. The network required 630,000 trials to learn the 120 events in the general corpus (330,000 trials to learn all but the most irregular events). On the other hand, the network required only 100,000 trials to learn the 2000 events of the syntactic corpus. The syntactic corpus, of course, is extremely regular, and the regularities are compositional. Given the model's good generalization results on the syntactic corpus, it is possible that the model will scale well to very large corpora if their regularities are composable.

One final deficiency of the model is its tendency to activate fillers for roles that do not apply to a particular frame. This tendency could perhaps be overcome by explicit training that there should be no output for a particular role, but this seems inelegant and impractical, especially if we are correct in believing that the set of roles is open-ended. The absence of roles seems somehow implicit in events, rather than explicitly noted. Perhaps event representations that preserved more detail of the real-world event would provide the relevant implicit constraints.

5. Conclusion

The SG model represents another step in what will surely be a long series of explorations of connectionist models of language processing. The model is an advance in our view, but there is still a very long way to go. The next step is to find ways to extend the approach to more complex structures and more extensive corpora, while increasing the rate of learning.

Appendix A. Input and Output Representations

Input

surface locations:
pre-verbal, verbal, post-verbal-1, post-verbal-n

words
consumed, ate, drank, stirred, spread, kissed, gave, hit, shot, threw, drove, shed, rose

someone, adult, child, dog, busdriver, teacher, schoolgirl, pitcher, spot
something, food, steak, soup, ice cream, crackers, jelly, iced-tea, kool-aid
utensil, spoon, knife, finger, gun
place, kitchen, living-room, park, bat, ball, bus, fur
gusto, pleasure, daintiness
with, in, to, by
was

Output

roles:
agent, action, patient, instrument, co-agent, co-patient, location, adverb,
   recipient

actions and concepts:
ate, drank, stirred, spread, kissed, gave, hit, shot, threw(tossed),
   threw(hosted),   drove(transported),   drove(motivated),   shed(verb),
   rose(verb)
busdriver, teacher, schoolgirl, pitcher(person), spot
steak, soup, ice cream, crackers, jelly, iced-tea, kool-aid
spoon, knife, finger, gun
kitchen, living-room, shed(noun), park
rose(noun), bat(animal), bat(baseball), ball(sphere), ball(party), bus,
   pitcher(container), fur
gusto, pleasure, daintiness

action features:
consumed, passive

concept features:
person, adult, child, dog, male, female
thing, food, utensil
place, in-doors, out-doors

Appendix B. Sample Sentence-Frame

Hit

In the sentence-frame below, superior numbers 1, 2, 3, 4 have the following
meaning:

   [1] Include a role in the input with this probability.
   [2] Choose this filler with this probability.
   [3] Choose this word with this probability.
   [4] The word appears in this prepositional phrase.

agent 100[1]
  25[2] busdriver 70[3] adult 20 person 10
    verb 100
      100 hit 100
    patient 100
      25 shed-n 80 something 20
        instrument 50
          100 bus 80 something 20 with[4]
      40 ball-s 80 something 20
        location 50
          100 park 100 in
        instrument 50
          100 bat-b 80 something 20 with
      10 bat-a 80 something 20
        location 50
          100 shed-n 100 in
        instrument 50
          100 bat-b 80 something 20 with
      25 pitcher-p 70 child 20 person 10
        location 50
          100 park 100 in
        instrument 50
          100 ball-s 80 something 20 with
  25 teacher 70 adult 20 person 10
    verb 100
      100 hit 100
    patient 100
      34 pitcher-c 80 something 20
        location 50
          100 kitchen 100 in
        instrument 50
          100 spoon 80 something 20 with
      33 pitcher-p 70 child 20 person 10
        location 50
          100 living-room 100 in
        instrument 50
          100 pitcher-c 80 something 20 with
      33 schoolgirl 70 child 20 person 10
        location 50
          100 kitchen 100 in
        instrument 50
          100 spoon 80 something 20 with
  25 pitcher-p 70 child 20 person 10

verb 100
  100 hit 100
patient 100
  40 ball-s 80 something 20
    location 50
      100 park 100 in
    instrument 50
      100 bat-b 80 something 20 with
  10 bat-a 80 something 20
    location 50
      100 shed-n 100 in
    instrument 50
      100 bat-b 80 something 20 with
  25 bus 80 something 20
    location 50
      100 park 100 in
    instrument 50
      100 ball-s 80 something 20 with
  25 busdriver 70 adult 20 person 10
    location 50
      100 park 100 in
    instrument 50
      100 ball-s 80 something 20 with
25 schoolgirl 70 child 20 person 10
  verb 100
    100 hit 100
  patient 100
    34 pitcher-c 80 something 20
      location 50
        100 kitchen 100 in
      instrument 50
        100 spoon 80 something 20 with
    33 spot 80 dog 20
      location 50
        100 kitchen 100 in
      instrument 50
        100 spoon 80 something 20 with
    33 teacher 70 adult 20 person 10
      location 50
        100 kitchen 100 in
      instrument 50
        100 spoon 80 something 20 with

REFERENCES

1. R.C. Anderson and A. Ortony, On putting apples into bottles: A problem of polysemy, *Cognitive Psychol.* **7** (1975) 167–180.
2. F.C. Bartlett, *Remembering: An Experimental and Social Study* (Cambridge University Press, Cambridge, 1932).
3. P.A. Carpenter and M.A. Just, Reading comprehension as the eyes see it, in: M.A. Just and P.A. Carpenter, eds., *Cognitive Processes in Comprehension* (Erlbaum, Hillsdale, NJ, 1977).
4. W.G. Chase and H.A. Simon, Perception in chess, *Cognitive Psychol.* **4** (1973) 55–81.
5. G.W. Cottrell, A connectionist approach to word sense disambiguation, Dissertation, Computer Science Department, University of Rochester, NY (1985).
6. G.W. Cottrell and A.L. Small, A connectionist scheme for modeling word sense disambiguation, *Cognition and Brain Theory* **6** (1983) 89–120.
7. J.L. Elman, Finding structure in time, CRL Tech. Rept. 8801, Center for Research in Language, University of California, San Diego, La Jolla, CA (1988).
8. T.D. Erickson and M.E. Mattson, From words to meaning: A semantic illusion, *J. Verbal Learn. Verbal Behav.* **20** (1981) 540–551.
9. C.J. Fillmore, The case for case, in: E. Bach and R.T. Harms, eds., *Universals in Linguistic Theory* (Holt, New York, 1968).
10. L.R. Gleitman and E. Wanner, Language acquisition: The state of the state of the art, in: E. Wanner and L.R. Gleitman, eds., *Language Acquisition: The State of the Art* (Cambridge University Press, Cambridge, MA, 1982).
11. G.E. Hinton, Implementing semantic networks in parallel hardware, in: G.E. Hinton and J.A. Anderson, eds., *Parallel Models of Associative Memory* (Erlbaum, Hillsdale, NJ, 1981).
12. G.E. Hinton, Learning distributed representations of concepts, in: *Proceedings Eighth Annual Conference of the Cognitive Science Society*, Amherst, MA (1986).
13. G.E. Hinton, Connectionist learning procedures, Tech. Rept. CMU-CS-87-115, Computer Science Department, Carnegie-Mellon University, Pittsburgh, PA (1987).
14. G.E. Hinton, J.L. McClelland and D.E. Rumelhart, Distributed representations, in: D.E. Rumelhart, J.L. McClelland and the PDP Research Group, eds., *Parallel Distributed Processing: Explorations in the Microstructure of Cognition* **1**: *Foundations* (MIT Press, Cambridge, MA, 1986).
15. M.I. Jordan, Attractor dynamics and parallelism in a connectionist sequential machine, in: *Proceedings Eighth Annual Conference of the Cognitive Science Society*, Amherst, MA (1986).
16. A.H. Kawamoto, Distributed representations of ambiguous words and their resolution in a connectionist network, in: S.L. Small, G.W. Cottrell, and M.K. Tanenhaus, eds., *Lexical Ambiguity Resolution: Perspectives from Psycholinguistics, Neuropsychology, and Artificial Intelligence* (Morgan Kaufmann, San Mateo, CA, 1988).
17. B. MacWhinney, E. Bates and R. Kliegl, Cue validity and sentence interpretation in English, German, and Italian, *J. Verbal Learn. and Verbal Behav.* **23** (1984) 127–150.
18. M.P. Marcus, *A Theory of Syntactic Recognition for Natural Language* (MIT Press, Cambridge, MA, 1980).
19. W. Marslen-Wilson and L.K. Tyler, The temporal structure of spoken language understanding, *Cognition* **8** (1980) 1–71.
20. J.L. McClelland and J.L. Elman, Interactive processes in speech perception: The TRACE model, in: J.L. McClelland, D.E. Rumelhart and the PDP Research Group, eds., *Parallel Distributed Processing: Explorations in the Microstructure of Cognition* **2**: *Applications* (MIT Press, Cambridge, MA, 1986).
21. J.L. McClelland and A.H. Kawamoto, Mechanisms of sentence processing: Assigning roles to constituents, in: J.L. McClelland, D.E. Rumelhart and the PDP Research Group, eds., *Parallel Distributed Processing: Explorations in the Microstructure of Cognition* **2**: *Applications* (MIT Press, Cambridge, MA, 1986).

22. J.L. McClelland and D.E. Rumelhart, An interactive activation model of context effects in letter perception: Part 1. An account of basic findings, *Psychol. Rev.* **88** (1981) 375–407.
23. G. McKoon and R. Ratcliff, The comprehension processes and memory structures involved in instrumental inference, *J. Verbal Learn. and Verbal Behav.* **20** (1981) 671–682.
24. R. Miikkulainen and M.G. Dyer, Building distributed representations without microfeatures, Tech. Rept., Artificial Intelligence Laboratory, Computer Science Department, University of California, Los Angeles, CA (1988).
25. L.G. Naigles, H. Gleitman and L.R. Gleitman, Syntactic bootstrapping in verb acquisition: Evidence from comprehension, Tech. Rept., Department of Psychology, University of Pennsylvania, Philadelphia, PA (1987).
26. W.V. Quine, *Word and Object* (Harvard Press, Cambridge, MA, 1960).
27. D.E. Rumelhart, colloquium presented to the Department of Computer Science, Carnegie-Mellon University, Pittsburgh, PA (1987).
28. D.E. Rumelhart, G.E. Hinton and R.J. Williams, Learning internal representations by error propagation, in: D.E. Rumelhart, J.L. McClelland and the PDP Research Group, eds., *Parallel Distributed Processing: Explorations in the Microstructure of Cognition* **1**: *Foundations* (MIT Press, Cambridge, MA, 1986).
29. D. Servan-Schreiber, A. Cleeremans and J.L. McClelland, Encoding sequential structure in simple recurrent networks, Tech. Rept. CMU-CS-88-183, Department of Computer Science, Carnegie Mellon University, Pittsburgh, PA (1988).
30. M.F. St. John and J.L. McClelland, Reconstructive memory for sentences: A PDP approach, *Proceedings Inference: OUIC 86*, University of Ohio, Athens, OH (1987).
31. R. Taraban J. McDonald and B. MacWhinney, Category learning in a connectionist model: Learning to decline the German definite article, in: R. Corrigan, ed., *Milwaukee Conference on Categorization* (Benjamins, Philadelphia, PA, to appear).
32. G. Tesauro, Scaling relationships in back-propagation learning: Dependence on training set size, Tech. Rept., Center for Complex Systems Research, University of Illinois at Urbana-Champaign, Champaign, IL (1987).
33. D.S. Touretzky and S. Geva, A distributed connectionist representation for concept structures, in: *Proceedings Ninth Annual Conference of the Cognitive Science Society*, Seattle, WA (1987).
34. T.A. van Dijk and W. Kintsch, *Strategies of Discourse Comprehension* (Academic Press, Orlando, FL, 1983).
35. D.L. Waltz and J.B. Pollack, Massively parallel parsing: A strongly interactive model of natural language interpretation, *Cognitive Sci.* **9** (1985) 51–74.

Index